Voice in the Wilderness

S

Corliss Lamont

Voice in the Wilderness

Collected Essays of Fifty Years

ℙℬ *Prometheus Books*
BUFFALO, N.Y. 14215

Published by PROMETHEUS BOOKS
923 Kensington Avenue, Buffalo, New York 14215

Library of Congress Catalog Card Number 74-75351
ISBN 0-87975-060-X

Printed in the United States of America

ACKNOWLEDGMENTS

All articles and reviews in this volume are reprinted by permission of the journal, newspaper or publisher that originally printed them.

Beyond Freedom and Dignity by B. F. Skinner. Review article, *Science & Society*, Summer, 1973.

Bill of Rights Fund, The, *The Churchman*, April, 1962.

Cassandras in America, The, *The New York Times*, July 25, 1971.

Critical Examination of the Belief in a Life After Death, A, by C. J. Ducasse. Review article, *British Journal for the Philosophy of Science*, Vol. XIII, No. 51 (1962), published by Cambridge University Press.

Enduring Impact of George Santayana, The, Basic Pamphlet, 1964. In this article Sonnet XI, "The Poet's Testament" (Copyright 1953 Charles Scribner's Sons), "Epitaph" (Copyright 1952 Charles Scribner's Sons) and excerpts from various books by Santayana are used by permission of Charles Scribner's Sons.

How To Be Happy—Though Married, Basic Pamphlet, 1973. This essay has been considerably expanded and revised from an article in *The Humanist* bearing the same title. Parts of the essay have also appeared in *The New York Times*.

Interview with Chile's President Allende, An, *The Churchman*, October, 1971.

It All Began in the Yard, *Bill of Rights Journal*, December, 1969.

Mistaken Attitudes Towards Death, *The Journal of Philosophy*, January 21, 1965.

Mission to Mexico, *New World Review*, January, 1962.

More on *Heroes and Heretics*, *Monthly Review*, April, 1965.

New Light on Dewey's *Common Faith*, *The Journal of Philosophy*, January 5, 1961.

Open Letter to President John F. Kennedy, An, *The New York Times*, April 11, 1962.

Ordeal of Soviet Russia, The, *New World Review*, February, 1958.

Philosophy in Revolution by Howard Selsam. Review article, *Science & Society*, Winter, 1958.

Right To Read, The, by Paul Blanshard. Review article, *Science & Society*, Summer, 1956.

South American Sidelights, *The Churchman*, December, 1971.

Undeclared War, The: The U.S. Army vs. the People of South Vietnam, *New World Review*, May, 1962.

Why I Believe in Socialism, *Monthly Review*, October, 1949.

Why the Bomb Was Dropped, *New World Review*, November, 1965.

Contents

II. CIVIL LIBERTIES

III. WORLD PEACE AND SOCIALISM

IV. EPILOGUE

Introduction

The essays and reviews in this volume cover a period of fifty years. Reading them over brings back memories of many struggles and controversies that I had all but forgotten. During my last two years at Harvard College (1922-24), I was already concerned with various fundamental social issues of the time and was arguing about them at the Harvard Debating Union and the Harvard Liberal Club. As a student, I was active on behalf of some of the main causes that I am still supporting in 1974. While an undergraduate, I decided that I wanted to work for a better America and a better world; and I became an inveterate seeker of Utopia.

After graduating from Harvard in 1924, I went to New College, Oxford, to study for a year, and I soon decided to concentrate in the field of philosophy. I began to work for a degree in that subject at Columbia University under two outstanding philosophic naturalists, Professors John Dewey and Frederick J. E. Woodbridge. I took my Ph.D. in 1932 after writing a thesis entitled *Issues of Immortality*, which was published in book form. During my studies and research at Columbia my thinking led me to adopt the general position of naturalistic Humanism. Humanism is simply another and more appealing name for the naturalism of Dewey, Woodbridge and others.

The humanist philosophy rejects belief in any form of the supernatural and regards our supreme ethical commitment as seeking the happiness and progress of all humanity in this natural world. *Humanist Manifesto I*, issued in 1933 and signed by eminent philosophers such as

John Dewey and John H. Randall, Jr., strengthened my conviction that mature individuals, relying on reason and science, should adopt Humanism as their way of life.

About the same time, with the United States still in the throes of the Great Depression, I reached the conclusion that the best solution for the economic ills of America and the world was some form of democratic socialism. This led me to an interest in what was going on in Soviet Russia. I visited that country in 1932 and 1938 and found that it was making great economic and social progress. After my trip in 1938 I wrote: "It is my own feeling that the Soviet people are well-nigh invincible in an economic, moral and military sense. From without, Soviet socialism can undoubtedly be set back, but hardly destroyed." Very few Americans agreed with me.

When Nazi Germany attacked the USSR in June of 1941, I predicted that the Soviet Union would withstand the assault and defeat Hitler's legions. "The Soviets," I said, "will never yield. They will fight on their plains, they will fight in their cities, they will fight along their rivers, their lakes and their seas, till the trampling march of Nazi power dies away into the silence of history."

In 1942 George E. Sokolsky, a bitter anti-Soviet columnist on the *New York Sun*, stated: "So even those of us who are not given to seeing any good in Russia are faced by the very cold facts of the moment, and until we are proved right about our prognostications and doubts, we have to bow to such superior prophets as Corliss Lamont, who always said that the Bolshies would do it."

Yet, in regard to the development of Soviet democracy, I admittedly was not a superior prophet, but something of a wishful thinker ever longing for Utopia. I had thought for many years that the Soviet Union would steadily advance towards political democracy and that the dictatorship would gradually wither away. In 1974, however, fifty-seven years after the Communist Revolution of 1917, the Soviet Union still lags, lamentably, in the establishment of democratic procedures and in the implementation of the civil liberties guaranteed in its own creditable constitution.

My biggest mistake was to underestimate the extent of Stalin's terrible tyranny and to defend the Moscow Trials of 1936-38 as genuine. I was led astray here by my belief that hardened revolutionaries, such as the defendants in the Trials, could not be forced to make false confessions. Since Premier Nikita Khrushchev's speech to the Congress of the Soviet Communist Party in 1956, we can hardly doubt that the Trials constituted judicial frame-ups.

The lack of democracy in the Soviet Union and China need not and does not prevent the United States from cooperating in a number of ways with these countries, as President Nixon's policy of détente has clearly demonstrated. And if we are aware of historical relativity, we must realize that nations such as the USSR and China, which have had little or no tradition of political democracy, necessarily take a long time to develop democratic institutions. The same holds true of the underdeveloped countries of Africa, Asia and Latin America.

As columnist Max Lerner said in commenting on the Middle East and Southeast Asia: "The deeper truth is that most of the new Asian nations simply do not have the economic, political, administrative and social base on which a functioning democracy can yet be built. We are learning these days that a lasting democracy is the end-product of a long process of development, in which men learn in their daily lives to value and trust each other as equal persons, and leaders and admini-strators are trained to give them direction."(*New York Post,* October 3, 1959).

The future of democracy seems quite doubtful in the world at large. A Freedom House study released in January of 1973 found that two-thirds of the earth's people were "without freedom." On the whole African continent, the report pointed out, tiny Gambia, with a popula-tion of about 400,000, was the only country that possessed a fully func-tioning democracy. Later in 1973, both the Philippines and Chile changed from democratic republics into dictatorships. Chile had been one of the few nations in South America that had maintained demo-cratic institutions. In September a military junta violently overthrew the Chilean Government headed by President Salvador Allende, whose Administration had been attempting to establish a socialist economy. The junta immediately put into effect a reign of terror, in which thou-sands of Chilean liberals and leftists were executed. The right-wing coup in Chile inevitably raised the question as to whether full-fledged socialism could ever be achieved through peaceful and democratic means.

Democratic government has functioned most successfully in the Anglo-Saxon countries, especially Great Britain, and in Scandinavia. In the United States, democracy has been continually thwarted or negated by various large-scale violations. The greatest of these was the Civil War, when the Southern states took up arms rather than submit to the democratically arrived at enactments of the Federal Government regarding slavery. The preservation of free expression and civil liber-ties, as guaranteed in the United States Constitution with its Bill of Rights, is an integral part of the democratic process in America. Yet civil liberties have continually been tossed aside by the powers-that-be, especially during periods of hysteria such as that following World War I and the anticommunist witch-hunt led by Senator Joseph Mc-

Carthy in the 1950s.

The power of money in elections, corruption in government and disregard for the law by elected officials are other important factors in the subversion of American democracy. Notorious examples of government corruption have been exposed in the conduct of political machines and political bosses in some of our larger cities. However, the worst instance in our history of government actions that combine corruption and the flouting of law has been in the Watergate case and other misdeeds of the Nixon-Agnew Administration.

Another menace to American democratic institutions has been the unbridled and unconstitutional extension of executive power by our presidents since the end of World War II, particularly by Presidents Lyndon B. Johnson and Richard M. Nixon. These two Chief Executives went far beyond their constitutional prerogatives in waging and continuing the American war of aggression in Indochina—in both South and North Vietnam, in Cambodia, in Laos. Such conduct transforms the President of the United States into a semidictator in foreign affairs, able to involve the nation in wars without the approval of Congress.

Although our republic was founded almost two hundred years ago and has had the advantage of drawing upon the English democratic experience initiated in 1215 with the signing of the Magna Carta, my critique of American democracy shows how far we are from having attained the democratic ideal. Americans, then, should have some sense of humility and restraint in criticizing countries, underdeveloped in the art of politics, where evolution towards democracy is slow or even nonexistent. As our own shortcomings make clear, complete democracy is an ideal most difficult to achieve.

Yet I am optimistic about the future of democracy in the United States. The disclosure of the Watergate scandals, the prosecution of almost all the guilty parties, the repeated revelations pointing to Nixon's own involvement, the dismissal of the Pentagon Papers case against Daniel Ellsberg, the forced resignation of Vice-President Agnew, the open, unrepressed campaigns for President Nixon's impeachment or resignation—all these developments demonstrate that our democratic procedures and judicial institutions possess considerable efficacy in dealing with governmental crisis.

Like many other observers, however, it is my opinion that a parliamentary system such as that of Great Britain is more flexible than the American system, and better able to react speedily to changing situations. In Britain a prime minister who had been proved as dishonest and sinister as Richard Nixon would have been voted out by the House of Commons in short order. It is significant that the major democracies on the continent of Europe and elsewhere in the world have adopted some form of parliamentary government.

The history of politics in America shows a pervasive lack of decent ethical standards on the part of elected officials and large sections of the electorate itself. For every official who accepts a bribe there is at least one dishonest citizen who offered him the bribe. As a Humanist I wish to make clear that while I reject Christian theology, I accept much of the Judeo-Christian ethic as set forth in the Old and New Testaments. In America today we need nothing so much as a renewed allegiance to precepts of the Ten Commandments such as "Thou shalt not steal," "Thou shalt not bear false witness," and "Thou shalt not kill." In my writings I, for one, have not stressed sufficiently the cardinal importance of plain, simple old-fashioned honesty in every walk of life.

I have been discussing political democracy. But we must remember that there are also at least six other important forms of democracy: *racial or ethnic democracy,* wherein all racial or national minorities have equality with other ethnic groups in every sphere of life; *economic democracy,* which means the right of every adult to a useful job at a good wage and to a proportionate voice in the conduct of economic affairs; *organizational democracy,* that is, the implementation of democratic principles and practices in and by the thousands of non-governmental organizations, professional associations, trade unions, societies and committees that function in a country; *social democracy,* in which every person recognizes the inherent worth and dignity of every other person as a fellow citizen or member of the human family; *educational and cultural democracy,* which provides for the right of all children and adults to share equally in the educational and cultural, the artistic and intellectual life of the community; and *democracy between the sexes,* meaning equality between men and women in all relevant ways, and the freeing of the female sex from traditional discriminations and the operation of male chauvinism. All of these democracies I, as a Humanist and democrat, vigorously support and strive to bring into actuality.

Various people, especially newspaper columnists, have habitually tried to make a mystery out of my beliefs and actions owing to the fact that my father, Thomas W. Lamont, was a successful banker. But both my father and mother were warm, sympathetic, generous individuals who were liberals on most issues of importance and shared with me the aim of seeking the greatest good for the greatest number. Early in my youth my father told me, "The way to be happy is to make others happy." At the family dinner table I met and talked with such men as John Masefield, British Poet Laureate; H. G. Wells, author and socialist; Marshal Smuts, philosopher and Prime Minister of South Africa; and Lord Robert Cecil, English expert on the League of Nations. In a real sense, I have carried on in the spirit of my parents, though thinking their goals would be more likely achieved through leftist solutions.

My career has been neither unique nor remarkable. Throughout America and the world thousands, indeed tens of thousands, of sons and daughters from affluent capitalist families have in this twentieth century joined radical or liberal organizations to fight for progressive causes. All of us have endeavored to follow the dictates of reason in working out the best solutions for the enormous economic and political problems that confront humankind today. And in disagreeing with our elders we have exercised our precious freedom of choice (free will), rejecting the common assumption, stemming from philosophic determinism, that sons and daughters necessarily adopt the opinions of their parents.

In my own case, I deny that an Oedipus complex involving hate for my father, or other psychological complexes have been operative. Just as intellectual analysis over a number of years led me to adopt the philosophy of Humanism, to become active in the defense of civil liberties, and to work for international peace, so it was that reason induced me to believe that a planned socialist system was the best way out for the United States and the world. In my support of these various causes my emotions have, of course, been deeply involved because of my allegiance to the great overall aim of humanity's well-being. I have proceeded, then, on the basis of my intellect operating conjointly with my strong feeling of compassion for my fellow humans.

I have chosen *Voice in the Wilderness* as the title of this book, because during the greater part of my adult life I have been a dissenter on most of the important economic, political, philosophic and international issues. This means that usually I have sided with the minority and have been involved in constant controversy and struggle. I have always enjoyed a good debate and a good fight against the forces of evil. My successful battle against Senator Joseph McCarthy and his Senate investigating committee was surely one of the high points of my career and one of my happiest experiences.

When I appeared under subpoena before the McCarthy Committee in 1953, the Senator repeatedly implied in his questioning that I was some sort of secret communist, or a member of the Communist Party itself. Of course I had never even dreamed of joining the Communist Party, because I disagree with so much of its tactics and program. But the wacky charge that I was an undercover communist became widely accepted in the United States. Sometimes I merely laughed at the red-baiting, as when the reactionary columnist Westbrook Pegler wrote that I was "as red as a fire engine." And another columnist of the same breed, Benjamin DeCasseres, paid me the high compliment of assertng: "The 'intellectuals' from Plato to Karl Marx and Corliss Lamont are he bane, the pests of the human race." However, it was not funny vhen the communist smear led many radio and TV stations to perma-1ently blacklist me.

Despite many defeats in the campaigns and causes I have supported, remain optimistic about the future of America and of the human race. 'erhaps my optimism stems from a certain buoyancy of temperament. Thus I do not share the pessimism of such Humanists as Thomas Hardy 1nd A. E. Housman, although I agree with them that a large amount of tragedy and unhappiness is inherent in human existence. There is the bitter paradox of sex love, which can bring to men and women 3upreme happiness, but which so often explodes into heartache and 1nguish. And there are always death and dying, which inevitably cause 3train and sorrow.

While I do not believe in any kind of personal immortality, I think that the immortality of the human race is worthwhile and possible. Humankind's existence is threatened by the piling up of tremendous armaments that include nuclear weapons. However, I do not think that 1ny one of the chief nuclear-bomb Powers is going to be insane enough to start a nuclear war. Small wars may well go on for some time, but 3urely we possess sufficient intelligence and moral restraint to avoid another world war.

If man, then, does not destroy himself, he can probably live fairly comfortably upon this earth for billions of years into the future. Reli-able astrophysicists tell us that the sun will continue to radiate suf-ficient heat to maintain life for at least five billion years. When that time has passed, science may well be able to deal with the resulting 3roblem. Already scientists are talking of "artificial suns" that could revolve around the earth. And ultimately it is possible that human beings will be emigrating to other planets and solar systems.

In this Introduction I have stressed my reliance on reason or intelli-gence. And it is my belief that the essays in this book illustrate the method of intelligence in dealing with some of the fundamental prob-lems of America and mankind. I do not claim infallibility and admit-tedly have made serious mistakes in my conclusions from time to time. Be that as it may, I am still trying to think things through and to imple-ment in action the decisions I reach. And I am still a seeker after Utopia.

Corliss Lamont

New York City
April 1974

I

THE HUMANIST PHILOSOPHY

THE HUMANISTIC PHILOSOPHY

The Humanist Tradition

Twentieth-century Humanism is a philosophy which rejects all belief in the supernatural and which sets up as its supreme aim the happiness, freedom and progress of all humanity in this one and only life. No less important than the goals of Humanism are its *methods*; and it insists that in solving their problems men should rely upon the methods of reason, science and democracy.

It is sometimes thought that modern Humanism is a new and radical viewpoint which has no roots in the past of Western civilization. This is not true. For in the West there have been outstanding humanist thinkers and writers in every era. And the humanist tradition goes back at least as far as the Golden Age of Greek culture from the sixth through the fourth centuries B.C. In this tradition there are five main strands which Humanism tries to weave into an integrated whole. I shall describe them very briefly.

First, there is the contribution of philosophy as such. Here the two philosophies closely allied in thought with Humanism—naturalism and materialism—both stem from ancient Greece. Aristotle, who believed that nature constitutes the totality of things, was the first great naturalist and had no faith in either immortality or God as properly defined. In seventeenth-century Holland Spinoza revived the naturalism of Aristotle in a rigorously worked-out system based on the newly established facts and laws of fast-developing modern science. Like Aristotle, Spinoza brought in highly abstruse and redefined concepts of God and immortality, but they bore no similarity to the personal God and per-

Source: Basic Pamphlet, 1952.

sonal immortality of Christian theology.

We must remember that philosophers throughout history have constantly indulged in a drastic and frequently misleading redefinition of basic terms. Some thinkers have done this because they sincerely considered it intellectually justified; others clearly because they could avoid social, religious or political pressures, and perhaps even preserve their lives, by the strategy of using some of the time-honored words. I am convinced that one of the keys to Western thought is the well-known dictum: "All wise men have the same religion, but wise men never tell." The basic idea behind this saying is, of course, to be applied to all controversial fields, whether religion, philosophy, biology, economics, politics or anything else. And we know that today in America "wise men" are becoming more discreet than ever in giving public utterance to what they really believe.

In the twentieth century John Dewey has brought naturalism up to date and developed it in precise and scientific terms. He is the great contemporary philosopher of scientific method and actually knows more about the fundamental assumptions and implications of science in general than do most specialized scientists. Dewey has an enthusiastic and influential following among younger philosophers in the United States, although in Europe the tendency is to neglect or misunderstand him.

The general philosophy of materialism, stressing the fact that the foundation stuff of the universe is matter in motion, was also first formulated in ancient Greece. There the brilliant Democritus, the so-called laughing philosopher, propounded the theory that the ultimate constituents of existence are tiny atoms whirling through the void and interacting according to a definite causal sequence. As we know, science verified this general theory some 2300 years later. Epicurus, another Greek thinker, further developed the materialistic viewpoint, especially in an ethical sense; and Lucretius, the versatile philosopher-poet of ancient Rome, gave, in his *On the Nature of Things,* the greatest philosophical poem ever written, a detailed and fully rounded version of materialism.

The materialistic philosophers of the French Enlightenment, such as Diderot and Holbach, were too mechanical in their approach; but their errors were corrected by the dynamic or evolutionary materialism characteristic of nineteenth-century Germany and represented by Feuerbach and Marx. Marx, of course, called his philosophy dialectical materialism. In its general attitude towards the universe and the destiny of man, it is close to naturalism and Humanism; but Marxist materialism departs from these two philosophies in the radical economic and political views associated with it, as well as in its strict determinism and militant antireligious position.

The second strand in the humanist tradition comes from the great religions of mankind. Humanism is antitheological and antisupernatural, but it incorporates in its philosophy many of the ethical teachings of outstanding religious leaders like Jesus, Confucius and William Penn. Any humane philosophy must include such New Testament ideals as the brotherhood of man, peace on earth and the abundant life. There is much ethical wisdom, too, in the Old Testament and its Ten Commandments. Without accepting any ethical principle as a dogmatic dictum never to be questioned, the Humanist certainly adheres in general to a Biblical commandment such as, "Thou shalt not bear false witness against thy neighbor."

In the modern evolution of Christianity the Unitarians have come closest to the humanist viewpoint and in twentieth-century America have given considerable stimulus to the humanist cause. Many Unitarian ministers and churches in the United States definitely support Humanism. Like a number of other Humanists, these Unitarian Humanists call Humanism a *religion* rather than a philosophy. Another important religious group humanistic in outlook is the American Ethical Union, with separate Ethical Societies in New York, Brooklyn, St. Louis and other cities.

A third and most significant strand in Humanism is the scientific. The Humanist insists that his inclusive philosophy must be consistent throughout with the established facts and laws of science. Modern astronomy has of course blasted the old theory that man and his earth were the focal point of the universe in space and time. We know that our entire solar system represents only a tiny splotch of light in a great spiral nebula or galaxy containing some one hundred billion stars; and that throughout the infinitely vast cosmos there are billions of other such flaming galaxies. Nature, it seems, has no particular regard for man and is neutral towards his welfare and what he considers the good.

Modern physics has demonstrated that matter, far from being an inert and base substance as the ancients thought, is a thing of the most tremendous dynamism, complexity and potentiality. We need no supernatural intervention in terms of Divine creation and guidance to explain why such remarkable stuff has flowered into whirling suns and planets and life itself, including the human species. Modern biology comes to complete the story and to chart convincingly man's long evolution upward from lower forms of life and according to natural law. Death, instead of being man's greatest enemy, is seen in this picture to be as necessary a part of natural processes as birth, an essential factor in the evolution which produced the human race, and a basic condition for continuing progress and for giving future generations

5

their full chance to enjoy the sweetness of life.

Humanism believes that death marks the end of the conscious human individual and that therefore there is no personal immortality. The sciences of biology, psychology and medicine all lend support to this viewpoint by showing the intimate and inseparable relation between the human body and the human personality, which includes mind and memory. Body and personality are born together, they grow together, and they die together. The human being is an interfunctioning oneness of the body, mind and spirit which must attain its happiness and fulfillment in this world and not in some mythical realm beyond the grave.

More important for Humanism, however, than any scientific fact or series of facts is the modern scientific *method* of experimentation and verification. The Humanist claims that scientific method represents reason or intelligence at its most precise; and that men should rely upon it as the best way of solving their individual, social and international problems. This method judges whether an idea is true or not in terms of its *consequences,* and it applies to the sphere of ethical decision as well as to all other fields of human conduct. True scientific method forswears dogmatism and always leaves the door open for new facts and sounder reasoning to prove that some currently accepted view is wrong.

It is scientific method, too, which has brought about the invention of the machine and the enormous development of modern technology. This machine technology in industry, agriculture and the arts of communication has made possible the attainment of the humanist aim of an abundant life, both material and cultural, for all people in every nation. But the achievement of this goal may be immeasurably set back by worldwide atomic war and ruin caused by the failure of statesmen and governments to carry over into international affairs the cool and objective procedures of reason and science.

Enriching the humanist tradition, fourth, are the contributions of literature and art. Again, we start with ancient Greece and note that the leading dramatists—Aeschylus, Aristophanes, Euripides and Sophocles—wrote in a distinctly humanist vein. From the Bible, viewed as literature, we take two great humanist documents, *The Song of Solomon,* with its superb love passages, and *Ecclesiastes,* with its central theme of enjoying life to the full while one is able, even though all human happiness and achievement seem transient.

Passing quickly to modern times, we find much of a humanist nature in the work of the bold, witty, all-encompassing Voltaire in eighteenth-century France. In England of the nineteenth century the militant genius of Shelley denounced in verse the evils of religious supernaturalism and gave us a magnificent humanist poem in *Prometheus Unbound*. Shelley, too, together with Keats, Byron and Wordsworth, constituted a school of English Nature poets outstanding in the history of literature. These poets all stressed the beauty and splendor of the external world—a motif most important in the humanist philosophy. In nineteenth-century America Bryant and Whitman also wrote memorable nature poetry, while today Robert Frost is the foremost figure in his field.

In his *Earth Is Enough* the American poet Edwin Markham put into simple language the key ideas of Humanism. Thus the poem starts:

> We men of Earth have here the stuff
> Of Paradise—we have enough!
> We need no other stones to build
> The Temple of the Unfulfilled—
> No other ivory for the doors—
> No other marble for the floors—
> No other cedar for the beam
> And dome of man's immortal dream.

There have been many novelists who in general have supported a humanist position in their writings. In England this was true of George Eliot, Thomas Hardy, John Galsworthy and H. G. Wells; in America, of Theodore Dreiser and Sinclair Lewis. In France after the middle of the nineteenth century the names of Gustave Flaubert, Émile Zola, Alphonse Daudet, Guy de Maupassant and Anatole France stand out as preeminently humanist. The great German novelist, Thomas Mann, has repeatedly affirmed his humanist beliefs.

In the sphere of music Beethoven's Fifth Symphony, portraying the triumph of man over fate, and his Ninth Symphony, assertive of the brotherhood of man, are humanist in spirit. And Wagner treats of a central humanist concept in his series of operas *The Ring of the Nibelung*, which tells the story of disintegrating godhead and humanity supplanting it. The final opera of the tetralogy, *The Twilight of the Gods*, brings this theme to a dramatic culmination as Valhalla crashes down in flames. In sculpture, the stirring statuary of the Frenchman Auguste Rodin perhaps brings out best the humanist affirmation of the radiant actualities of life on earth. In painting, the most effective expression of the humanist attitude is to be found, I believe, in the incomparable murals of the Mexican painters Orozco, Siqueiros and Rivera. They have done some of their best work in the United States.

The fifth strand in the humanist tradition, and absolutely essential to it, is the idea of democracy and democratic procedures as developed down the ages. Here again we start with ancient Greece, where Athenian democracy, even though it was severely limited in scope, laid down some of the main patterns. After the downfall of the Greek city-states the idea and practice of democracy fell pretty much into disuse until the modern era. Following the American Revolution of 1776 and the French Revolution of 1789, democracy again came into its own, particularly in the new American Republic. In the American Bill of Rights the Humanist sees the greatest state document on free speech and civil liberties in history.

The humanist insistence on democracy necessarily follows from its stress on the use of reason and scientific method. For reason and science cannot reach their full flower unless they are able to develop in a democratic atmosphere where it is understood disagreements will be settled through the competition of ideas in the marketplace and through resort to the ballot box instead of violence. The scientific method constantly encourages the trying out of new ideas and the questioning of the most basic assumptions in every field. It therefore demands a completely democratic society where all thinkers can feel free to dissent without fear of reprisals from fellow citizens, the government or private organizations.

Humanism's supreme goal of the welfare of all mankind requires democratic institutions and attitudes, not only in one's own country, but also throughout the world. In this progressive age the humanist concept of democracy includes not only *political* democracy, but likewise *racial* democracy, and equality for women everywhere. Humanists are militantly opposed to discrimination or prejudice on the grounds of race, color or physiognomy. Such discrimination and prejudice, often leading to horrible persecution and outright slaughter, are among the vilest attributes of the fascist state.

I have tried to give a compact summary of the chief elements that make up the long and illustrious humanist traditon in philosophy. Naturally I have been able to mention only the highlights in this venerable tradition. Humanism is frankly eclectic and incorporates in its overall viewpoint whatever relevant truths it can discover in other philosophies or in any realm whatsoever of human thought and cultural achievement. Most of the persons mentioned in my summary were not complete and consistent Humanists in my sense of the word; nor did they use the term "humanist" to describe their position. Nonetheless, because of what they actually thought and wrote, they can legitimately be placed in the humanist tradition. By the very nature of their beliefs, Humanists feel not only a sympathetic association and intellectual bond with millions of their fellowmen today, but also with many of the eminent thinkers, writers and artists of the past.

In my judgment Humanism, presenting an inclusive, consistent and scientifically based view of man and the universe, is a philosophy peculiarly appropriate to the mature and inquiring modern mind. Although neither now nor at any future time can there be any finality in the humanist synthesis, it will always remain, I believe, a philosophy that appeals to intelligent and socially minded persons and that tends to bring unity among the different nations and races of mankind.

Naturalistic Humanism

Humanism is such a warm and attractive word that in the twentieth century it has been adopted by various groups, often diametrically opposed in ideology. Some usages of this term are most questionable. For instance, the Catholics, who still adhere to many outworn myths of Christian supernaturalism, promote what they call Catholic Humanism; while the communists, who reject in practice political democracy and civil liberties, continually talk of socialist Humanism. But the Humanism that has become increasingly influential in this century, in English-speaking countries and throughout the noncommunist world, is naturalistic Humanism. This is the Humanism that I have supported through the written and spoken word for some forty years.

To define naturalistic Humanism in a nutshell: it rejects all forms of supernaturalism, pantheism and metaphysical idealism, and considers man's supreme ethical aim as working for the welfare of all humanity in this one and only life, using the methods of reason, science and democracy for the solution of problems.

To become more specific, I shall enumerate the chief elements in my understanding of Humanism.

First, Humanism believes that nature or the universe makes up the totality of existence and is completely self-operating according to natural law, with no need for a God or gods to keep it functioning. This cosmos, unbounded in space and infinite in time, consists fundamentally of a constantly changing system of matter and energy, and is neutral in regard to man's well-being and values.

Source: The Humanist, *September/October 1971.*

Second, Humanism holds that the race of man is the present culmination of a time-defying evolutionary process on this planet that has lasted billions of years, that man exists as an inseparable unity of mind and body, and that therefore after death there can be no personal immortality or survival of consciousness.

Third, in working out its basic views on man and the universe, Humanism relies on reason, and especially on the established facts, laws and methods of modern experimental science. In general, men's best hope for solving their problems is through the use of intelligence and scientific method applied with vision and determination. Courage, love and perseverance provide emotional drive for successfully coping with difficulties, but it is reason that finds the actual solution. Science and technology are to be considered instruments for the service of mankind and must always be controlled in the light of ecological, ethical, economic and other values.

Fourth, Humanism is opposed to all theories of universal determinism, fatalism or predestination, and believes that human beings possess genuine freedom of choice (free will) in making decisions both important and unimportant. Free choice is conditioned by inheritance, education, health, the external environment (including economic conditions) and other factors. Nonetheless, it remains real and substantial. Humanism rejects alike Christian theistic determinism, Marxist economic determinism and the determinism of the behaviorist psychologists. It places on the human individual full responsibility for his decisions and actions.

Fifth, Humanism advocates an ethics or morality that grounds all human values in this-earthly experiences and relationships, and that views man as a functioning unity of physical, emotional and intellectual faculties. The Humanist holds as his highest ethical goal the this-worldly happiness, freedom and progress—economic, cultural and material—of all mankind, irrespective of nation, race, religion, sex or economic status. Reserving the word "love" for his family and friends, he has an attitude of compassionate concern towards his fellowmen in general.

Sixth, in the controversial realm of sex relations, Humanism entirely rejects dualistic theories that separate soul from body and claim that the highest morality is to keep the soul pure and undefiled from physical pleasure and desire. The Humanist regards sexual emotions and their fulfillment as healthy, beautiful and nature's wonderful way of making possible the continued reproduction of the human race. While Humanism advocates high standards of conduct between the sexes, it rejects the puritanism of the past and looks upon sex love and sex pleasure as among the greatest of human experiences and values.

Seventh, Humanism believes that the good life is best attained by an individual's combining the more personal satisfactions with significant work and other activities that contribute to the welfare of one's city, nation, university, trade union or other social unit. Worthwhile work is likely to make a person happier. At the same time everyone must exercise a considerable amount of self-interest, if only to keep alive and healthy. Normal and legitimate self-interest can be harmoniously united with ethical idealism and altruistic endeavors on behalf of the community.

Eighth, Humanism supports the widest possible development of the arts and the awareness of beauty, so that the aesthetic experience may become a pervasive reality in the life of man. The Humanist eschews the artificial distinction between the fine arts and the useful arts and asserts that the common objects of daily use should embody a fusion of utility and grace. The mass production of industrial goods by machinery need not necessarily defeat this aim. Among other things, and particularly in America, Humanism calls for the planned architectural reconstruction of towns and cities, so that beauty may prevail in our urban life. (In other countries, Humanism cries out against destructive reconstruction.)

Ninth, Humanism gives special emphasis to man's appreciation of the beauty and splendor of nature. The Humanist energetically backs the widespread efforts for conservation, the extension of park areas and the protection of wildlife. Long before sound ecology and anti-pollution measures became widely accepted as national goals, he was campaigning for these very things. The Humanist's keen responsiveness to every sort of natural beauty evokes in him a feeling of profound kinship with nature and its myriad forms of life.

Tenth, for the actualization of human happiness and freedom everywhere on earth, Humanism advocates the establishment of international peace, democracy and a high standard of living throughout the world. Humanists, in their concern for the welfare of all nations, peoples and races, adopt William Lloyd Garrison's aphorism "Our country is the world; our countrymen are all mankind." It follows that Humanists are strongly opposed to all forms of racial and nationalist prejudice. Humanism is international in spirit and scope, as evidenced by the activities of the International Humanist and Ethical Union.

Eleventh, Humanism believes that the best type of government is some form of political democracy, which includes civil liberties and full freedom of expression throughout all areas of economic, political and cultural life. Reason and science are crippled unless they remain unfettered in the pursuit of truth. In the United States, the Humanist vigorously supports the democratic guarantees in the Bill of Rights and the Constitution.

Twelfth, Humanism, in accordance with scientific method, encourages the unending questioning of basic assumptions and convictions in every field of thought. This includes, of course, philosophy, naturalistic Humanism and the twelve points I have presented in this attempt at definition. Humanism is not a new dogma, but is a developing philosophy ever open to experimental testing, newly discovered facts and more rigorous reasoning.

I do not claim that every Humanist will accept all the twelve points I have suggested. There will be particular disagreement, I imagine, on the fourth point; that is, the one concerning free choice.

Not every Humanist wants to use the phrase "naturalistic Humanism." Some prefer the term "scientific Humanism," "secular Humanism" or "democratic Humanism." There is also a large group who consider Humanism a religion and who therefore prefer the phrase "religious Humanism." For my own part, I prefer to call naturalistic Humanism a philosophy or way of life.

The Philosophic Needs of Today:
The Humanist Answer

Unquestionably what most distinguishes the modern era from all past eras in human history is the development and extension of experimental science over the last four hundred years. Science and scientific method have enormously extended the boundaries of knowledge and have given to twentieth-century man unprecedented powers for both good and evil. Unfortunately, the philosophic and ethical growth of modern man has not kept pace with the rapid evolution of science.

We can gain some understanding of the enormous changes wrought by modern science by looking at its impact in various specific fields.

Astronomy. The prescientific view was that of a neighborly bandbox universe, created quite recently by the Almighty, in which the earth was the center of things with the sun and other stars revolving around it. Copernicus, Galileo and their successors utterly reversed this conception and showed that the earth revolves around the sun; that the sun is just a minor star toward the edge of the great galaxy we know as the Milky Way; that this galaxy is but one of millions and perhaps billions of immense star clusters or nebulae scattered throughout a cosmos of stupendous dimensions; and that galaxies, stars, sun and the earth itself are the result of an evolutionary process lasting over billions of years.

Physics. The prescientific view was that matter was a base, inert and uncreative thing. Modern physics has proved, however, that matter in its every manifestation is made up of unceasingly active units of restless energy. It is a dynamic substance full of complexity, versatility and

Source: *American Humanist Association Pamphlet, 1957.*

potentiality, as atomic research has more and more demonstrated in recent times. And we can no longer consider it mysterious that life and finally human beings should have arisen out of such altogether remarkable stuff.

Biology. The prescientific view, and the orthodox Christian conception until the second half of the nineteenth century, was that a supernatural God brought into being all the myriad forms of life upon this planet through a great magnanimous act of miraculous creation. Modern biology, with Charles Darwin as its outstanding figure, has demonstrated that man and all the higher species have evolved over aeons of time from lower forms of life; and that the relatively greater complexity of the brain, and especially the cerebral cortex, in man has led to the incomparable faculty of human thought.

Psychology. The prescientific view, still widely held today, was that man is a dualistic compound of physical organism and some sort of supernatural soul, including the mind, that entered the body at the moment of conception. The science of psychology has found increasing evidence that the human being is an *inseparable* unity of body on the one hand and personality (soul) and mind on the other. The personality and mind are functions of a physical organism of prodigious intricacy, its multitudinous parts adjusted to one another to the last degree of nicety and its billions upon billions of cells normally working together in perfect harmony. A mysterious soul from out of the blue is completely unnecessary and superfluous to explain the marvelous powers and accomplishments of the human mind-body in action.

Medicine. Relics of the prescientific era remained in the discipline of medicine for a long time. For example, well into the nineteenth century it was commonly accepted that insanity and hysteria were caused by devils and demons entering into the human frame. The science of medicine today has banished all such conceptions of intervening supernatural agencies. Likewise it has gotten away from traditional religious controls that prevented the use of anesthetics or the practice of dissection on the vague ground that they were contrary to the will of God.

Machine Techniques. The prescientific era could hardly conceive of a life of abundance for the masses of the people because the necessary instrumentalities of economic production and distribution did not exist. With the advance of science, a multitude of labor-saving inventions and intricate machines came into being and changed the face of the globe. Today we can safely state that mankind possesses the scientific and mechanical means to create a relatively high standard of living for every nation.

Method of Solving Problems. In the prescientific era men in general and most philosophers relied upon such methods as revelation, authority, intuition, prayer, divination or magic for the solution of individual and group problems. These procedures were obviously inadequate and untrustworthy. Now, the most important thing of all that modern science has brought to mankind is a reliable method of discovering the truth: the method of painstaking checking up on any idea or hypothesis by experiment and verification. This *is* modern scientific method. And it is nothing more nor less than human reason at its best and most precise, unaided and unimpeded by any alleged supernatural sources.

Social Sciences. Since the prescientific era, modern scientific method has attained its most notable success in the natural sciences and has not yet reached adequate precision and objectivity in the social sciences. The greatest need for the present critical period in human affairs is to carry over scientific attitudes and methods into the social sciences of economics, government, sociology and international relations. The lag between the natural and social sciences, and the application of intelligence and scientific method to social problems, is dramatically brought out by mankind's failure to control adequately the atomic energy which the advance of nuclear physics has made available.

As human civilization becomes more and more mature, it discards philosophic and religious myths which may have been useful in the childhood of the race but which can no longer be accepted by informed and intelligent persons. Those who have vested emotional, ideological or economic interests in outworn ideas naturally resisted the social *shedding* process which is essential to human growth and progress.

Happiness and progress, for the individual and society, are dependent upon the courage and intelligence which human beings demonstrate in continuously adjusting themselves to changing conditions and making use of the growing stores of knowledge and new scientific techniques. Millions of Americans fall short here because, while utilizing constantly the complicated machines and technological devices which science has made possible, they refuse to apply real scientific methods to their daily existence and to the formidable social and international problems that face them.

At the same time they fail to bring their philosophy or religion up to date by making it consistent all the way through with scientific fact and method. Yet they cannot give assent to the old beliefs based on prescientific concepts. So it is that multitudes of people, having lost the faith of their forebears, today wander uncertainly in a no-man's-land of doubt and distress over the ultimate problems of existence.

Humanism provides adequate solutions for these problems and satisfies the philosophic needs of today.

PHILOSOPHIC NEEDS OF THE MATURE MAN OF TODAY

First, the mature man of today, like the man of yesterday and tomorrow, needs a clear and consistent view of the universe, of human nature and of society, an inclusive and integrated philosophy or way of life which, like the great religions of the past, will pull together the various strands of his personality and give him a great purpose to work for beyond petty personal desires.

Humanism offers such a philosophy. It organizes into a compelling and consistent whole the chief elements of philosophic, religious and scientific truth in the past and present and dedicates itself to the full-hearted affirmation of life upon this earth. It is a dynamic philosophy of joyous service for the greater good of humanity in this natural world and according to the methods of reason and democracy.

Second, the mature man of today needs a philosophy which he can accept intellectually and which is completely consistent with the facts and principles of science. Furthermore, it must be a philosophy which weaves together the relevant materials from the major branches of science and constructs a broad overarching synthesis which is understandable by the average person.

Humanism is such a philosophy. It draws constantly on both the natural sciences and the social sciences, as well as on religion, art and literature. And while never closing the door to fresh knowledge, it has dared to construct a comprehensive philosophical system and to give a definite answer on the main issues in philosophy. Moreover, the chief points in Humanism can be simply phrased and are by no means difficult to understand.

Third, the mature man of today needs a philosophy which has grown beyond the outworn beliefs in supernatural beings and forces that supposedly control the course of nature and the destiny of humanity, beyond the naive faith in gods who interfere by means of miracles in the cause-effect sequences of natural law or who provide some sort of cosmic guarantee for the ultimate triumph of man and his values.

Humanism is such a philosophy. It believes in a naturalistic cosmology or metaphysics or attitude towards the universe that rules out all forms of the supernatural and that regards nature as the totality of being and as a constantly changing system of events existing independently of any mind or consciousness. There is no room in this picture for a properly defined Divine Providence.

Fourth, the mature man of today needs a philosophy which forthightly repudiates the otherworldliness of the past that set up salvation in a realm beyond the grave as the chief end of human life and called upon men to deny many of their most wholesome impulses and potentialities in order to keep their souls pure and undefiled for existence after death.

Humanism presents such a philosophy. Drawing especially upon the facts of science, it believes that man is an evolutionary product of the great nature of which he is part and that he is an inseparable unity of body and personality having no individual personal immortality. It claims that human thinking is as natural as walking or breathing and is indivisibly conjoined with the functioning of the brain. Humanism insists that the true good of man is a greater and greater enjoyment of happiness and beauty during his one and only life.

Fifth, the mature man of today needs a philosophy which no longer relies on prayer to an Almighty or revelation from some supernatural source for the solution of human problems. He requires a true and tested method of problem-solving which is thoroughly objective in its approach and which can be applied fruitfully to every field of human endeavor.

Humanism includes such a method, the method of reason and modern science that has already so enormously enlarged mankind's range of knowledge and control over the external world. Humanism believes that this method gives man the power and potentiality of solving his own problems successfully, whether in the realm of the natural sciences or in such fields as economics, sociology, international relations and ethics. Literally infinite are the possible achievements of human intelligence working on behalf of both the individual and society.

Sixth, the mature man of today needs a philosophy which, while recognizing fully the role of natural law upon this earth and throughout the universe, does not go to the extreme of contending that the existence of universal causality takes away from human beings their freedom of choice.

Humanism offers such a philosophy. It believes, in opposition to all theories of universal predestination, determinism or fatalism, that human beings possess true freedom of creative action and are, within reasonable limits, the masters of their own destiny. The human mind enables men to stand aside temporarily from the flux of existence, to reflect upon the different possibilities of action and to make genuine decisions where significant alternatives exist.

Seventh, the mature man of today needs a philosophy which is fully awake to the myriad forms of beauty and which stimulates the individual both to create and to enjoy art and literature.

Humanism responds to this need by helping to make the aesthetic experience a pervasive reality in the life of men. It believes that this experience properly includes the appreciation of external nature in all its beauty and magnificence and wonder. The humanist attitude leads to a feeling of kinship with the cosmos, of at-homeness upon this earth and in this universe where we live and move and have our being.

Eighth, the mature man of today needs a philosophy which, while rejecting any moral system based on supernaturalistic standards and hopes, presents an ethics inclusive of the highest ideals of past and present and one that continually grows in the light of new experience and knowledge. This ethics must also make provision for the emotional life of men and for their psychological security.

Humanism fulfills this need by setting up as the supreme ethical loyalty the this-worldly happiness, freedom and progress—economic, cultural and spiritual—of all mankind, irrespective of nation, race or religion. It embodies in its synthesis the relevant ethical teachings of great religious teachers like Jesus and Confucius. And it declares that human beings cooperating loyally together for common ends can feel a mutual warmth and solidarity that will stand them in good stead in the inevitable crises of living.

Humanism insists, furthermore, that each individual, in establishing his ethical standards and working out ethical problems, should not only exercise social sympathy and altruism but also follow strictly the method of intelligence. *For Humanism, neither the good heart nor the keen mind in itself is enough; good heart and keen mind must always function together for the attainment of the best.*

Ninth, the mature man of today needs a philosophy which offers a concrete prospectus for the achievement of human welfare on behalf of the individual, the nation and mankind.

Humanism provides such a philosophy. It believes in a far-reaching social program that stands for the establishment throughout the world of peace and democracy on the foundations of a flourishing and cooperative economic order, both national and international. It is convinced that the greater use of reason and scientific method in public affairs entails a much larger degree of social-economic planning, and on the international scene, of course, much closer cooperation between governments and peoples in such organizations as the United Nations. Humanism considers that in this twentieth-century world resort to violence for the settlement of disputes either within a nation or between nations constitutes a failure of both intelligence and morality.

Tenth, the mature man of today, while willing to strike out on bold new paths, prefers a philosophy which has some tradition behind it and which can summon some of the illustrious minds of the past in its support.

Humanism is such a philosophy, although few apparently realize this point. Since the philosophies of naturalism and materialism are closely akin to Humanism in their general outlook, we can consider their adherents as coming within the humanist tradition. So it is that in this tradition we roughly include great naturalists such as Aristotle in ancient Greece, Spinoza in seventeenth-century Europe, and John Dewey in twentieth-century America; and great materialists such as Democritus in ancient Greece, Lucretius in ancient Rome, Diderot in the French Enlightenment and George Santayana in contemporary thought. A number of eminent poets, novelists and dramatists have also made signal contributions to the humanist tradition. Humanism, then, while a minority viewpoint in every country and culture until this century, possesses one of the most vital and impressive traditions in the history of philosophy.

The preceding ten points constitute a brief, compact summary of the philosophy of naturalistic and scientific Humanism. Elsewhere I have given a more detailed treatment of this viewpoint, together with its historic background and its far-reaching implications for the present and future of the human race.

The philosophy of Humanism, or religion, as some choose to call it, enables the mature man of today to face the contemporary world with intellectual integrity and spiritual assurance; to enjoy wholeheartedly all the sweetness of living, all the simple pleasures of daily existence, all the manifold experiences that art and culture and science bring; and at the same time to give generously of himself on behalf of the on-going progress of his community, his country and humanity.

New Light on Dewey's *Common Faith*

John Dewey published his only book on religion, *A Common Faith* (Yale University Press, 1934), when he was seventy-five years of age. It was a short but pithy volume that outlined a new faith for modern man and that was severely critical of traditional religion because of its dependence on supernatural beliefs, theological dogmas and institutional rigidities. The book gave rise to considerable controversy, not only on account of its unorthodox approach, but also owing to a certain ambiguity in some of Dewey's formulations. In this article I intend to present unpublished materials that will throw fresh light on the debate that has continued for twenty-five years about Dewey, God and religion.

In his opening chapter, entitled "Religion versus the Religious," Dewey explains in some detail why he prefers the term "religious" to "religion." He writes: "The moment that we have a religion, whether that of the Sioux Indian or of Judaism or Christianity, that moment the ideal factors in experience that may be called religious take on a load not inherent in them, a load of current beliefs and institutional practices that are irrelevant to them. . . . It is conceivable that the present depression in religion is closely connected with the fact that religions now prevent, because of their weight of historic encumbrances, the religious quality of experience from coming to consciousness and find-

Source: The Journal of Philosophy, *Vol. LVIII, No. 1, January 5, 1961. This article is based on a lecture given by the author on November 19, 1959, in the University of Vermont John Dewey Centennial series.*

ing the expression that is appropriate to present conditions, intellectual and moral." (pp. 8-9).

Religious faith itself Dewey describes in ethical terms as "the unification of the self through allegiance to inclusive ideal ends, which imagination presents to us and to which the human will responds as worthy of controlling our desires and choices. . . . Understanding and knowledge also enter into a perspective that is religious in quality. Faith in the continued disclosing of truth through directed cooperative human endeavor is more religious in quality than is any faith in a completed revelation." (pp. 33, 26). Intelligent human action, Dewey points out, utilizing the available social forces and the experimental methods of modern science, is ever attempting to transform the ideal into the actual.

"It is," he states, "this *active* relation between ideal and actual to which I would give the name 'God.' " (p. 51). This is the new definition of God that has for a quarter of a century confounded equally the philosophers, the theologians, the clergymen, the educators, the students and the common man. I must admit that I, too, was confused for a while.

Expanding on his definition, Dewey goes on to say: "Whether one gives the name 'God' to this union, operative in thought and action, is a matter for individual decision. . . . I would not insist that the name *must* be given. There are those who hold that the associations of the term with the supernatural are so numerous and close that any use of the word 'God' is sure to give rise to misconception and be taken as a concession to traditional ideas." (pp. 51-52).

The qualms expressed in this last sentence were abundantly justified. No sooner had *A Common Faith* appeared in the spring of 1934 than a flood of misconceptions and misinterpretations swept philosophic and religious circles. Each reviewer and commentator gave his own opinion of what Dewey meant by the word "God," and naturally there was drastic disagreement. Protestant ministers and theologians tended to welcome Dewey as a new convert to theism, and the well-known religious journal *The Christian Century* ran a whole symposium titled "Is John Dewey a Theist?" with Dewey himself taking part.

In this lively discussion Dr. Henry Nelson Wieman, who has probably produced more redefinitions of deity than any other living person, insists that Dewey's definition locates in nature a power not ourselves that is concerned with furthering man's quest for ideal ends. Dr. Erwin A. Aubrey soberly disagrees and shows that Dewey is referring only to the power of creative human intelligence in the actualization of ideals, with reliance, of course, on scientific laws and techniques that enable man to use *some* processes in nature for his own advantage. In the

symposium Dewey himself explicitly supports Dr. Aubrey's interpretation.

In fact, Dewey believed that the cosmos as a whole is neutral
towards human aims and values, and suggested merely that "God" may
be a fitting term to sum up those activities of men that, turning to account certain forces in nature and society, seek to bring into being the
totality of human ideals. And he was perfectly clear that each individual must decide for himself whether he wishes to adopt this idea of
God. Now the question inevitably arises as to whether John Dewey was
himself incorporating this redefinition of God into his system.

Here again a hot controversy has raged over the years. Some of
Dewey's most brilliant students, able philosophers themselves, have
given an affirmative answer. I refer particularly to Professor Edwin A.
Burtt of Cornell in his book *Types of Religious Philosophy*, Professor
George R. Geiger of Antioch in *John Dewey in Perspective*, and Professor Sidney Hook of New York University in *John Dewey: An Intellectual Portrait*.

Professors Geiger and Hook express some misgivings as to Dewey's
wisdom in taking over the word "God." Dr. Hook writes: "There are so
many misconceptions of Dewey's philosophy it seems a pity that his
language at this point should invite more." (*John Dewey: An Intellectual Portrait*, New York: John Day, 1939, p. 221). But none of these
scholars seems to doubt that Dewey, whose main work on metaphysics, *Experience and Nature,* did not even include the word "God" in the
index, had finally brought into his system a naturalistic interpretation
of deity.

I myself became increasingly skeptical on this point, and, since
Dewey did not resolve the matter in *The Christian Century* symposium,
I accordingly initiated a correspondence with him on the subject on
May 8, 1935. On May 27 he responded to my inquiry in a letter that
states: "What I still don't get about your reaction to my book . . . and
the same is true of reviews from the conventional religious angle—is
why there is so much more concern about the word 'God' and so little
attention to that which I said was a reality to which the word *might* be
applied."

On July 28 I answered Dewey's note as follows: "You ask why both
myself and the church people gave so much attention to your use of
the word 'God' in *A Common Faith*. I think it was because this was the
unexpected thing in the book, the point that gave it news value, as it
were. Everybody knew that you were opposed to supernaturalism and
the old-time religion. But your support of 'God,' at least as a word—
that was new and startling. . . . The parsons . . . saw in your definition
of 'God' their one chance to make capital out of you on behalf of *their*

religion. The discussion in *The Christian Century* showed this, as well as reviews by such intelligent theologians as Reinhold Niebuhr."

On August 16 Dewey replied from his summer place at Hubbards, Nova Scotia: "Thanks for your note which explained something I hadn't been able to understand. I suppose one of the first things I learned in grammar was the difference between *will* and *shall*, and the consequent difference between *would* and *should*. But nevertheless I made a bad slip which accounts for the fact that you thought I was making a recommendation. The meaning in my mind was essentially: If the word 'God' is used, this is what it *should* stand for; I didn't have a recommendation in mind beyond the proper use of a word." And in a further comment Dewey adds: "I got my auxiliary verbs mixed."

Now isn't it splendid to know that John Dewey, the founder of our much-maligned progressive education, believed in grammar? But let us go back and look again at the key sentence Mr. Dewey and I were talking about: "It is this *active* relation between the ideal and actual to which I would give the name 'God.'" Dewey says the "would" ought to have been "should," so that the meaning he assigns here to "God" is merely a recommendation for a proper definition. It is as if I told my young niece that a centaur is to be defined as a horse with a human head. This statement would not imply that I thought centaurs actually existed, or that I was making "centaur" a significant word in my philosophy.

Dewey did not ascribe the same importance as I to the issue I have been raising about "God." In his final communication to me on the subject, May 23, 1941, he chides me for "squeamishness" about the use of the word "God," and states: "I think it important to help many people to realize that they can save what it actually meant to them free from superstitious elements."

To sum up, I feel justified in asserting that Dewey's letters to me constitute decisive evidence for settling the long argument as to his use of the term "God." He did not incorporate that word into his "common faith" or into his philosophy, as outstanding naturalist philosophers have often done—Aristotle and Spinoza, for example—to the lasting befuddlement of their readers for centuries, and indeed right down to the present day. John Dewey was not, then, in any sense a theist, but an uncompromising naturalist or humanist thinker, who saw the value of a shared religious faith free from outworn supernaturalism and institutional fanaticism.

It is no mere quibbling over words when we try to assign correct and unequivocal definitions for basic terms in a philosophy or religious faith. I like that old Chinese proverb, "The beginning of wisdom is calling things by their right names." In a real sense the whole philosophic enterprise starts with what various thinkers have called the ethics of words, or, as Dewey himself phrased it, "the integrity of language."

Furthermore, the facts of life compel us to realize that the competition between different philosophies and religions is so keen that those whom I would describe as the fundamentalists or traditionalists are forever trying to claim for their camp eminent persons who actually belong in some other ideological camp. In an article, "John Dewey in Retrospect," in *The Christian Century* of September 30, 1959, Professor Arthur W. Munk of Albion College repeats the mistakes about John Dewey and God to which I have called attention. He asserts that Dewey believed in a God that is "an impersonal, value-producing process" in nature, and even ascribes to Dewey a "theology." Such interpretations point up the danger of Dewey's being written down as another notable philosopher who came around to theism in his old age. (See also "The Faith of John Dewey," by Professor Nolan Pliny Jacobson, in *The Journal of Religion,* July 1960.)

It is relevant at this point to ask what we should *call* the faith for mature and intelligent men that John Dewey presented. Merely to term it, in his own words, "a common faith," leaves it too vague to appeal to the common man. I don't think he would have cared for the term "Deweyism," and we know he did not like the word "religion." Perhaps he would have accepted the formula "a way of life." Yet that, too, is rather vague.

This semantic problem leads me to cite another exchange in my correspondence with Professor Dewey. On August 30, 1940, I wrote him: "Since in 1933 you signed the *Humanist Manifesto* . . . I am wondering why you have not used the word 'Humanism' more to describe your own philosophy. Though I realize this term 'Humanism' is open to misconception, it is certainly far less formidable for the average person, whom you wish philosophy to reach, than the term Pragmatism or Instrumentalism or even Naturalism. And of course these latter words have also given rise to plenty of misunderstanding."

A week later, on September 6, Dewey answered me from Northport, Long Island: "There is a great difference between different kinds of 'Humanism,' as you know; there is that of Paul Elmer More, for example. I signed the humanistic manifesto . . . because it had a religious context, and my signature was a sign of sympathy on that score, and not a commitment to every clause in it.

"'Humanism,' as a technical philosophy is associated with Schiller; and while I have a great regard for his writings, it seems to me that he gave Humanism an unduly subjectivistic turn. He was so interested in bringing out the elements of human desire and purpose neglected in traditional philosophy that he tends . . . to a virtual isolation of man

27

from the rest of nature.

"I have come to think of my own position as cultural or humanistic Naturalism. Naturalism, properly interpreted, seems to me a more adequate term than Humanism. Of course I have always limited my use of 'instrumentalism' to my theory of thinking and knowledge; the word 'pragmatism' I have used very little, and then with reserves."

Deciding to argue a bit with my revered teacher, I mailed Dewey another and longer letter on September 12 in which I said: "Though Naturalism is probably clearer to professional philosophers, it is certainly confusing to the average person, who considers a Naturalist one who, like John Burroughs, makes a specialty of birds and flowers. Also, since Humanism as a word has real warmth and on the face of it indicates concern with humanity, I firmly believe that it would be more appealing and intelligible to the plain man. . . . You have always been in favor of bringing philosophy out of the confines of academic discussion and university circles so that it would mean something to the ordinary citizen. And I think you would have the best possible chance of succeeding in this aim with your own philosophy by calling it 'Humanism' or perhaps 'naturalistic Humanism.'

"Furthermore, even for philosophers you would be able to make your meaning of 'Humanism' clear and to drive its association with people like More and Schiller into the background. As a matter of fact, you are actively involved in the Humanist movement by being a member of the Advisory Board of Dr. [Charles F.] Potter's First Humanist Society."

Dewey sent his reply two days later, on September 14, 1940 (he always answered my letters quite promptly): "I don't see I have anything to add to what I wrote you the other day. I note that you prefer the word 'Humanism' as a name for my philosophy. I do not, and have definite objection to it save as an adjective prefixed to Naturalism, and I suppose I must be the judge in the case of my own philosophy.

"Since it is a philosophy in question and since philosophers from the time of Aristotle—and before—have used the word 'Nature' in a fundamental sense, I can't see the force of your objection about Naturalism having a philosophic sense. As to the Humanistic Society, as I told you before, I limit my acceptance of Humanism to religious matters where its meaning in opposition to supernaturalism is definite in significance. . . ."

I did not win the argument, but Dewey's two letters served to clarify his position to a considerable degree.

As to his connections with humanist groups, from 1933 until his death in 1952 Dewey was on the Advisory Board of the First Humanist Society of New York. This was a religious organization that held regular

Sunday services at which he spoke two or three times. John Dewey maintained even closer relations with the American Humanist Association (AHA), another non-ecclesiastical religious group founded in 1941 to carry on educational activities in the United States for the advancement of naturalistic Humanism. He was a member of the AHA from the day of its founding until he died, made frequent financial contributions to it, and occasionally wrote an article for its official periodical, *The Humanist*. He also carried on a lively correspondence with Edwin H. Wilson, the editor of that magazine and Executive Director of the Association, giving him constant encouragement.

In *A Common Faith* Dewey states: "A humanistic religion, if it excludes our relation to nature, is pale and thin, as it is presumptuous, when it takes humanity as an object of worship." (p. 54). But clearly the mainstream of religious Humanism in the United States has not been guilty of either of these errors. It has always laid much stress on "cosmic piety," a keen sense of man's natural community of being with the earth and universe that constitute his home. In fact, American Humanism is thoroughly in accord with the chief principles enunciated by Dewey in his study of religion.

Let me quote again from Dewey's letter to me of September 14, 1940: ". . . I limit my acceptance of Humanism to religious matters . . ." That statement, the contents of *A Common Faith*, and Dewey's active interest in humanist organizations all lead me to say that it would be both enlightening and legitimate to call his faith a *humanist* faith. There is no doubt, however, that he prefered the term "naturalism" to denote his general philosophy.

John Dewey
and the American Humanist Association

ew centenaries of eminent personalities have stimulated such a vast
number of meetings, addresses, articles, symposia, books and other
tributes as that of John Dewey in 1959. Philosophers, educators and
critics throughout America and the world have been reevaluating his
philosophy, assessing its relevance for our modern age, and trying to
clarify it so that the average educated person can comprehend its
various aspects.

In this review of Dewey's voluminous creative work, it is important
to establish precisely what his relation was to Humanism and to the
American Humanist Association (AHA). In 1933 Dewey became actively involved in the humanist movement when he signed *A Humanist
Manifesto,* first published in *The New Humanist* for May-June of that
year. This *Manifesto* summed up the position of religious Humanism in
fifteen brief but comprehensive propositions. Thirty-four leading
Unitarian ministers, college teachers, Ethical Culture leaders and other
intellectuals signed this vigorous document, a landmark in the evolution of Humanism in the United States.

The Humanist Press Association (HPA), precursor of the AHA, came
into existence in 1934 and took over the publication of *The New
Humanist.* In 1935 the Press Association asked John Dewey to become
one of its directors. He declined on the ground that he was trying to
reduce his organizational commitments, but sent in $5 as an associate
member.

At a meeting early in 1936 the HPA elected Dr. Dewey as an honor-

Source: The Humanist, *January/February 1960.*

ary member. In notifying him of this action, the Secretary-Treasurer of the organization—the Reverend Edwin H. Wilson, a Unitarian minister who had signed the *Humanist Manifesto*—wrote Dewey: "Under our new By-laws we plan to name as Honorary Members from time to time those who have given particularly distinguished service to the Humanist cause. At the dinner your service was mentioned as that of 'giving philosophical direction and social consecration to the Humanist movement.'"

In April 1936, Professor Dewey also became a member of the Advisory Board of the First Humanist Society of New York, a religious organization founded in 1929 by the Reverend Charles Francis Potter, another Unitarian clergyman. The Society held regular Sunday services at which Dewey spoke on two or three occasions. He remained on the Advisory Board as long as he lived. Other notable members of this Board were Harry Elmer Barnes, Albert Einstein, Julian Huxley and Thomas Mann. The First Humanist Society became inactive as a functioning group several years ago.

THE FOUNDING OF THE AHA

John Dewey maintained closer relations, however, with the American Humanist Association, a non-ecclesiastical religious group founded in 1941 to take the place of the HPA. Its purpose was to carry on educational activities in the United States for the advancement of naturalistic Humanism and "to serve the religious and educational needs of its members and others of humanistic, scientific and naturalistic outlook." Dewey was a regular member of the AHA for twelve years—from its founding until his death in 1952. He also made frequent financial contributions and joined the New York chapter as its first member when it was organized in 1950.

Thus for more than a decade towards the end of his career, John Dewey cooperated actively with the Humanist Association. During that time he wrote several articles for its official publication, *The Humanist,* and carried on a lively correspondence with Edwin H. Wilson, editor of the magazine and Executive Director of the Association. Dewey gave him much sage advice and once intervened successfully with some college professors who were attacking *The Humanist,* although he himself was critical of the magazine in relation to the controversial issue at stake.

I have recently read through Mr. Wilson's fat Dewey file, which is a veritable storehouse of information concerning Dewey's attitude towards Humanism. One of Dewey's first letters to Wilson was dated June 14, 1941, and was a comment on a communication the AHA had received from William J. McDonald, Executive Secretary of the American Education Association, a Catholic group. Mr. McDonald asked permission to quote the sentence from the *Humanist Manifesto* that read: "We are convinced that the time has passed for theism, deism and modernism." By showing that Dewey subscribed to this statement, he hoped to discredit Dewey's educational theories.

Dewey said in his letter: "McDonald is one of the extreme right wing Catholics—he has made several attacks on my educational philosophy and this move is doubtless for another one. He attacked the 'Activity Program' as anti-religious, etc., which evoked a reply from some other Catholics that the Activity Program in education wasn't necessarily connected with my philosophy and heresies! I'm willing to stand by what I have written, however, even as the basis of an attack. So he can quote anything I've signed."

THE EARLY *HUMANIST*

On October 8, 1942, Dewey wrote to Wilson: "I want to congratulate you and the editors on the recent issues of *The Humanist*. The articles have a stimulating variety of contents, and unity of direction and drive. I am moved to ask whether you have much of a circulation in college libraries and reading rooms. If not, I think an appeal for special funds to send copies for a year might be successful. At the end of a year a certain number of institutions might subscribe for themselves."

Here is another letter from Dewey to Wilson dated March 3, 1944, and written from Key West, Florida, where the Deweys used to go during the winter months. Dewey declared: "I think your idea of an educational series of articles an excellent one. I'm sorry I can't get anything for you for the next issue. If you will send me a copy of it here . . . I am pretty sure I can get something to you for a subsequent number."

Every few months there was an exchange of communications between John Dewey and Edwin Wilson. Sometimes Dewey sent only a postcard, as on May 16, 1944, when the message was simply: "The title of my article is 'The Penning in of Natural Science.'" That article appeared in the July 1944 issue of *The Humanist*.

Wilson mentioned Dewey's next article, "The Revolt Against Science," in a letter of October 18, 1945: "Please accept my congratulations and best wishes on your birthday. The autumn issue of *The* · *Humanist* with your article will soon be off the press. Your encouragement in the work I endeavor to do through the American Humanist Association and its quarterly is one of the things that helps to keep me going. Gradually we are finding support and with this issue are printing 2500 copies."

Wilson followed up this note to Dewey with another one on October 24, which stated: "I enclose tear sheets from the *Catholic Digest* for October 1945, which is now on the news stands. Will it serve any purpose for me to write to this in our Winter issue and what would you suggest I say?"

Dewey answered as follows on October 27:

> Thanks for the birthday greeting and your note with the enclosure of the 24th. I think the printer got captions mixed. "Flights of Fancy" should have been over the piece on me. The article doesn't even attain the dignity of falsehoods, since falsity implies some touch of intellectual traits. However, it is serious as a sign of the times if not in its personal reference. It is a curious phenomenon that just at the time when dogmatism is generally letting up the Roman Church is making so much headway.
>
> However, they wouldn't call it curious, but two sides of the same fact. The fact that the Church promises security and makes so little demand upon its subjects, save creedal conformity, helps explain the phenomenon, I think. Whether it is worth notice in *The Humanist* I don't know—perhaps as a sign of the times but not in its personal bearing. . . . Glad to hear your circulation is going up. I enclose a check for ten dollars.

On June 21, 1949, John Dewey sent a short note to Curtis Reese, President of the American Humanist Association: "I enclose a minor contribution. $10. Perhaps I can do more later. I am happy to get the news contained in the communication today. Dr. Wilson has done wonders considering his two jobs. Now that he can give his time to editorial activity, I am sure *The Humanist* will be better. Yellow Springs is an excellent location, I believe."

The reference to Wilson's work in this letter requires some explanation. Humanism as an organized movement began in the United States in 1928 with the formation of The New Humanist Associates, which evolved into the Humanist Press Association, which in turn gave way to the American Humanist Association. Edwin Wilson, over a span of twenty-one years and on a voluntary, unpaid basis, had carried on the main organizational work for these three groups and had likewise edited their publications. Throughout this long period he had also been working full time as a Unitarian minister in various cities. That is why Dewey wrote of "his two jobs." In 1949 Wilson withdrew as minister of the First Unitarian Church in Salt Lake City to devote his entire energies to the AHA and *The Humanist*.

THE QUESTION OF RELIGION

Early in the fall of 1950 Edwin Wilson asked John Dewey and several others to help draw up a new Humanist Manifesto, an up-to-date declaration that would stress Humanism's allegiance to democracy and democratic procedures. [For various reasons this project was not completed.] Dewey, who was ninety years old at the time, typed out his answer on October 4, 1950:

I haven't been in good shape as concerns writing and haven't managed to put together anything in reference to yours of the 29th last. My own feeling would be to emphasize the need people have—not for a religion, much less for anything that pretends to be *the* religion—but for the qualities of experience that make it religious, morally and aesthetically supporting, which association of religion with the supernatural turns many away from; but which humanism makes provision for with no shock to nor strain upon intellectual integrity or moral self-respect; and which, as the very word suggests, instead of making a separate and isolated entity out of the religious, uses it to tone or temper and color all worthwhile aspects of human life and relations of human beings to one another. Personally, I'd be inclined to make reference to freedom as exemplifying an aspect of this intrinsic dignity and value of the human as human.

In a letter to Wilson a few weeks later, on October 29, Dewey again took up the question of religion:

Today's literary section of the *N.Y. Times* has a review of Fromm's recent book on *Psychoanalysis and Religion.* According to Harry Overstreet, the reviewer, Fromm holds that while everyone has some sort of a religion, psychoanalysis that is true to its principles must treat "authoritarian" (i.e., supernaturalistic) religion as having nothing in common with itself, since the precise object of the latter is to free human beings of dependence from the tensions that are bred of dependence on irrational authority, while psychoanalysis has everything in common with humanistic religion.

This seems to be a cue for the Humanist journal—a review of Fromm with emphasis on this point; and in addition perhaps Overstreet can be enlisted if not already a member of the Association [Professor Overstreet has been a member of the AHA since 1944] or if he is a member, to participate actively—writing, etc. For he is in full sympathy in the review with Fromm, saying that he "has put his finger on the central issue of religion."

35

THE FIRST HUMANIST PIONEER

Besides exchanging frequent letters with Dewey, Wilson went to see him occasionally and always received a cordial welcome. There are a number of additional Dewey-Wilson letters. I have cited enough of the correspondence to show that John Dewey took a deep and abiding interest in the American Humanist Association and *The Humanist*. It was natural for the AHA to honor Dewey posthumously in 1954 with its first Humanist Pioneer Award. These Pioneer awards are made annually by the Humanist Association to two individuals who have contributed materially to the development of Humanism in America. Of course it was also entirely fitting for the AHA to be one of the organizations that celebrated Dewey's centennial in 1959.

Although John Dewey preferred to call his technical philosophy naturalism, it is evident that his religious faith was humanist. His signing of the *Humanist Manifesto*, his connection with humanist organizations, the correspondence to which I have referred, a few letters he wrote to me, and the contents of his only book on religion all point in this direction.

A COMMON FAITH

This brief study, *A Common Faith*, was published in 1934 and aroused much controversy. In it Dewey distinguishes carefully between religion and "the religious," discarding religion as discredited, but taking the position that he has a religious faith. At the same time he suggests, for those who still wish to use the term "God," a new definition of the word as meaning the process by which human beings actualize their ideals. Dewey, however, by no means intended to incorporate the word "God" into his own system.

A thorough reading of *A Common Faith* makes very clear that Dewey is presenting an integrated way of life whose main facets are all humanist in their significance.

First, his book stresses the religious quality of man's ceaseless striving towards ideal ends for the fulfillment of the good life in this-earthly existence.

Second, this common faith, unlike any of the traditional religions, teaches that reason and scientific method, with their insistence on keeping the door open for future findings, must be man's chief reliance in solving problems and bringing about progress.

Third, science and intelligence lead cultivated men and women to reject all forms of supernaturalism and to realize that this historic encumbrance of traditional religions is an obstacle to the achievement of essential and valid aims.

Fourth, Dewey's faith always views the individual in his social setting and regards democratic sharing, democratic procedures, and cooperation for democratic goals as the essence of civilized living.

Fifth, Dewey's religious faith, ever sensitive to the cosmic matrix that forms the background for all living things, looks beyond man to the abundant earth with its infinite resources and possibilities, and beyond this whirling planet to the whole vast universe with its billions of shining stars and galaxies stretching out into endless space. This adds up to the "cosmic piety" that George Santayana thought so important.

Sixth, on the very last page of his book Dewey brings out a final point of universal significance:

> The things in civilization we most prize are not of ourselves. They exist by grace of the doings and sufferings of the continuous human community in which we are a link. Ours is the responsibility of conserving, transmitting, rectifying and expanding the heritage of values we have received that those who come after us may receive it more solid and secure, more widely accessible and more generously shared than we have received it. Here are all the elements for a religious faith that shall not be confined to sect, class, or race. Such a faith has always been implicitly the common faith of mankind. It remains to make it explicit and militant.

In this memorable passage Dewey bequeaths his common faith to all humanity. It is to be international, cutting across all lines of race and nation, above all theological, political and economic creeds. So John Dewey—the tough-minded philosopher of scientific method and stern fact, yet the tender-hearted idealist of the democratic dream—in the end proposes a humanistic way of life that could encompass the entire world and that expresses the human race's ages-long aspirations towards a brotherhood of men, of nations and of peoples.

The Enduring Impact of George Santayana

The centenary of the birth of philosopher George Santayana (1863-1952) occurred on December 16, 1963. Several magazines and professional organizations gave due recognition to this important anniversary, with *The Humanist* and *The Journal of Philosophy* both publishing special Santayana issues.

The question naturally arises at this time as to whether Santayana is likely to attain a permanent place in the history of philosophy and culture. While there will undoubtedly be considerable disagreement on this matter, I believe that his name and influence will indeed be lasting, for three main reasons: first, because of the wide-ranging nature and general excellence of his work; second, because he gives a sound, telling and comprehensive presentation of one of the great living philosophies—naturalism or Humanism; and third, because his superb literary style makes him a joy to read and will continue to attract people whose specialty is not necessarily philosophy.

SANTAYANA'S GREAT CREATIVITY

As to my first point, George Santayana undeniably was a writer of enormous creativity, covering not only the whole vast field of philosophy, but also producing poetry, plays, essays such as those in *Soliloquies in England*, a first-rate novel, *The Last Puritan*, and a volume of fascinating letters. In his youth at Harvard Santayana

Source: Basic Pamphlet, 1964.

showed genuine artistic promise in his sketches. From his earliest books, such as *The Sense of Beauty* and *The Life of Reason,* he maintained the highest standards of literary quality and displayed marked intellectual mastery of relevant subject matter. It is only the last volume published during his lifetime, *Dominations and Powers,* a collection of somewhat rambling and disjointed essays, that seems to me to fall below par.

The massive corpus of Santayana's work is broader in scope than that of John Dewey, for example, in that the latter published no poetry, drama, literary essays or fiction. But Santayana's reach was narrower than Dewey's in that, while he accepted and relied upon the facts and methods of science, he did not in his writings go thoroughly into the specifics of scientific method, as did Dewey in *How We Think* and *Logic: The Theory of Inquiry.* Also unlike Dewey, Santayana wrote little on the theory and techniques of education.

Regarding my second point, George Santayana's exposition of naturalism, which he sometimes prefers to call "materialism" and which I prefer to call "naturalistic Humanism," is in my opinion outstanding among modern philosophers. This fundamental naturalist viewpoint runs through all of his books on philosophy and through much of his other work. Furthermore, in his revised, one-volume edition of *The Life of Reason* Santayana presents an integrated and inclusive summary of the naturalist philosophy that can be understood by the average educated person. The broad sweep of this classic work becomes clear from its main divisions: "Reason in Common Sense," "Reason in Society," "Reason in Religion," "Reason in Art" and "Reason in Science."

This sort of philosophic synopsis is something that John Dewey, for one, never achieved. Towards the end of his life Dewey was working on such a book, but lost the only copy of his manuscript when it was about two-thirds finished. In the English-speaking world at least, comparatively few of that minority group known as naturalists, materialists or Humanists have taken the trouble to write overall outlines of their philosophies that could serve to educate the public. The fact that Santayana *has* done this, brilliantly and within the pages of a single book, constitutes another reason why his fame will not soon fade.

SUPERNATURALISM A POETIC MYTH

In his elucidation of naturalism, Sanayana is at his best in demonstrating that religious supernaturalism, taken literally, is simply bad physics and misleading science, but that taken poetically it becomes significant myth and symbol with moral overtones. "Reason in Religion" embroiders upon this theme in detail and stands out as one of the most able and convincing books ever written in showing that mature and educated individuals cannot accept as fact the existence of supernatural gods, spirits, powers or immortalities of any sort. Just because this volume treats traditional religion with understanding and restraint, it is especially persuasive. For as one of Santayana's characters in *Dialogues in Limbo* observes, "You will never enlighten mankind by offending them." (p. 181).

It is important to note that Santayana's father, Don Agustin, early gave encouragement to the familiar naturalistic analysis of religion that his son later developed. I have recently read over the revealing letters, in Columbia University's special Santayana collection, that Agustin Santayana wrote from Spain to George, who was living near Boston, between 1873 and 1893. The elder Santayana repeatedly expressed his agnostic and anticlerical views regarding religion. One passage, written when his son had just turned twenty-one, struck me especially: "I am firmly convinced that the time is not far off when man will no longer be able to believe in anything supernatural, and that all religions are the inventions or creations of man—like *poems*. Then there will be no cults, nor priests. There will be only a feeling of wonder at what is beyond our comprehension."

Santayana died in 1952 at the age of eighty-eight; and while there are some inconsistencies in his philosophic system, particularly in relation to his doctrine of essences, he maintained his basic naturalism to the end. Unhappily, however, there are a few critics who claim that he compromised in his old age, and who purport to prove their point by special reference to the book he brought out in 1946 when he was eighty-three years old—*The Idea of Christ in the Gospels or God in Man, A Critical Essay.*

A good example of this type of approach is to be found in a recent study, *Santayana: Saint of the Imagination,* by Professor of English M. M. Kirkwood of the University of Toronto (University of Toronto Press, 1961). Mrs. Kirkwood starts out well in her book by combining in interesting fashion a running biography of Santayana with a survey of the main features of his philosophy. But towards the end of her volume she goes far astray in her interpretation.

MRS. KIRKWOOD'S MISUNDERSTANDINGS

Using as her text *The Idea of Christ in the Gospels,* she writes about Santayana: "He views the universe as significant largely because it operates mysteriously so as to glorify the Good." (p. 207). Mrs. Kirkwood blithely makes this colossal *faux pas* in the teeth of numberless assertions elsewhere by Santayana to the contrary. Sufficient to refute her is a single dictum from *Reason in Common Sense:* "Only in its relative capacity can the universe find things good, and only in its relative capacity can it be good for anything." (p. 37).

Mrs. Kirkwood buttresses her unfortunate misunderstanding of Santayana by the following passage from *The Idea of Christ in the Gospels:* "But when God personifies *The Good,* the heart loves him already without having named him, and the new revelation comes only in the miracle that *The Good* should prove to be also the power that ultimately governs everything." (p. 80).

Taken by itself, this quotation might seem to support Mrs. Kirkwood's transformation of Santayana from a complete naturalist into a Christo-Platonic saint. But the very next sentence in his book reads: "Such is the atavistic message, the glad tidings, brought by Christ." By entirely omitting this statement, Mrs. Kirkwood gives entirely the wrong impression.

Mrs. Kirkwood repeats this unscholarly procedure at the conclusion of her chapter "A Philosopher Completes His Task," where (p. 230) she quotes with a grand flourish from Santayana's *Dialogues in Limbo:* "Religion in its humility restores man to his only dignity, the courage to live by grace. Admonished by religion, he gives thanks, acknowledging his utter dependence on the unseen, in the past and in the present; and he prays acknowledging his utter dependence on the unseen for the future." (p. 67).

Again, Mrs. Kirkwood leads the reader to think that the quotation represents Santayana's own position, failing to point out that these words were uttered by the shade of "Democritus." For, of course, *Dialogues in Limbo* constitutes a philosophical discussion among seven different characters, each one of whom speaks for himself and none of whom necessarily expresses Santayana's ultimate opinions.

Curiously enough, so far as *The Idea of Christ in the Gospels* is concerned, the chief offender besides Mrs. Kirkwood is the Catholic Government of Spain. After he died in September 1952, Santayana was buried in the special Spanish section—the Tomb of the Spaniards—of Rome's big Catholic cemetery, Campo Verano. In 1959 I visited this Pantheon, with cypress trees shading it on one side, and took detailed notes.

Santayana's grave stands out noticeably because it is the only one which has a raised marble slab, and his name and dates are incised on this in letters much larger than those in the other inscriptions. It is evident that the Spanish Ambassador to Italy, who is in charge of the Pantheon, wished to give Santayana preferred status in it. The Ambassador also had a passage from Santayana translated into Spanish and placed in bold block letters on a concrete wall next to his grave.

BETRAYAL AT SANTAYANA'S GRAVE

The legend reads: "*Cristo ha hecho posible para nostros la gloriosa libertad del alma en cielo.*" ("Christ has made possible for us the glorious liberty for the soul in heaven.") After some research I discovered that the words in question are a free translation of the first two lines on page 167 in Santayana's chapter "The Resurrection" in *The Idea of Christ in the Gospels*. In this chapter the author explains what the story of the resurrection means to Christians. Again, a statement is disingenuously lifted out of context and utilized on behalf of a supernaturalstic ideology in which Santayana definitely disbelieved.

Shortly after his study of the Gospels was published, Santayana became aware that it was being widely misinterpreted. Thus in July 1946 he wrote David Page, an American editor: "Now nobody—not even good critics—seem to gather what my books say. . . . They report what they themselves dreamt while their eyes perused the pages. This is particularly true of *The Idea of Christ*. This book is a perfect illustration of the view of religion that I formulated in 1900 in a Preface to *Interpretations of Poetry and Religion*." (George Santayana Collection, Columbia University Libraries.)

In 1951 Santayana wrote a letter to Warren Allen Smith, an American Humanist, explicitly repudiating any notion that in *The Idea of Christ* he was tending towards theism. He asserted: "My Naturalism is fundamental and includes man, his mind, and all his works, products of the generative order of Nature. Christ in the Gospels is a legendary figure." *The Letters of George Santayana*, ed. Daniel Cory, New York: Scribner's, 1955, p. 408).

Santayana was also well aware of certain ages-long peculiarities of the Catholic Church. Amid the vicissitudes of World War II, he had retired at the age of seventy-seven to a Catholic nursing home in Rome administered by English nuns. It was called the Convent of the Blue Sisters of the Little Company of Mary. About two years before his death, when his health had become increasingly delicate, Santayana expressed some misgivings about the Blue Sisters. In Daniel Cory's words:

> He said that in case I happened to be away when a final relapse overtook him, I was not to be misled by any reports that were circulated about his last hours. I must remember that he was living in a Catholic nursing home where it was more or less expected that a man should die like a Christian. So if I ever heard reports that there had been a sudden "change of heart" at the end, I was not to believe, for instance, that he had requested "extreme unction"; but perhaps

it might be difficult to avoid receiving it, especially if he were in a semi-unconscious state. (*Santayana: The Later Years*, New York: Braziller, 1963, p. 304).

Santayana repeated this warning to Cory several times. And sure enough something of the kind *was* attempted during the philosopher's last days, although the episode is not described in Cory's book. What happened was that a Catholic nurse suddenly refused to administer morphine, which the patient, very ill from cancer, required to ease his pains, unless he called in a priest to confess him. Santayana rebuked the nurse and murmured, "I shall die as I have lived." Fortunately, Cory was in constant attendance during the philosopher's terminal illness and was able to prevent any religious hoax from going through.

In spite of his basic naturalistic position concerning the chief problems in philosophy, Santayana always remained sympathetic to the Christian church as an institution and particularly to the Catholic Church, whose majestic and colorful rituals had an aesthetic appeal for him. As the late Professor William Pepperell Montague of Barnard College put it, there can be both "anti-clerical theists," like himself, and "clerical atheists." Obviously Santayana belonged in the latter class. And there is some pertinency in the quip of a fellow-philosopher, reputed to be Bertrand Russell, "Santayana thinks there is no God and that Mary is his mother."

CONVERSATION WITH SANTAYANA

In August of 1950, two years before Santayana's death, I had the privilege of visiting him in Rome. About four o'clock on a Friday afternoon I walked halfway up the ancient, narrow, cobblestoned Via Santo Stefano Romano, on Celian Hill near the Coliseum, and entered the outside gate of the Convent of the Blue Sisters. I went on past cypress trees and a well-groomed, typically English lawn to the front door, which was opened by one of the Sisters. She ushered me into a sitting room. Santayana in his dressing gown shuffled in and took me down to the end of the hall to show me the view of the old city wall. Then we went into his own simply furnished room for tea.

We talked for two hours without interruption, as I asked him question after question about his philosophy. Santayana was eighty-seven at this time and not in the best of health, but he seemed to me exceptionally keen intellectually. Throughout our conversation I was impressed by how alert and sparkling were his eyes.

"I was brought up on English philosophy," he said, "but it never suited me. Then when I read the Greeks, I knew that was *it*. The way I think is the way Aristotle and the pre-Socratic philosophers thought, in a different idiom and in a different civilization. Socrates too much moralized philosophy and prepared it only too well for the topsy-turvy system of Christianity. When I was an undergraduate at Harvard, I used to carry around a pocket copy of Lucretius's *On the Nature of Things*, which a friend had given me. I would read it on the horse car. As for modern philosophy, I think that perhaps my greatest inspiration was Schopenhauer. I like his pessimism."

Santayana spoke of how much he loved to write. "That is why I have written for myself," he continued, "rather than for any public. I believe that some of my best writing was done when I was preoccupied, as during the First World War in England. I would go out walking alone all day, taking along a notebook, and would lunch on bread and cheese. That is how *Soliloquies in England* came into being."

When I got up to go, I did not expect to see Santayana again, but he suggested that I come back when convenient. So I returned Sunday afternoon for another rewarding talk. This time he was dressed in a brown cassock and looked a bit like a monk.

We soon got on the subject of Santayana's essences. For him, he told me, they were really ideas and sensations respectively intuited and felt by human beings. When he describes the essences as eternal, he does not mean that they are everlasting, but that they are outside of and above time, like the defined concepts of the triangle and the oddity of the numeral three.

As we chatted, Santayana made caustic comments about some of his opponents in philosophy and amusing personal observations on various people he had known. Two of his great-nephews had come to see him in Rome, one of them a brilliant boy who had been head of his class at Harvard. But, added Santayana scornfully, "this promising lad has gone into the manufacture of soap!" Our philosopher even censured the Pope, remarking that perhaps he had been foolish to declare the dogma of the bodily Assumption of the Virgin Mary to heaven. Was it any better, Santayana asked, than the big lies of the Russians, who now claimed that they had made practically all the great scientific discoveries?

When I said my final goodby, Santayana told me he had been glad to see me and that it seemed to wake him up. His parting words were: "I shall be right here next year if I am still alive."

Though Santayana became distinctly a sort of hermit philosopher during the last half of his life, he always appeared happy to have serious-minded visitors from America and elsewhere come to call. After the U.S. invasion of Italy during the Second World War, he welcomed the numerous American soldiers and officers who interrupted his solitude. I was, then, only one of many persons who had long and fruitful talks with him. However, as Professor Horace M. Kallen, who was Santayana's Assistant at Harvard, once remarked, "Santayana is like the Pope; he does not return calls." The point is that despite his retirement from teaching and social life, he remained a friendly and understanding human being. And his bachelor isolation enabled him to find the time to produce a galaxy of thought-provoking books that will continue to interest and inspire intelligent individuals for a long time in the future.

Coming finally to my third point—Santayana's literary style—I believe that his prose, which I regard as the most beautiful in philosophy since Plato, will be an important factor in making his influence a lasting one. His command of English is all the more remarkable because he learned the language well only after he was fourteen, his native tongue being Spanish. I am aware of course that some critics, of whom Father Thomas N. Munson is typical, claim that Santayana's style is "florid" (*The Essential Wisdom of George Santayana*, New York: Columbia University Press, 1962, p. 45). I do not find it so. Santayana not only ranks with Bertrand Russell as one of the twentieth century's most readable philosophers, but also frequently delights us with brief nuggets of wisdom that in a single sentence brilliantly sum up a deep and complex thought. I have never known a philosopher who produced so many genuine aphorisms.

Some thirty-five years ago when I first began the intensive study of philosophy I started a notebook, continued up to the present day, in which I recorded usable short quotations from the era of ancient Greece down to contemporary times. The entries from Santayana far exceed in number those from any other thinker. I here give some typical examples that afford considerable insight into Santayana's basic tenets:

TYPICAL SANTAYANA EPIGRAMS

That rare advance in wisdom which consists in abandoning our illusions the better to attain our ideals. (*Interpretations of Poetry and Religion*, p. 250)

In Aristotle the conception of human nature is perfectly sound; everything ideal has a natural basis and everything natural an ideal development. (*Reason in Common Sense*, p. 21)

Love would never take so high a flight unless it sprung from something profound and elementary. (*Reason in Society*, p. 32)

The fact of having been born is a bad augury for immortality. (*Reason in Religion*, p. 240)

A string of excited, fugitive, miscellaneous pleasures is not happiness; happiness resides in imaginative reflection and judgment, when the *picture* of one's life, or of human life, as it truly has been or is, satisfies the will and is gladly accepted. (*The Middle Span*, p. 8)

The truth is cruel, but it can be loved, and it makes free those who have loved it. (Introduction to Everyman's Edition of Spinoza's *Ethics*, p. xix)

Like Polonius's cloud, she [nature] will always suggest some new ideal, because she has none of her own. (*Reason in Art*, p. 201)

Trifles, as Michael Angelo said, make perfection, and perfection is no trifle. (*Soliloquies in England*, p. 43)

The dark background which death supplies brings out the tender colours of life in all their purity. (*Soliloquies in England*, p. 99)

Reason is not a force contrary to the passions, but a harmony possible among them. Except in their interests it could have no ardour, and, except in their world, it could have no point of application, nothing to beautify, nothing to dominate. (*The Realm of Matter*, p. 147)

Those who cannot remember the past are condemned to repeat it. (As quoted in *The American Treasury*, Clifton Fadiman, ed., p. 734)

PROFESSOR EDMAN'S OPINION

As Professor Irwin Edman of Columbia has said, Santayana's gift "for the sentence that distills a life, an argument, or an adoration becomes unmistakable. One does not need to have these jewels in their setting to note the brilliance with which each one of them shines. . . . One would like to examine the way in which adjectives that seem merely a surface felicity, serve really to carry on the argument, while the reader is pausing over their flagrant charm. . . . Lovers of literature are enchanted (and it is a good guess that they always will be) by a prose as supple and picturesque, as musical and as just as exists in our time." (*The Saturday Review of Literature*, December 16, 1933).

In the same article Professor Edman states that Santayana "cannot avoid the perfect cadence and the image at once glamorous and distracting in its beauty." Here I must disagree with Edman. For while I am deeply stimulated aesthetically by the rhythmic march of Santayana's prose, I am no more distracted by it than by the melody of Lucretius's verse in *On the Nature of Things*. In other words, Santayana's style carries along with it his intended meanings in all their purity and implication, making him more rather than less easy to understand. The grace of that style extends even to Santayana's letters, as can be seen in the large volume edited by Daniel Cory that I have cited. I myself received some of those marvelous letters, the first one back in 1935 and the last in 1951.

I have been discussing here primarily Santayana's prose style, but I would like to add a word about his poetry, which includes some of the finest poems in the English language. There are four volumes of verse, almost all of it written during the first part of Santayana's career, while he was still a teacher at Harvard University. They are: *Lucifer*, a drama in verse; *The Hermit of Carmel and Other Poems; Poems*, including most of the sonnets; and *The Poet's Testament*, published posthumously and containing a delightful play in verse about Plato and other Greek philosophers at the court of Dionysius the Younger in ancient Syracuse.

There follow three of my favorite Santayana poems, the first a sonnet that brings out the above-the-battle quality of his character:

SONNET XI

Deem not, because you see me in the press
Of this world's children run my fated race,
That I blaspheme against a proffered grace,
Or leave unlearned the love of holiness.
I honour not that sanctity the less
Whose aureole illumines not my face,
But dare not tread the secret, holy place
To which the priest and prophet have access.
For some are born to be beatified
By anguish, and by grievous penance done;
And some, to furnish forth the age's pride,
And to be praised of men beneath the sun;
And some are born to stand perplexed aside
From so much sorrow—of whom I am one.

EPITAPH

O Youth, O Beauty, ye who fed the flame
That here was quenched, breathe not your lover's name.
He lies not here. Where'er ye dwell anew
He loves again, he dies again, in you.
Pluck the wild rose, and weave the laurel crown
To deck your glory, not his false renown.

THE POET'S TESTAMENT

I give back to the earth what the earth gave,
All to the furrow, nothing to the grave.
The candle's out, the spirit's vigil spent;
Sight may not follow where the vision went.

I leave you but the sound of many a word
In mocking echoes haply overheard.
I sang to heaven. My exile made me free—
From world to world, from all worlds carried me.

Spared by the Furies, for the Fates were kind,
I paced the pillared cloisters of the mind;
All times my present, everywhere my place,
Nor fear, nor hope, nor envy saw my face.

Blow what winds would, the ancient truth was mine.
And friendship mellowed in the flush of wine,
And heavenly laughter, shaking from its wings
Atoms of light and tears for mortal things.

To trembling harmonies of field and cloud,
Of flesh and spirit, was my worship vowed.
Let form, let music, let the all-quickening air
Fulfill in beauty my imperfect prayer.

In this essay I have not had the space to analyze in depth the different aspects of George Santayana's work. I have given only a brief outline of why I believe that the renown of this thinker and writer will long survive the corrosive ordeal of time. He clearly stands out as one of the greatest naturalist or humanist philosophers who has so far emerged in the United States.

As Santayana's co-teacher and friend in the Harvard Philosophy Department, the late Professor Ralph Barton Perry, has written: "When all is said, there is no denying Santayana's genius and his place among the immortals. It is not difficult to disagree with his opinion, or to withhold the affection which he seemed not to ask, but it is impossible not to esteem him, and pay him homage as a great mind and a great spirit. To posterity his life and work will appear as one of the redeeming features of his troubled age."

Freedom of Choice

When the fatalistic Mohammedan fighters in the motion picture *Lawrence of Arabia* wanted to persuade Colonel Lawrence of the impossibility of one of his proposed military ventures, they said, "It is written." To which Lawrence's spirited answer was always, *"Nothing* is written." And the film in each case proceeds to show how he carried out the venture against immense odds.

Actually, Lawrence was not right, nor were the Arabs. The truth is that in human life there is a great deal that is inexorably determined ("written") and a great deal that springs from man's free choice ("free will" in traditional terminology). Both Lawrence and the Arabs made the mistake of considering these concepts, freedom of choice and determinism, to be mutually exclusive, as if there must be universal determinism *or* absolute freedom. Philosophers, too, have sometimes made the same error.

In modern times man has gained enormous control over nature by discovering a multitude of scientific laws and then using them to his own advantage. Those laws represent determinism and are always the expression of if-then relations or sequences. *If* the temperature drops to 32 degrees Fahrenheit, *then* water freezes into ice. Fortunately, many human functions, such as breathing and the circulation of the blood, are automatic and deterministic. At the same time an individual functioning on the level of intellectual deliberation can exercise true freedom of choice in deciding between two or more genuine alternatives that confront him.

Source: The Humanist, *March/April 1965.*

When a man wishes to go somewhere in his car, he relies on its built-in determinisms of self-starter, accelerator, steering wheel and brakes. But it is he, not the automobile, that makes the decison as to precisely what road he will take or what his destination is to be. This is an everyday example of how freedom utilizes determinism. In fact, successful human living is built upon this basic principle, which reaches its apex in a machine civilization like that of the United States. There is, then, in human existence a constant, interlocking pattern of *both* freedom and determinism.

Human freedom of choice always operates, of course, within definite limits. It is conditioned by natural law, by the past, by the present environment, by economic circumstance and other factors. All men are governed by the law of gravity and yet have very wide liberty of movement. To cite another familiar example, persons who play chess abide ordinarily by its established rules, which represent determinism; but within that broad framework a tremendous variety of moves are possible, and they represent freedom. The same principle holds true for all competitive games and sports.

The *if* of every if-then law points to the fact that chance or contingency is involved in the occurrence of any *if*. When such occurrence is initiated, by a human being or by a nonhuman force, certain specific consequences will necessarily follow. But nature does not decree when and how any particular causal law will come into effect. As Professor Sterling P. Lamprecht states in his brilliant book *Nature and History*: "Necessity and contingency, so far from being unconnected ideas to be taken, one wholesale and the other retail, are supplementary ideas which belong together in the analysis of every separate event."

Contingency occurs when two independently initiated event-streams, with no common cause behind them, meet at a definite point in space and time. We must say that the more than four hundred persons killed by lightning annually in the United States are victims of chance in the form of very bad luck. To analyze an instance of contingency in more detail, let us look at the collision in midair over Chesapeake Bay on November 23, 1962, between a United Airlines Viscount and two whistling swans weighing some eight pounds each. When the bodies of the birds penetrated the tail mechanism of the plane, the pilot lost control and the Viscount plunged to earth. All seventeen aboard were killed.

It is my claim that no matter how far back into the past we are able to trace the event-stream represented by the Viscount and the event-stream represented by the swans, we shall find no relevant common cause that started both causal series on their respective ways so that they inevitably intersected on that November day. This was the first airplane accident involving whistling swans in the records of the Federal Aviation Agency.

If contingency really does exist as an ultimate and pervasive trait of the universe, then the thesis of universal necessity cannot be logically upheld and the hard-core determinist is proved wrong. His position is that the great cosmic juggernaut rolls on inexorably and that each event and thing of the present down to its last detail, including his own argument and my answer, has been predetermined since the beginning of time. The existence of contingency undermines that position and opens the door for freedom of choice, without guaranteeing that it will come into being.

For only thinking creatures such as men have freedom of choice. They possess this capacity because they usually do not need to react immediately to a challenge or problem in a speedy stimulus-response manner. They are able instead to stand aside temporarily from the flux of events and to delay a decision while they reason concerning the advantages or disadvantages of the different alternatives that may be followed. It is well to remember that the word "intelligence" originates in the Latin *inter* (between) and *legere* (to choose). "Choosing" means making up one's mind.

In the intellectual process that leads to a decision, the individual ordinarily employs general concepts or "universals," as they are called in philosophy. As Professor Charles Hartshorne puts it, "our very power to form general conceptions (in a sense in which these are beyond the reach of other animals) is the same as our not being determined by irresistible impulse, habit or antecedent character, to but one mode of acting in a given case . . . Freedom in the indeterministic sense is thus inherent in rational understanding as such, understanding through universals."

Suppose that you are living in a fairly large city and that you want to go with your wife on a Saturday night to a good motion picture. Going to the movies is, then, your general idea, and under it can be subsumed the various possibilities, the particular instances, listed in the leading newspaper or some magazine like New York's *Cue*. You talk the plan over carefully with your wife and finally select five pictures that you both agree would be worth seeing. Then you check on the time when each movie begins and how long it will take to get to each theater. Finally, you make your choice and take a bus to the theater in question.

I insist that a complex thought process such as I have just described is not mere play-acting for setting up an evening's entertainment that was predetermined prior even to one's general desire to see a movie. On the contrary, such a weighing of pros and cons is a serious exercise in deliberation that in itself all but implies freedom of choice. The determinist argument that even human thinking and its results are all decided in advance turns thought into an incomprehensible and superfluous appendage of Homo sapiens.

That argument also robs the concept of potentiality of its fundamental meaning. For "potentiality" means the presence of *plural* possibilities in nature and in the lives of human beings. If universal and absolute determinism rules the world, then there is always and everywhere only one potentiality, namely, the potentiality of that which actually occurs. This doctrine runs counter to logic, common sense and human experience.

A potent reason for the widespread acceptance of the determinist thesis is a rather common misunderstanding of the operation of cause and effect. Many individuals look upon the present as merely the effect of preceding causes and forget that the present in its multitudinous forms is itself an active cause. It is the spearhead of all activity, the great forward thrust of universal being. In truth, the past, which is dead and gone, does not create the present; it is the present which creates the past. For the present alone exists, and the past has efficacy only as embodied in the substance or structure of some present event or object. As the dynamic present forges ahead, it leaves its past behind it, making a trail as it were, as a skier gliding downhill through the snow, or a boat producing a foamy wake.

Human beings, functioning as causes themselves, constitute the surging crest of an ongoing and unending wave of the present. And now we return to the theme of contingency. When man-as-cause acts upon some subject matter external to himself, there occurs, unless a regular pattern has been previously established, a conjunction between two separately initiated event-streams. This is why freedom of choice is inextricably linked with contingency. When I decide one evening to drive to the movies in my car, I am the immediate cause-stimulus for the event-stream that is myself intersecting with the event-stream represented by my automobile.

In that situation true freedom of choice is possible for me owing to the open world of contingency, as compared with the closed world of omnipotent determinism. So it is that a free choice becomes a free cause. The human individual, a thinking, initiating, choosing agent, can be and frequently is the free cause of his actions. This knowledge, I believe, helps to build up the morale of a man and stimulates him to greater creativity. It also gives deeper meaning to human ethics, for awareness of freedom of choice brings home to every individual that he must take full responsibility for his actions.

Now at the end of my analysis I raise an issue that is usually mentioned at the start of discussions on freedom of choice: the very strong intuition native to most men that they are not slaves of fate, but are free to make the choices they do. This feeling is not to be considered conclusive, but only as a hint or hypothesis. It must be checked and double-checked against the available evidence. When this is done, I am convinced that the intuition of free choice emerges as an important truth buttressed by reason.

To summarize, we find eight main points in support of the case for freedom of choice. First, the central issue is not that of freedom *versus* determinism, since human beings constantly utilize the if-then, deterministic laws of nature. Second, there is no absolute free choice, since it always functions within limits. Third, the existence of chance or contingency as an ultimate trait of nature negates the thesis of universal determinism or necessity. Fourth, human thinking continually goes on in terms of general conceptions or universals under which many different particulars or potentialities may be considered; and the reality of these potentialities shows that no one line of action has been foreordained. Fifth, to take seriously the meaning of *potentiality* as signifying plural possibilities in itself controverts the determinist position. Sixth, the fact that only the present exists and that it creates the past makes impossible the determining of present and future by the past. Seventh, freedom of choice encourages ethical behavior. And, eighth, most human beings possess a powerful intuition of free choice.

B. F. Skinner's *Beyond Freedom and Dignity*

In this book, one of the most controversial in recent years, Professor B. F. Skinner at the outset makes the enormous assumption that absolute determinism rules throughout the universe, the earth and human life. He goes on from there to outline how individuals and society would function on a purely deterministic basis. The author does not make the slightest effort to come to grips with the underlying question of freedom of choice and determinism, one of the most hotly and widely debated issues in history and at the present time.

It is Professor Skinner's thesis that every action, every thought, every emotion of every human being is completely determined by his genetic inheritance and the external environment. The logic of this position is that every sentence, word and punctuation mark in Skinner's own book was preordained in strict cause-effect sequence not only yesteryear, but at the time of the American Revolution and some five billion years ago when our planetary system was probably born. This is a *reductio ad absurdum* Skinner can't escape.

As the argument proceeds in *Beyond Freedom and Dignity*, the author hardly mentions the genetic factors and places overwhelming emphasis on how the outside environment determines and controls what men and women do. "A scientific analysis of behavior," states Skinner, "dispossesses autonomous man and turns the control he has been said to exert over to the environment" (p. 205); "a scientific analysis shifts the credit as well as the blame to the environment" (p. 21);

Source: This review of Beyond Freedom and Dignity (*New York: Knopf, 1971*) *was first published in* Science and Society, *Summer 1973.*

"a scientific analysis shifts both the responsibility and the achievement to the environment" (p. 25); "abstract thinking is the product of a particular kind of environment, not of a cognitive faculty" (p. 189).

These statements by Skinner are one-sided and overlook the fact that the human individual and the external environment are always *interacting*. He talks as if man were an entirely passive creature, reacting automatically to outside pressures, whereas man is an active, initiating and forceful being who often controls or alters the environment to a considerable extent. This point does not in itself disprove determinism, but it shows that Skinner has not really thought through the problems he discusses.

My quotations from *Beyond Freedom and Dignity* underline Skinner's repeated insistence that we ought not to praise persons for their achievements or blame them for wrongdoing, since all of their actions were predestined before they were born. According to Skinner nobody is responsible for what he does or does not do; the environment bears *all* the responsibility. Of course the environment bears much of the responsibility, but the implication of Skinner's position is that we ought not to condemn the war criminals in Washington who have been guilty of waging a cruel and immoral war of aggression against Vietnam that has included the wholesale shooting of peasants and terror bombing of civilian centers.

Skinner constantly makes the assertion that "scientific analysis" and science support his position that free choice does not exist and total determinism does. But as Professor Noam Chomsky conclusively demonstrated in *The New York Review of Books* (December 30, 1971), Skinner's "science" is of a most questionable variety. And Skinner himself bewails the fact (p. 19) that "almost all" the specialists in political science, law, economics, anthropology, sociology, psychotherapy, education, child care and linguistics still believe in "autonomous man" (the author's phrase for a human being having free choice or free will). Skinner, then, refutes his own claim that science in general sustains his thesis.

In Skinner's deterministic Utopia the efficacy of the far-reaching controls he would establish depends on what he describes as "the predictability of human nature." Indeed, that alleged predictability is a major premise in his philosophy of determinism. Here, again, I must challenge him. The key organ in human choice is the thinking brain, which possesses 10^{11} (100 billion) neurons or nerve cells and 10^{14} synapses. A few minutes of intense thought may involve intricate interneuronic connections all but infinite in number. The sheer complexity of human thought—not to mention its internal privacy—must always prevent an outside observer from making a 100 per cent prediction as to what an individual is going to think or choose. This complexity renders it impossible to prove that any human being is completely subject to determinism. And perhaps in the complexity of the brain with its cerebral cortex—through vast quantity giving rise to a new quality—lies the secret of free choice in humans.

Skinner keeps implying that the theory of "autonomous man" bestows on the individual almost absolute freedom of choice. This is a caricature concocted by the author to make his own theories seem more plausible. Free choice is always *relative*, and limited by one's genetic endowment, upbringing, education, knowledge, economic situation and the environment in general. Human choice, then, is conditioned, but not determined, by a number of factors. An acceptable theory of free choice does not, as Skinner implies, rule out determinism (or necessity) in the world, but finds that determinism, as exemplified, for instance, in the if-then laws of science, coexists with chance (or contingency) and human freedom. We constantly utilize the determinism embodied in natural law and in a thousand and one mechanical devices. When I drive my car, I rely on its deterministic functioning, but it is I, not the automobile, that decides where to go.

If my analysis is correct, those who wish to build a better society (and Skinner is definitely among them) can adopt many of the author's suggestions for improving human behavior, without accepting his overall determinism. For instance, he believes that "reinforcers" (his special word for "rewards" or "incentives") are more effective for educating children and reeducating criminals than punitive measures. Most educators and sociologists agree with Skinner here.

Again, Skinner strikes an enlightened note when he speaks in favor of "the intentional design of a culture." What he clearly means is the purposeful planning of a society, with "*planned* diversification, in which the importance of variety is recognized" (p. 162). Much of his discussion in this connection is consistent with socialist planning. But while socialist planning entails general directives for economic production and distribution, Skinner's "design of a culture" goes to an impossible extreme by proposing that there be detailed rules for the behavior of every last person in the community.

It is true, as some critics have suggested, that Skinner's program could be easily utilized by a fascist state, but in my opinion it could be used by any kind of state that decides to institute for its own purposes propaganda and brainwashing to the nth degree.

Much as I disagree with *Beyond Freedom and Dignity*, I think the book is valuable for three reasons: First, as I have pointed out, many of Skinner's ideas for the improvement of present-day society are valid; second, the book represents an interesting and stimulating *tour de force* by pursuing to a logical extreme the social implications of hard-core determinism; and, third, this volume, which has become something of a best seller, has evoked widespread and animated discussion concerning the significant issue of free choice and determinism.

Self-Determinism and Freedom of Choice

Articles are seldom reviewed, but Professor Frederick Ferré of Dickinson College has written such an illuminating essay on the issue of free choice and determinism that I think it warrants special comment—all the more so because humanism is, in my judgment, committed to an ethic of human freedom. Professor Ferré ascribes to human beings the power of self-determinism, but it seems to me that his concept is essentially what I have elsewhere called freedom of choice or free will.

Ferré defines philosophical determinism as "the view that all events are uniquely and regularly assured, in principle, by prior events—the earlier events standing as sufficient conditions for the later ones." Recognizing that a large proportion of human choices and actions are governed by prior cause-effect determinants, he suggests that in some human happenings "the sufficient condition is supplied by the conscious agent himself and that his exercise of this determination is not simply fixed by prior events." In such situations, a human being can make determinations, "not within a regress of caused causes but as an agent: a creative initiator of events within a limited and evanescent nexus of open possibilities."

Professor Ferré then proceeds to the decisive point in his argument: ". . . under these conditions, the person, not prior determining factors, would be the 'end of the line' for inquiries into the causes of consequent behaviors. Without such a stopping place, every event would be entitled to 'pass the buck' to its predecessors *ad infinitum*; self-determination provides a basis for saying (sometimes) 'the buck stops here,'

Source: This review of "Self-Determinism" (American Philosophical Quarterly, July 1973) was published in The Humanist, *May/June 1974.*

61

and in this sense establishes, in a way impossible either for philosophical determinism or for simple indeterminism, the foundations of human responsibility."

When Ferré says that "every event would be entitled to 'pass the buck' to its predecessors *ad infinitum*," he is referring to the fact that if universal determinism were true, then our choices and actions of today were predestined not only yesterday, but a year ago, one hundred years ago and indeed from the moment that the earth came into existence. Self-determinism makes this infinite regress irrational and irrelevant and at the same time undermines the thesis that all of a person's faults and mistakes can be ascribed to antecedent causes, such as the genes handed down to him by his parents, grandparents or great-grandparents. Thus, Ferré's concept of self-determinism knocks out the use of the theory of overall determinism as the great alibi for human weakness and misconduct.

Of course, as Ferré makes clear, cause-effect sequences in the long process of evolution have created living forms upon this earth, including human beings. But once a complex organism like man, with his unique power of thought, has been caused, there emerges the ability under some circumstances for that organism to break free from the strict control of prior causes and to exercise self-determination. Man can make choices among genuine alternatives and put them into effect through the conscious control of the organism's relevant structures and potencies. Such self-determinism is equivalent, in my opinion, to what is usually meant by freedom of choice.

Spiritualism and Reincarnation

Throughout all crises and developments in human society, throughout war, revolution and the exploration of outer space, the question of whether the personality survives death remains perennially one of the most significant issues in religion and philosophy. Hence we are fortunate that Curt J. Ducasse, Professor Emeritus of Philosophy at Brown University, has in his latest book given an able and wide-ranging analysis of arguments and evidence for and against the reality of life beyond the grave.

He makes clear at the outset that he is not talking about a post-mortem existence based on the orthodox Christian doctrine of a literal resurrection of the body, but is discussing survival in psychological terms as meaning a continuance of the human "center of consciousness" with its memory and awareness of self-identity essentially intact. He states that the New Testament stories about the appearances of Jesus after his crucifixion "make sense only if interpreted as reports of what are commonly called 'apparitions' or 'phantasms' of the dead."

The author also eliminates the idea of *immortality* from his study: "For immortality, strictly speaking, is incapacity to die, which, as ascribed to a human consciousness, entails survival of it *forever* after bodily death. But survival for some indeterminate though considerable period, rather than specifically forever, is probably what most persons actually have in mind when they think of a life after death. Assurance of survival for a thousand years or even a hundred, would for those of

Source: This review of A Critical Examination of the Belief in a Life After Death *(Springfield, Ill.: Charles C. Thomas, 1961) was published in the* British Journal for the Philosophy of Science, *Vol. XIII, 1962.*

us who desire survival, have virtually as much present psychologica value as would assurance of survival forever." (p. 6).

Professor Ducasse takes the position that "neither religion no theology really provides any evidence that there is for man a life afte death." But his philosophic analysis leaves the door open for evidence and proof of *discarnate* survival through various types of paranorma phenomena, including those brought to light by hypnosis and psychi cal research, and those offered by mediums as messages from the deac or materializations of their spirits. He has obtained first-hand informa tion about Spiritualism not only by carefully studying the vast litera ture of this religion, but also by attending mediumistic séances.

At one of these, described in a chapter on "Occurrences *Prima Facie* Indicative of Survival," he tells how:

> . . . some eighteen fully material forms—some male, some female, some tall and some short, and sometimes two together—came out of and returned to the curtained cabinet I had inspected beforehand, in which a medium sat, and to which I had found no avenue of sur- reptitious access. These material forms were apparently recognized as those of a deceased father, mother, or other relative by one or another of the fourteen or fifteen persons present, and some touch- ing scenes occurred, in which the form of the deceased spoke with and caressed the living. One of those forms called my name and when I went up to her and asked who she was, she answered "Mother."

But, alas, she did not, according to Ducasse, "in the least resemble" his mother! (p. 167).

The author, troubled over the old adage, "If ghosts have clothes, then clothes have ghosts," makes the following comment: "If one assumes that the clothing the apparition or materialization wears is materialization only of a memory image of the deceased's clothing, then would not consistency dictate the conclusion that the now tem- porarily perceptible parts of the deceased's body are materialization likewise only of a memory image of his appearance and behavior?" (p. 169).

After considering the hypothesis that telepathy could explain the extraordinary communications offered by mediums which apparently divulge information known only to a dead person or somebody ac- quainted with him whom the medium has not known, Ducasse claims that the quality, quantity and diversity of evidence "we get over the mediumistic telephone" dictates the conclusion that "the balance of the evidence so far obtained is on the side of the reality of survival."

The author devotes a whole chapter to criticism of scientists in general, the majority of whom, he declares, are ready to dismiss without investigation, on a priori grounds, the objective existence or evidential value of paranormal phenomena such as the séance described above and many other occurrences. He quotes with approval as applying today the words of Professor James H. Hyslop, founder of the American Society for Psychical Research, in his book *Contact with the Other World*, published in 1919: "Science, content, without thorough inquiry, to confine its investigations to the physical world in which it has achieved so much, will not open its eyes to anomalies in the realm of mind and nature and so degenerates into a dogmatism exactly like that of theology!" (pp. 145-6). Yet for the last half-century neurologists, psychiatrists, psychoanalysts, and physicians practicing psychosomatic medicine have occupied themselves tirelessly with "anomalies in the realm of mind."

The scope of this volume is seen in the fact that a full third of it is concerned with theories of reincarnation, metempsychosis or transmigration. The author reviews the various religious and philosophic doctrines on this subject and recounts several unusual episodes in which a person supposedly recalls his former life under the influence of hypnosis. Concerning one of these, the widely publicized case of Bridey Murphy, Ducasse painstakingly endeavors to refute those who rejected it as an authentic instance of reincarnation.

In trying to establish his thesis that both discarnate survival and reincarnation are possible, the author argues at length to disprove the chief theories of mind that make it dependent on or a function of the activities of the body, nervous system and brain. In this section of his book, I do not think he gives sufficient attention or importance to the numberless facts from the sciences of biology, physiology, psychology and medicine that demonstrate an apparently indissoluble connection between the functioning of the physical organism, especially the cerebral cortex, and such mental processes as reasoning, imagining and remembering.

The preservation of memory is, of course, indispensable to any future life that maintains the self-identity of the personality. But it is impossible to understand how a man's memory patterns—millions upon millions of them—imbedded in the interneuronic pathways of the cortex, could possibly continue to exist after the dissolution, decay or destruction of the living brain where they had their original locus and being. And those stored-up psycho-physiological memories that we call habits are likewise inseparably connected with the physical organism.

In the humanist or naturalist philosophy, stemming from Aristotle,

65

that supports this general position, a human being has ideas, feelings or emotions only with the occurrence and concurrence of "certain complex physico-chemico-physiological events and structures." From this viewpoint the abstraction "mind" always connotes an activity or function of the brain-body. It would be better to say "mind*ing*" or "reason*ing*" to show that thinking, without exception, is an activity of the physical organism as natural as breathing or digestion, and equally based on bodily processes. To oversimplify for the sake of emphasis, just as bad digestion can play havoc with effective thinking, so "bad" thinking in the form of extreme worry or mental depression can adversely affect digestion and even lead to ulcers. In both cases, within the complex and integrated whole that constitutes a man, the malfunctioning of one organ has deleterious effects on the functioning of another.

A fundamental difficulty in this entire problem is, as John Dewey has pointed out, that "when we talk of the relations of mind *and* body, and endeavor to establish their unity in human conduct, we still speak of body *and* mind and thus unconsciously perpetuate the very division we are striving to deny. . . . In just the degree in which action, behavior, is made central, the traditional barriers between mind and body break down and dissolve. . . . What the facts testify to is not an influence exercised across and between two separate things, but to behavior so integrated that it is artificial to split it up into two things." (*Philosophy and Civilization,* New York: Minton Balch, 1931, pp. 302-3).

Disregarding Dewey's admonition, Ducasse treats mind and body as two different substances, agents or entities. He writes: "Had not the word 'substance' so chequered a philosophical history, we could say that a mind is as truly a psychical substance as any material object is a physical substance. Let us, however, avoid the misunderstandings that this might lead to, and say that a mind, no less than a tree or sugar, is a *substantive*—using this word . . . for the kind of entity to which the part of speech called a 'noun' corresponds." (p. 56). Thus, in his effort to pave the way for an afterlife, the author, while not employing the traditional language, adopts a species of Cartesian dualism, although he does not say so specifically in this volume. He is much more definite in his earlier essay, "In Defense of Dualism," published in the symposium, *Dimensions of Mind* (Sidney Hook, ed., New York University Press, 1960).

In attempting to disprove the monistic psychology that regards personality (including mind) as the activity of the body (as cuttingness is to the axe, in Aristotle's analogy), Ducasse spends considerable time on my book, *The Illusion of Immortality.* He contends that I have set up an "ontological dualism" (p. 111) of my own when I state that the

ind, in its manipulation of meanings, which are certainly not material
bjects, can and does influence the body. But mind, as I have
epeatedly noted in this review, is always *man thinking*, the body-
rain-cortex carrying on the function of apprehending, developing,
nagining, recollecting, synthesizing, putting into effect ideas. And
hese ideas or meanings do not originate or exist in some supernatural
r other-than-natural realm. They are not apart from nature, but *a part*
f nature, and they operate through the language, signs, communica-
ion that complexly structured and thoroughly this-worldly organisms
uch as Homo sapiens are able to establish.

For Ducasse to describe this well-known naturalistic position as an
ontological dualism" is a radical misuse of terms. At the same time we
an admit that there are completely naturalistic dualisms—if one
refers that word—within a man: for instance, between the distinctive
unctioning of the brain and the rest of the body; or, within the brain
tself, between the different functioning of the cortex and of the thala-
nus, cerebellum and brain-stem.

At one point Ducasse becomes a bit polemical and accuses me of
'turning aversions into disproofs" (p. 118). Yet I must state that far
rom having an aversion to a life beyond death, I, who have now
eached sixty years of age, would like very much to awake after my
demise to another existence, to see again the many dear friends and
relatives I have lost, and to be able to believe in some dualistic psychology that makes all of this possible. In truth, I am one of those
perhaps old-fashioned persons who desire immortality in the traditional sense of living on forever and ever. But trying to follow faithfully
where facts and logic have led, I have been forced regretfully to give
up my former faith in personal survival and to conclude that the probabilities against it are overwhelming.

My simple desire for immortality leads me to clash again with the
author. For he evidently agrees with the dictum of Professor James B.
Pratt that "some sort of belief in at least the possibility of the object is
a condition for any real desire for it." I realize that many psychologists
have the same opinion, but I am convinced they are wrong. Quite
frequently I wish for things that I know cannot possibly be attained,
and I think that most people have similar wishes.

I do not intend that my criticisms of Professor Ducasse's volume
should seem to negate in any way the fact that he has mounted here
one of the most powerful arguments I have encountered for the possibility of postmortem survival. Although I have been unable to agree
with some of his fundamental theses, I found his book fascinating to
read and can recommend it to students of philosophy, religion and
eschatology as a most interesting and useful work.

Mistaken Attitudes Towards Death

The preoccupation of existentialist thinkers with death and their painful agonizing over it have lately brought about something of a revival in philosophic reflection on human mortality. In his stimulating but erratic book *The Faith of a Heretic* (New York: Doubleday Anchor Books, 1963), Walter Kaufmann sharply criticizes the views on death of Kierkegaard and Heidegger, of Sartre and Camus. While I agree with much in these criticisms and in Kaufmann's volume as a whole, he finally reaches conclusions about death that I consider almost as unacceptable as those of the existentialists. I quote:

If one lives intensely, the time comes when sleep means bliss. If one loves intensely, the time comes when death seems bliss. . . . The life I want is a life I could not endure in eternity. It is a life of love and intensity, suffering and creation, that makes life worth while and death welcome. There is no other life I prefer. Neither should I like not to die. . . . For most of us death does not come soon enough. Lives are spoiled and made rotten by the sense that death is distant and irrelevant. One lives better when one expects to die, say, at forty, when one says to oneself long before one is twenty: whatever I may be able to accomplish, I should be able to do by then; and what I have not done then, I am not likely to do ever. One cannot count on living until one is forty—or thirty—but it makes for a better life if one has a rendezvous with death. Not only love can be deepened

Source: The Journal of Philosophy, *Vol. LXII, No. 2, January 21, 1965.*

and made more intense and impassioned by the expectation of impending death; all life is enriched by it (p. 372-3).

In some forty years of reading in the religious and philosophic literature concerning death, I have rarely found a statement that seems so perverse as the one just cited. If what Kaufmann says about loving intensely is not just poetic extravagance and is to be taken seriously, then I must seriously retort that it runs counter to common sense and human psychology. Just why should the rapture of love make us "welcome" the nothingness of death? Why not the continued rapture of love? Kaufmann's sleep-death metaphor is just as misleading in the year 1963 A.D. as in the year 463 B.C. when the ancient Greeks were already toying with it. Death is about the last thing to occupy the thoughts of a man and woman passionately in love; and the more intense their feelings, the more unlikely it is that they regard the complete extinction of themselves and their love as some sort of "bliss."

As for Kaufmann's assertions, "For most of us death does not come soon enough" and "One lives better when one expects to die, say, at forty," I am frankly dumbfounded. For these remarks imply that it is preferable to die in the very prime of life. According to Kaufmann, I ought to feel rather ashamed that I am nearing sixty-three and am still in good condition. Evidently, Kaufmann expects the generality of mankind to be youthful geniuses and accomplish all their best work by the time they are forty. Yet the briefest glance at the history of highest literary, artistic and cultural achievement shows what an enormous proportion of it has resulted from the energies of persons well beyond that age.

Apparently, too, for Kaufmann the science of medicine has for a long time been on the wrong track by concerning itself with individuals over forty and by gradually increasing the span of life, so that today in the United States the average life expectancy is more than seventy years. If he is consistent, Kaufmann should prefer the situation in India, still a country of appalling poverty, starvation, overpopulation, ill health and lack of medical facilities, where the average life expectancy is only forty-two.

"Whatever I may be able to accomplish," avers Kaufmann, "I should be able to do by then" [by forty]. Not a word about enjoyment or pleasure, or the leisurely delights of retirement, old age or perhaps being a grandparent. Kaufmann adds: "What I have not done then [by forty], I am not likely to do ever."

The plain facts do not bear out this judgment. Consider the thirty-six Presidents of the United States: not one of them became chief executive until after he was forty, and the three greatest—Jefferson,

Lincoln and Franklin D. Roosevelt—were not inaugurated until they were over fifty. Moreover, the truly creative individual, no matter what his age, rarely feels that his work is done; new tasks, new vistas keep opening up for him. I think especially of three active nonagenarians, all philosophers, whom I have been privileged to know personally: William Ernest Hocking, Alexander Meiklejohn and Bertrand Russell. These persons all happen to be well known, but there are thousands of others in the same age group who have carried on with useful work. These various considerations lead me to say that the ideal should be to live to at least twice forty, thus increasing by a decade the traditional goal of three-score years and ten.

Finally, I take issue with Kaufmann's assertion that "all life is enriched" by "the expectation of impending death." The joys and values of human living are valid and worthwhile in and of themselves; they stand on their own feet and need no ratification, either by some supernatural god or through comparison with the realm of death. The great consummatory experiences, the moments and moods of exaltation that come from knowing beauty or love, do not depend in the slightest on any sense of imminent death. Psychologically, an individual who is constantly aware of impending death is usually saddened by the thought in a way that hardly enriches his day-to-day existence. When Kaufmann declares that "it makes for a better life if one has a rendezvous with death," he is suggesting an exaggerated consciousness of death that is only too reminiscent of the Christian viewpoint. He reminds me here of the story about the man who reread his will every night before retiring, fearing that he might not survive until morning.

All in all, then, Kaufmann's attitude towards death, in the passages I have cited, appears to me fantastically out of joint. Even if in these comments he intended merely to strike a poetic pose, it does not come off and remains essentially a strained and lugubrious meditation on man's fate.

II

Charles Hartshorne is another philosopher with whose views on death I emphatically disagree. He writes in *The Personalist* (Autumn, 1958, p. 387):

No animal endowed with much power of memory ought to live forever, or could want to, I should maintain; for the longer it lives, the more that just balance between novelty and repetition, which is the basis of zest and satisfaction, must be upset in favor of repetition, hence of monotony and boredom. Old animals, and old people, in principle (exceptions are in degrees only) are bored animals and bored people. This is not essentially a glandular or circulatory phenomenon. It is psychological: one has felt and done most of the things that must be felt and done so many times before.

As Jefferson wrote to a friend: "I am tired of putting my clothes on every morning and taking them off every evening." Thus, he concluded, the Creator prepares us for death. Thus indeed. That many old people are spry and eager only proves that their chronological age gives but a rough index of psychological age. Thus all complaint against death itself seems misguided. Death is needed for the solution of an aesthetic problem, how memory is to be reconciled with zest.

I must take issue with Hartshorne's analysis from start to finish. I am an animal with a pretty good memory and in full control of my mental faculties. And though I wrote a book, *The Illusion of Immortality* (New York: Ungar, 1965), in order to show that there can be no survival of the human personality after death, I nonetheless *do* want to live forever, provided I maintain fairly good health and a satisfactory economic standard of existence. Obviously, nobody would desire the eternal life of a senile mind and decrepit body.

Many people commit suicide because they feel too unhappy to go on living, or because they meet some shattering setback, or because they are mentally abnormal. I suppose that some individuals kill themselves out of sheer boredom. However, I cannot accept for a moment the claim that human beings in general are bound to become so bored with life that they are glad to have it end. Jefferson's remark about dressing and undressing was, with all due respect to that great man, a trivial one to support the solemn conclusion he drew from it. Dressing and undressing, and many other routine actions needful for day-to-day existence, ought ordinarily to become habits that require but little conscious effort.

Hartshorne asserts: "Old animals, and old people, in principle (exceptions are in degree only) are bored animals and bored people." This could be true of beasts, fish and birds, but the possession of mind in man does make quite a difference. Owing to the immense progress of medicine and health over the last hundred years, old age in the more highly developed societies does not usually now begin until a man is, say, seventy. Yet I have known so many individuals between seventy and ninety who never got bored with life, that I refuse to admit they were all exceptions "in degree" or in any other way. On the other hand, I have known a few people who were bored with well-nigh everything at the age of twenty-three, thirty-three or fifty-three. Such individuals will find their existence tedious if they reach old age, since they always did.

Actually, this pleasant earth and the many different countries and cultures that have developed upon it provide endless varieties of experience for an alert and vigorous person. How many centuries would it take for an educated man to learn all the world's languages and read all the good books in every field that have been published since the invention of the printing press? How many aeons would a lover of nature require to view and explore all the scenic beauties of this planet, including those of America's national and state parks? Such questions show how easily the imagination can conceive of unlimited opportunities for human beings to enjoy the continued novelty and zest that are needed, according to Hartshorne, to make life worthwhile.

For the sake of argument, I have been assuming that Hartshorne is correct when he asserts that zest and satisfaction are dependent on a "just balance between novelty and repetition." However, I now wish to say that I think his psychology here is unsound. In the first place, much that is novel is unpleasant; any new type of pain, for example, is hardly the sort of experience one would seek in order to give life zest.

In the second place, I deny that repetition *as such* leads necessarily to "monotony and boredom." Consider, for instance, the basic biological drives of thirst, hunger and sex. Pure, cool water is the best drink in the world, and I have been drinking it for sixty-two years. If we follow through with Hartshorne, I ought to be so tired of water by this time that I seek to quench my thirst solely by wine, beer and coca cola! Yet I still love water. By the same token, the average person does not fall into a state of ennui through the satisfaction of hunger or sexual desire.

Hartshorne states: "Death is needed for the solution of an aesthetic problem, how memory is to be reconciled with zest." Here again I must disagree. *My* memories of happy experiences—whether of listening to a Beethoven symphony, reading poetry or philosophy, rejoicing in the play of my grandchildren, skiing down a snow-covered slope in Vermont or viewing beautiful vistas of forest, stream and mountain—such memories do not make me feel "How dreadfully tired I am of all that!" Instead, they give me a zest for encores.

What Hartshorne forgets, it seems to me, is that while constant repetition of the identical experience may well cause boredom, a repeated *cycle of variety* does not have the same effect. Characteristic human activities such as eating, traveling, making love, writing books, reading books, going to plays and concerts, painting pictures, dancing, working creatively and exercising in the open air can be carried on in patterns of variety that seldom give rise to monotony.

73

These, then, are some of the reasons why, despite Hartshorne's re-marks, I would rejoice in living on as an immortal upon our earth or in some other place equally attractive. Now either he or someone else is going to call these sentiments of mine extremely egoistic. Yet they are mainly an extention of the innate urge for self-preservation; and in any case a large degree of self-interest is ethically legitimate in the motiva-tions of any human being. I suggest, however, that my position stems primarily from a profound sense of the sweetness and splendor of life.

III

In a thoughtful and provocative paper, "Pragmatism and the Tragic Sense of Life," Sidney Hook tells us that the essence of tragedy in hu-man life resides in the moral conflict of choosing between two ethical goods, between the good and the right (with the right representing obligation or duty) or between two rights. He discusses the implica-tions of death for his theme and concludes that "death as such is not a tragic phenomenon and that its presence does not make the world and our experience within it tragic." (*Proceedings and Addresses of The American Philosophical Society, 1959-1960*, Yellow Springs, Ohio: Antioch Press, p. 13).

Of course, death *as such* in the economy of nature and the course of biological development is clearly neither an evil nor a tragedy. Man would never have evolved had not the great institution of death given strictest meaning to the survival of the fittest in evolution and elimi-nated unprogressive species from the earth. Death has served man in another way. For ever since he appeared on this planet, he has depended preponderantly upon the death of animal, plant and vege-table forms for food, clothing, fuel, housing, and many other essentials of living.

Hook's discussion, however, pertains solely to the death of human beings. Life having brought them into existence, is it tragic that death should terminate that existence? I certainly agree with Hook that death for human beings, despite all the grief and anguish it evokes, does not in itself justify the conclusion that man's life as a whole is tragic. But this does not logically rule out the judgment that death for some men or all men is "a tragic phenomenon."

With my disbelief in any sort of personal immortality, a position that Hook shares with me, I have come to think over the years that death, with all its implications, is a blow of such magnitude and finality that it is always a thing of tragic dimensions—to the person who dies, or his intimate survivors, and usually to both. If the deceased was widely known and beloved in the community, his death can be a tragedy for many people—indeed for millions or tens of millions—who were not personally acquainted with him. Such was the case when President John F. Kennedy was assassinated in November 1963. Even when death is a relief from painful and incurable illness, it seems tragic that the only remedy should be the total obliteration of the personality. obviously, when death strikes someone who is young or in the prime of life, the tragedy is worse.

For me there is tragedy, too, in the death of the old, even of those in their eighties and nineties. Some of the greatest scenes in literature concern the death of aged persons, throwing a searchlight on the living, such as that of the grandmother in Proust's *Remembrance of Things Past* and of the central character in Tolstoy's *Death of Ivan Ilyich*. As I said in my comments on Walter Kaufmann, I know a number of individuals over ninety who are still carrying on with wonderful vitality and mental acumen. Mankind can ill afford to lose such wise and useful citizens. And the death of anyone whom we love, no matter how advanced his age, stabs deep into the heart and leaves a lasting pang.

It is evident that, although I am in agreement with Hook's conception of the tragic insofar as it goes, I would extend the definition in accordance with more popular usage to include events that give rise to great suffering and sorrow. It is revealing that *Webster's New International Dictionary* includes "death" in the very meaning of "tragic." Its second definition of "tragic" reads: "Characterized by, or involving, death or calamity or the suffering implied in tragedy; terrible; calamitous."

In my opinion, death is additionally a tragedy because it represents a clash—and this is more in line with Hook's analysis—between two goods or values that are basically inconsistent with each other. Death is a genuine value in that it ensures room upon this earth for the on-flowing, ever newborn generations of humanity. And as Hook observes, "it gives us some assurance that no evil or suffering lasts forever. . . . It washes the earth clean of what cannot be cleansed in any other way." (p. 12).

At the same time, non-death is hypothetically a value in that it would preserve human individuals with their almost limitless possibilities for growth, achievement and happiness, would avert the wholesale waste of men and women of widest experience who have reached the peak of their social functioning, and would prevent the deep shock and enduring sorrow, often of a traumatic character, that come from the loss of loved ones.

IV

In my view, death is simply one of the many different kinds of tragedy that human beings encounter; yet it is unique because it is inevitable and universal. The mature philosopher never attempts to mask the tragic aspects of death. But he is not preoccupied with death; nor does he permit it, on account of the heartache and crisis it causes, to overshadow in his philosophy the other phases of human existence. Nor does he cry out against death in the manner of Dylan Thomas in his lines:

> *Do not go gentle into that good night.*
> *Rage, rage against the dying of the light.*

No, the wise man, be he philosopher or otherwise, looks at death with honesty, dignity and calm, recognizing that the tragedy it brings is inherent in the great gift of life.

The Crisis Called Death

No philosophy, religion or overall way of life can be judged complete or adequate unless it includes a definite position on whether or not the human personality can surmount the crisis called death and continue its career in another and immortal realm of existence. Without being dogmatic about it, naturalistic Humanism does give an answer on this issue.

Humanism, in line with its rejection of belief in any form of the supernatural, considers illusory the idea of personal immortality, or the conscious survival of the self beyond death for any period of time whatsoever. The basic reason for regarding a hereafter as out of the question is that since a human being is a living unity of body and personality, including the mind, it is impossible for the personality to continue when the body and the brain have ceased to function.

The sciences of biology, medicine and psychology have accumulated an enormous amount of evidence pointing to the oneness and inseparability of personality and the physical organism. And it is inconceivable that the characteristic mental activities of thought, memory and imagination could go on without the sustaining structure of the brain and cerebral cortex. The only possible way for a man to achieve immortality is to carry out its original meaning, "not-death," by keeping alive his natural body forever. Although such an outcome is extremely improbable, the average span of life, at least in the United States, has been increasingly extended during this century. I can imagine my own this-earthly "resurrection" taking place some twenty

Source: The Humanist, *January/February 1967.*

years hence at about the age of eighty-five, when I shall go for a week or so to the hospital and have my tiring natural heart replaced by an inexhaustible mechanical heart.

Paradoxically enough, traditional Christianity supports the humanist position on the unity of body and personality by insisting that man can gain immortality only through the literal resurrection of the physical body. The promise of this resurrection was, according to the New Testament, the wonderful, world-shaking message that Jesus brought. Undoubtedly the best chance for personal survival after death is precisely through this resurrection route of old-time religion. The trouble here for Humanists is that they cannot possibly accept the resurrection doctrine.

Since the Humanist thinks that his one and only life is in the here and now, he aims to make the best of it in terms of attaining happiness for himself, his family, his countrymen and all mankind. Accordingly, the Humanist is a militant fighter for social justice, racial equality, higher living standards and world peace. And he remembers that faith in immortality has often cut the nerve of effective action for improving the lot of humanity on this earth.

For example, during this crucial era when the folly, horror and tragedy of international war continue to afflict mankind, we find the following gem of supernaturalist apologia in *The New York Times* of September 11, 1950, at the height of the Korean War: "Sorrowing parents whose sons have been drafted for combat duty were told yesterday in St. Patrick's Cathedral that death in battle was part of God's plan for populating the kingdom of heaven." A Catholic prelate, Monsignor William T. Greene, offered this extraordinary form of consolation, but both Pope John XXIII and Pope Paul VI would surely have winced at it.

The Humanist faces his own death and that of others with more equanimity than the average person, because he realizes that in the processes of nature death is a necessary corollary of life and has played an indispensable role in the evolution of the higher animals, including man. Death has rid the earth of unprogressive species and has given full meaning to the Darwinian doctrine of the survival of the fittest. Without our good friend death, the race of man would never have come into being at all.

Biologically speaking, nature's method with the more complex forms of life is to discard the old and faltering organism at a certain stage to make way for newborn and lustier vitality. As the American novelist Anne Parrish said, each one of us "must die for the sake of life, for the flow of the stream too great to be dammed in any pool, for the growth of the seed too strong to stay in one shape. . . . Because these bodies must perish, we are greater than we know. The most selfish must be generous, letting his life pour out to others. The most cowardly must be brave enough to go." So it is that death gives the opportunity for the largest number of human beings, including our own descendants, to experience the joys of living. And in this sense, death acts as the firm ally of future and unborn generations, through the simple procedure of making room for them upon this planet.

To philosophize about man's mortality, as I have been doing, or to take seriously religious promises of an afterlife, may soften slightly the impact of death, but in my opinion nothing can really counteract its bitter sting. The Humanist believes that death is a blow of such magnitude and finality that it is always a tragedy, either for the deceased or for the survivors who were close to him, or for both. Even when dying puts an end to a painful and incurable illness, it remains tragic that extinction of the individual should be the only "cure." Of course, the tragedy is greater when a person dies in youth or the prime of life.

But it is always too soon to die, even if you are three-score years and ten, even if you are four-score years and ten—indeed, no matter how young or old you may be. Hotspur's cry in *Henry IV* resounds across the ages, "O gentlemen! the time of life is short." I myself am almost sixty-five and have the familiar experience of looking back on my life and finding that it has all gone by with appalling swiftness. Days, years, decades have slipped by so quickly that now it seems I hardly knew what was happening. Have I been daydreaming all this time?

Today more than ever, I feel the haunting sense of transiency. If only time would for a while come to a stop! If only each day would last one hundred hours and each year one thousand days! I sympathize with everyone who ever longed for immortality, and I wish that the enchanting dream of eternal life could indeed come true. So it is that as a Humanist I deeply regret that death is the end. Frankly, I would like to go on living indefinitely, providing that I could be assured of continued good health and economic security. And I would be most happy if anybody could prove to me that there actually is personal survival after death.

Humanists try to look death in the face—honestly, courageously, calmly. They recognize that it is one of the basic tragedies inherent in the great gift of life. We do not agonize over this fact, nor are we preoccupied with it. Our main antidote for death is *preoccupation with life*, with the manifold enjoyments that it brings and with creative work that contributes to the progress of our country and the welfare of humanity. We know there can be no individual immortality, but we have hopes that once global peace is permanently established, international cooperation and the steady advance of science will secure the immortality of the human race in this infinitely varied and beautiful world of nature.

Philosophy in Revolution: A Review

Dr. Howard Selsam is the former Director of the Jefferson School of Social Science, an educational institution which concentrated on the teaching of Marxism. Selsam and his board fought long and courageously against the shameful antifreedom prosecutions of the United States Government, but finally had to close down the school in 1956.

Selsam, himself a teacher of philosophy, has for many years been a close student of Marxist theory. This little book is a polemic on behalf of Marxism in philosophy rather than a scholarly analysis of the subject. It is not up to the standard of the author's earlier works such as *What Is Philosophy?* The new book, however, does deal with the main issues in a forceful manner; and I am glad to continue in the pages of *Science and Society* the stimulating philosophical discussions that I have carried on with Howard Selsam for many years.

In my opinion *Philosophy in Revolution* brings out some of the typical mistakes in contemporary Marxist analyses of philosophy. Selsam's biggest mistake, which runs right through the book, is that he claims far too much for Marxist materialism. He talks as if it were the only philosophy of the present which states forthrightly that matter in motion is the underlying stuff of the universe, which relies on the facts and methods of science and which is interested in seeing the workers of the world attain happiness and the abundant life.

Here, for example, is one of the author's exaggerations: "It is dialectical materialism as the philosophy of the working class which *alone*

Source: This review of Philosophy in Revolution *(New York: International Publishers, 1957) was published in* Science and Society, *Winter 1958.*

carries forward the one great idea of progressive philosophy, the idea, namely, that through our sense experience and reason, by the methods of the sciences, we humans can know ever more about the nature of things, and so knowing, achieve ever greater mastery of our world." [p. 23—*Italics mine*—C.L.]

In this statement, as in other sections of his study, Selsam leaves out of account the scientifically based materialism of the 1949 symposium, *Philosophy for the Future: The Quest of Modern Materialism,* edited by Professors Roy Wood Sellars, V. J. McGill and Marvin Farber. He drastically misinterprets as "shame-faced idealism" the science-oriented school of naturalism as represented in the 1944 symposium, *Naturalism and the Human Spirit,* edited by Professor Y. H. Krikorian and dedicated to an outstanding naturalist, Morris R. Cohen. And Selsam nowhere mentions the important philosophy of naturalistic Humanism of which I myself am an exponent. In a review of my *Humanism as a Philosophy* in 1949 Selsam said that while my philosophy was incomplete from a Marxist viewpoint, nonetheless Marxists could accept the eight central propositions of Humanism that I had laid down. And he stated specifically that the book affirmed "man's ability to solve his problems by reason and scientific method and 'to enlarge continually his knowledge of the truth.'" Naturalism and non-Marxist materialism likewise hold that man's chief reliance for the solution of his problems should be on reason and the experimental method of modern science.

Selsam makes the same sort of oversimplification when he discusses the philosophies which reject the idealist thesis that all existence can be reduced to ideas or that spirit or mind has primacy over matter. (This latter position is most clearly expressed in the dualist tradition of Platonism, Christianity and Kantianism.) The author avers that the recognition that matter is primary "is the heart of the revolution the working class wrought in philosophy (p. 51). . . . Bourgeois philosophy from Hume on was willing to give up the luxury of proving God for the greater luxury of preventing anyone from proving the existence of matter. It was a strategic retreat which only dialectical materialism has seen through and fought." (p. 66).

These sweeping statements raise a number of different questions. But in any case contemporary non-Marxist materialism, naturalism and naturalistic Humanism all take the view that the material universe came first and that mind emerged in the animal man only after some two billion years of biological evolution upon this material earth. Many other modern philosophers, difficult to label precisely, have likewise held that matter is the primordial constituent of the cosmos.

Blithely refuting himself, Selsam acknowledges that a number of philosophers in ancient Greece—thinkers like Thales, Empedocles,

Democritus and Epicurus—"saw the general issues of materialism versus idealism as clearly as we do" and "were able to be basically materialist without benefit of modern science, as was Lucretius later." (p. 68). Furthermore, the author tells us that there were many materialists at Alexandria under the Ptolemies (300 B.C.-250 A.D.); and that during the French Enlightenment the brilliant d'Holbach and Diderot also believed in the primacy of matter. The "revolution" in philosophy that Selsam so stresses apparently first occurred some 2500 years ago; and it was later repeated several times before the modern working class took it over.

It is, then, all the more startling to read that "the primacy of matter *versus* mind never has been a pure question of objective evidence, of what we know or do not know about the world. It is a question ultimately, of class position." (p. 69). This statement is made without qualification. And it is very difficult for me to understand what "class position" led the Greek, Alexandrian, Roman and French thinkers mentioned above to materialism. Lucretius, for example, was an aristocrat and a member of Rome's ruling class.

What Selsam is implying is that today only those who support the working class against the capitalists can be depended upon to have the correct view of the metaphysical status of mind in relation to matter. This position is not tenable. There is no necessary logical connection between believing in a planned socialist society and believing in the primacy of matter. At most there may be a certain socio-psychological connection, since an individual who has radical tendencies in economics may also be radical in philosophy.

In any event there are millions of good theistic Christians in the world, many of them in Soviet Russia, who support a socialist program. We all know of many outstanding church leaders, men like Harry F. Ward and the Dean of Canterbury, who are heartily in favor of socialism and most sympathetic to the remarkable achievements of the Soviet Union. They stand in the long Christian tradition that interprets Jesus as a militant radical leader and that concentrates on the social gospel rather than on theology.

Nor is there a necessary logical connection between believing in the capitalist system and believing in God or some form of idealism. The naturalists, Humanists and non-Marxist materialists, most of whom are bourgeois in origin and sympathy, prove this point.

Among the non-Marxist materialists we have the horrible example of Mr. Charles Smith, who is aggressively pro-capitalist, pro-racist, antidemocratic and anticommunist. Smith is head of the American Association for the Advancement of Atheism and editor of a monthly journal, *The Truthseeker*. In its pages he preaches that the great movement on behalf of full democratic and educational rights for the Negro in the United States is not only pernicious in itself, but has been inspired principally by the Jews.

It is not surprising that Selsam, like other Marxists, vehemently denounces practically every aspect of John Dewey's philosophy and classifies him as an idealist instead of a naturalist. The author's method in this respect is quite remarkable. He says, "Dewey has, in two or three sentences, scattered through his scores of volumes, confessed his idealism." (p. 64). In other words, for Selsam two or three statements, perhaps vague in meaning, are more weighty than the whole massive corpus of Dewey's many books, which clearly show that he is an anti-idealistic naturalist or Humanist. Dewey's signing of the anti-supernaturalist *Humanist Manifesto* of 1933 unquestionably points to the same conclusion.

Now I freely admit that John Dewey's writings are not always easy to understand and that sometimes his style obscures what he is trying to say. Moreover, some of his statements on technical points in his theory of knowledge give the impression to the uninitiated that he is still caught in the toils of subjectivism. As Professor Irwin Edman once frankly asked Dewey, "*Why* do you write this way?"

Selsam has discovered an ambiguous sentence in which Dewey talks about a "genuine idealism" emerging in philosophy. A little farther on in the same paragraph Dewey makes an assertion that Selsam does not quote: "To magnify thought and ideas for their own sake, apart from what they do (except, once more, esthetically) is to refuse to learn the lesson of the most authentic kind of knowledge—the experimental—and it is to reject the idealism which involves responsibility." (*The Quest for Certainty*, p. 138). It is obvious from this second sentence that Dewey in both statements is referring to *ethical,* not metaphysical, idealism. It has been a source of constant confusion in philosophy that since the eighteenth century "idealism" has been used to describe a metaphysical or ontological system as well as an ethical tendency. The metaphysics should rightly have been called "ideaism."

When Selsam comes to Dewey's theory of knowledge, he again goes astray. As I have been pointing out for at least twenty years, the Marxist and Deweyan theories of knowledge are quite similar. When Lenin said, "Practice alone can serve as a real proof," he was taking the same general position as Dewey. Dewey would agree with Selsam's formulation in *Philosophy in Revolution*: "Knowledge arises out of practice, based in the first instance on needs and interests which must be satisfied if the race is to survive. And its test, the standard for determining its correctness and adequacy, is, again, human practice." (p. 109).

Selsam complains that the imperialists of American capitalism are able to utilize Dewey's pragmatic doctrines. This charge is true, but it only goes to prove that Dewey is right. The point is that *if a theory of knowledge is sound and scientific, then anybody and everybody can use it,* regardless of his nation, class, party or purposes. So it is with mathematics and with scientific laws in general, provided the individual or group wishing to use them has acquired the necessary know-how. If the Marxist theory of knowledge is correct, then capitalists as well as Marxists can put it to work. The Soviet Union does not throw overboard the laws of technological advancement discovered and utilized in capitalist countries, and there is just as little reason for it to discard a bourgeois theory of knowledge if that happens to be valid.

As to Dewey's social theories, Selsam also misjudges them. He asserts, for example, that Dewey denies "that change can be planned as well as that it can be revolutionary. 'Planned public policies,' he [Dewey] wrote, 'initiated by public authority, are sure to have consequences totally unforeseeable—often the contrary of what was intended.' It is amusing to note that Dewey can know only one thing about the future, namely, that it will be the opposite of what we plan." (p. 147).

But when we read the Dewey quotation in its context, a rather different impression results. "In fact," Dewey says, "there is one thesis of Herbert Spencer that could now be revived with a good deal of evidence in its support: namely, the economic situation is so complex, so intricate in the interdependence of delicately balanced factors, that planned public policies initiated by public authority are sure to have consequences totally unforeseeable—often the contrary of what was intended—as has happened in this country rather notably in connection with some of the measures undertaken for control of agricultural production." (*Freedom and Culture*, p. 62).

Dewey, writing in 1939, is plainly referring to some of President Roosevelt's New Deal planning measures, of which Selsam's fellow Marxists were likewise extremely critical. Dewey is not condemning all economic planning, but is saying that there is "a good deal of evidence" to show that a government plan may result in unforeseen by-products. This was certainly true of New Deal planning, and it has also been true, to a considerable extent of Soviet planning.

Dewey's basic position on planning is well formulated in his little book *Liberalism and Social Action:* "Organized social planning, put into effect for the creation of an order in which industry and finance are socially directed in behalf of institutions that provide the material basis for the cultural liberation and growth of individuals, is now the sole method of social action by which liberalism can realize its professed aims." (p. 55).

In the same book Dewey disposes of Selsam's comment that he is against revolutionary change: "The one exception—and that apparent rather than real—to dependence upon organized intelligence as the method for directing social change is found when society through an authorized majority has entered upon the path of social experimentation leading to a great social change, and a minority refuses by force to permit the method of intelligent action to go into effect. Then force may be intelligently employed to subdue and disarm the recalcitrant minority." (p. 87).

I have discussed the question of John Dewey in some detail because Selsam's treatment of him is typical of the way he deals with other modern philosophers from Locke and Hume to Bertrand Russell. At least one reason why Marxists have not been objective in judging the work of Dewey and Russell is that these thinkers have been strongly anticommunist and anti-Soviet.

In Selsam's study, however, I discern another and perhaps more powerful motivation. That is a wish to enhance the prestige of the working class and Marxism in general by asserting that the Marxists have discovered a world-shaking new philosophy of life that constitutes a veritable intellectual revolution. Yet it is significant that the only persons the author can cite by name as initiating and carrying forward this great revolution are Marx, Engels, Lenin, Stalin and Mao Tse-tung. None of these is to be classed as a professional philosopher. With the Soviet Union celebrating its fortieth anniversary, the Chinese Communist Revolution its eighth, and dialectical materialism a doctrine discussed throughout the world, it is astonishing that Selsam fails to mention a single practicing professional philosopher, besides himself, who adheres to this philosophy.

Now Marxism, as an inclusive theory of man, history and the universe, does make a unique contribution to thought—above all in its economics, but also in its political theory and its social theory (or philosophy of history) known as historical materialism. But I cannot agree that Marxism so far has offered anything of real originality in metaphysics (or ontology) and in theory of knowledge (epistemology), with the possible exception of dialectics in its post-Hegelian development.

This is surely no reflection on dialectical materialism. Admittedly its roots go far back into ancient Greece of the fifth century B.C., and it draws a great deal upon Hegel. Today, every philosophy that is worthy of the name must be eclectic to some degree. Marxists like Selsam would make more progress in the teaching and development of their subject if they would cease their inflated claims and acknowledge the main similarities between Marxist philosophy and other philosophies of the past and present. Then the peoples of non-socialist countries, instead of regarding Marxist philosophy as esoteric and totally alien to their cultural patterns, would be able to approach it with less apprehension as something half familiar.

I have emphasized in this review my criticisms of *Philosophy in Revolution*. But let me say in conclusion that there is much of merit in the book, especially when the author is describing the actual content of Marxist thought. And the study has value ipso facto because in a day when Marxism has become a term of opprobrium in the United States and many Marxists have been jailed merely because of their ideas, Selsam's work keeps the important subject of Marxism before the public and open for discussion.

How To Be Happy—Though Married

Marriage has been a prime subject for criticism throughout history. Especially in the United States during the second half of the twentieth century, attacks on this institution have been perhaps more drastic and widespread than ever before. Books, magazines, newspapers—the mass media in general—have frequently voiced such strictures. A growing number of young men and women who have not bothered with a wedding ceremony are living together, the divorce rate has steadily increased, and premarital and extramarital sex relations have become commonplace and more socially acceptable. At the same time it is reliably estimated that some 70 percent of American marriages are unhappy in a sexual sense. As Sir Julian Huxley says in *Memories II*, "Marriage poses as many problems as it solves."[1]

In spite of all this, I think that marriage continues to have an indispensable role in American life and throughout the world. I cannot believe that in general human beings would lead happier lives without the institution of matrimony, even with all its faults. The family remains the basic social unit in most civilized countries. Many critics of marriage do not give sufficient attention to the existence and welfare of children; and children need a stable, permanent home with loving parents. I wish it were possible for all men and women to experience the joys of having children and, indeed, grandchildren.

But marriage needs to be radically reformed, as the high incidence of American divorce shows. Again, keeping the well-being of children in mind, we must deplore the ever mounting rate of broken families.

Source: Basic Pamphlet, 1973.

For divorce in a family almost always has harmful effects upon the children, even if they are fully grown. I am convinced that certain changes in the attitude and behavior of married couples could make them happier and reduce the number of divorces.

I approach the problem of sexual relations with the scientifically grounded belief that man is a functioning unit of body, mind and emotion. Totally unacceptable is the traditional concept of Christian dualism, which regards a human being as divided into two parts, body and soul (including the mind). In this dualistic theory the soul possesses all the finer attributes of a person and, after death, goes marching on into the realm of immortality. The body, on the other hand, is steeped in sin and corrupted by base physical desires, the worst of which is sexual passion. And the mainstream of Christian thought, until recently, regarded sexual intercourse as evil because through it Adam's "original sin" was transmitted to every human being. It was a cardinal sin ever to stigmatize sex as sinful!

Man's sexuality is no more sinful than his need for food or drink. There is no sharp separation between the physical and the spiritual, and love at its best represents a pervasive intermingling of the two. George Santayana in *Reason in Society* expresses this beautifully: "Love would never take so high a flight unless it sprung from something profound and elementary."[2] Enduring romantic love between a man and a woman is, I believe, the greatest of all sexual experiences. True wisdom regards sexual activity, rationally controlled, as a unique combination of joy and beauty that can enhance the life of every human being and that contributes mightily to the supreme goal of happiness for all mankind. We can wholeheartedly rejoice that we live in an exciting world of male and female. As the French say, "Vive la différence!" And let us be grateful that nature has given us the power of preserving the human race through the marvelous means of making love! Yet, despite all this, we are faced with the bitter paradox that sexual activity and love, which can bring to human beings the greatest possible pleasure, often result in unhappiness and downright misery.

In this essay I wish to state categorically and without elaboration (1) that increasingly reliable methods of contraception, including the Pill, have made possible a freer and more joyous sex life for a large proportion of the human race; (2) that such methods have enabled husbands and wives to adopt careful and intelligent planning for the birth of children; (3) that abortion should ordinarily be permitted, as the United States Supreme Court has ruled, except during the last ten weeks of pregnancy; (4) that every state should legally allow either party in a marriage to obtain a speedy, no-fault divorce on the grounds of incompatibility alone; (5) that the double standard in sex relations must be eliminated, with women having complete equality with men, yet maintaining in full their femininity; (6) that men and women should rely on intelligence as well as emotion in choosing a marriage partner and in the general conduct of their marriage; and (7) that people differ so much in character, philosophy, sexuality and traditions that it is impossible to set up a code of sex ethics and conduct that will be acceptable to all Americans, let alone all mankind.

With these seven propositions as background, I shall discuss some other, more controversial questions about how to achieve a happy marriage.

Far-reaching reforms in the economic system, such as the guarantee of a decent living standard to everyone in the nation, will alleviate marriage problems that are particularly related to poor economic conditions. But such developments can never, in themselves, solve the overall difficulties of marriage or bring assured happiness to wedded couples. After all, in America affluent husbands and wives are likely to have as much marital trouble as those in lower economic brackets. And in the socialist society of the Soviet Union, despite enormous economic progress since the Revolution of 1917, I suspect that the majority of married couples are as dissatisfied with their sex lives as the majority in the United States. The divorce rate in the USSR is almost as high as in the USA. No revolution can be considered adequate or complete so long as a large proportion of the people are unhappy in their sexual relations.

A PREMARITAL TRIAL RUN

Many men and women who take the wedding vows do so without knowing each other well enough for a lasting relationship and without being certain that they are sufficiently compatible sexually and in other ways. I am of the opinion that an experimental period of living together for at least six months, with strict birth control in effect, would be desirable for all who are formally engaged or seriously contemplating matrimony. Such a trial period would give the couple ample opportunity to apply their intelligence to the question of whether they are in general well enough suited to each other to warrant the long-term commitment of marriage. The trial run would be the nearest thing possible to a scientific experiment in preparation for the responsibilities of marriage and would be an effective acknowledgement of William Congreve's classic warning, "Married in haste, we may repent at leisure." There is no guarantee, of course, that even after a congenial trial period a couple entering legal marriage, and probably having children, will make a success of their new relationship.

A "practice marriage" should at least enable a man and a woman to find out whether they are deeply in love or merely assuaging each other's sex hunger. As Bertrand Russell states in his *Marriage and Morals*: "If the girl is expected to be a virgin when she marries, it will very often happen that she is trapped by a transient and trivial sex attraction, which a woman with sexual experience could easily distinguish from love. This has undoubtedly been a frequent cause of unhappy marriages."[3] And men can be trapped in the same way. We have it on the authority of both Chaucer and Shakespeare that "Love is blind," but this is precisely what we want to guard against.

In the premarital stage of living together, a couple will presumably learn that sex for the sake of sex alone ignores the higher values of love and leads into the blind alley of mere sensuality. In America today, precisely this sort of dead-end relationship between men and women is widely encouraged. Cheap pornography assails us from every side, and much of the mass media has been transformed into a voyeur spectacle that affronts one's sense of decency. This perversion of sex, in my view, debases the relations between male and female and treats the physical aspect, especially intercourse, as if it were the sole raison d'être.

Such pressures are only too likely to result in the denigration of sexual union as no more important than a friendly handshake. At the same time "instant sex"—the quick and casual coming to orgasm between persons hardly acquainted—is a prime factor in the growing rate of venereal disease in the United States. Thus, promiscuity can lead to the ruination of sex, love, health and life itself. The practitioners of instant sex miss half the pleasure of love-making. They have no sense of the art of love, and bypass a whole range of emotions that may, with gentle tempo, come into play as a prelude to and accompaniment of the sex act. In fact, the greatest joy in sex relations is experienced only when a man and woman know each other well and share the full emotional quality of love.

In intimate sex relations, lovers are at their best when they combine a keen sense of beauty with a healthy eroticism and sexuality. This quality of *eroto-aesthetic sensitivity* is fundamental to successful marriage. Of equal significance is the deep awareness of tenderness and intimacy in sexual communion, the warm, wonderful sense of physical and spiritual oneness with the beloved, the feeling of exultation and exaltation at the same time. When love is experienced in these ways, it becomes a powerful antidote to the loneliness that at times besets the human creature.

"There is, finally," as psychiatrist Rollo May says in *Love and Will*, "the form of consciousness which occurs ideally at the moment of climax in sexual intercourse. This is the point when the lovers are carried beyond their personal isolation, and when a shift in consciousness occurs which they experience as uniting them with nature itself. There is an accelerating experience of touch, contact, union to the point where, for a moment, the awareness of separateness is lost, blotted out in a cosmic feeling of oneness with nature." [4]

Of utmost importance for a happy marriage is that a couple share, in addition to their romantic feelings for each other, basic interests—cultural, political, travel, sports, friends. The pursuit of such interests not only brings pleasure in itself, but draws husband and wife more closely together in an inclusive comradeship and makes them more appreciative of each other's qualities. They can become an effective team, both in recreation and in the more serious aspects of life. In *A Preface to Morals*, Walter Lippmann sums it up: "Love endures only when the lovers love many things together, and not merely each other." [5] In this connection, having children is of course helpful, but not in itself enough.

THE NEED FOR VARIETY

Now I come to a theme about which there is bound to be considerable disagreement—the place of variety in the enterprise of marriage. Of course the normal, life-loving couple will find much variety in the pleasures that they enjoy together. But beyond all that is the fact that most marriage partners need more diversity in sex interplay than they can give each other and should, therefore, have ample contact with friends of the opposite sex outside the family circle. For I am convinced that a very grave danger to marital happiness is that wives and husbands simply see, hear and have too much of each other. In his "Epipsychidion," Shelley makes the same point:

> I never was attached to that great sect,
> Whose doctrine is, that each one should select
> Out of the crowd a mistress or a friend,
> And all the rest, though fair and wise, commend
> To cold oblivion, though it is in the code
> Of modern morals, and the beaten road
> Which those poor slaves with weary footsteps tread,
> Who travel to their home among the dead
> By the broad highway of the world, and so
> With one chained friend, perhaps a jealous foe,
> The dreariest and the longest journey go.

My uncle, who was something of a wit, used to tell about a pair of newlyweds who chose to spend their honeymoon camping out alone on an island in Lake Sebago, Maine. A week after the wedding one of their friends remarked to my uncle, "I should think by this time they might be ready to see a friend." "Or even an enemy!" shot back my uncle.

The truth is that the variety principle applies not just to marriage, but to all sorts of other personal relations. For instance, in family life, parents and children, who are inevitably in close contact much of the time, need periods of separation. And friends, too, must guard against seeing too much of one another.

The high rate of divorce in the United States and other countries may be primarily due, not to essential incompatibility between marriage partners, but simply to their getting bored with each other. "After thirty years we had nothing left to talk about," a college classmate told me when he was seeking a divorce. This sort of trouble is especially likely if the children in a family go away to school or college, and later leave home to pursue their own careers. Recently an old friend told me that the main reason for her divorce was that after her four children had flown the family nest, she could not endure the prospect of facing her husband, whom she still loved, alone at meals and trying to make conversation with him. And a relative of mine, after her husband retired from business at sixty-six and was at home most of the time, remarked to me in some alarm that in her marriage vows she had promised to take him for better or for worse, but not for lunch every day!

EXTRAMARITAL RELATIONS

The question arises as to whether extramarital relations in the variety pattern should go further than Platonic friendship in sharing such amusements as dining, dancing, walking, the movies, the theatre. Naturally that depends on the temperaments of the individuals involved, their vitality, their sexuality, their life-style in general. There can be warm companionship between a man and a woman that involves but little physical contact. Yet since it is clear that one can be sincerely in love with at least two persons at the same time, a husband or wife should feel free to go the whole way with another person whom he or she truly loves. Many married couples find a certain monotony in monogamy; what they may need, as a sort of safety valve, is some diversity in love-making. To limit the supreme sexual experience to just one member of the opposite sex for an entire lifetime represents an unreasonable restraint and a killjoy ethics.

The traditional one-and-perfect-mate theory, always overly romantic and unrealistic, dissolves in the light of a little common sense. That theory assumes that the well-matched husband and wife are completely sufficient for each other for life and can fully minister to each other's every mood and need. But this is expecting and asking too much. As I stated in *The Independent Mind*, "No one woman can possibly combine all the virtues that are characteristic of women in general; no one man has all the excellences of men in general. Every sensitive and completely alive person has something to give every other sensitive and completely alive person."[6]

These considerations show how unreasonable it is to have the bride and groom, as in some of the traditional Christian wedding ceremonies, make the promise of "forsaking all others." Also the vow "until death do us part," always too absolute a pledge, made more sense in previous centuries when death was likely to part husband or wife sooner than now. As for the phrase "for better or for worse," that too ought to be eliminated from wedding services. For how much "worse" is either of the partners expected to endure? (For a new type of wedding service, see Corliss Lamont, *A Humanist Wedding Service*, Buffalo, N.Y.: Prometheus, 1972.)

One idea that rather appeals to me is to have marriage contracts limited to ten years and then renewable for the same length of time if both parties agree; or, if either party insists, the contract would be automatically dissolved without litigation or social stigma. Virginia Satir, a well-known family therapist, has suggested that the marriage contract be for five years, but I think that is too short a time.

D. H. Lawrence, in lines written a full century after those I have quoted from Shelley, gives his version of why variety is needed in sex relations:

> Since you are confined in the orbit of me
> do you not loathe the confinement?
> Is not even the beauty and peace of an orbit
> an intolerable prison to you,
> as it is to everybody?[7]

It is to be remembered that human beings are not instinctually monogamous. Most men and women possess strong polygamous tendencies, and in many countries those tendencies find lawful and socially approved expression. In the West one civilized example of the variety principle has been the traditional ménage à trois, in which an unhappy triangle is transformed into a congenial trio.

The drive for sexual variety is also clearly discernible in today's far-out experimentation, such as youth communes, wife-swapping and the antics of "the swingers." The swingers consist of dissatisfied couples who contact other dissatisfied couples and meet to exchange mates for a night of vigorous sexual activity. The two or more couples involved have usually had no previous acquaintance with one another. Curiously enough, swingers are likely to be rather conservative in politics and economics. Swinging couples rarely get together with another couple more than once, since they want to guard against becoming emotionally involved. In other words, swingers are concerned only with the physical aspect of sex; there is no real love-making because love is purposely ruled out. I find all this somewhat revolting.

LOVING MORE THAN ONE

Within certain limits of physical and emotional capacity, the amount of love an individual can feel—be it for relatives, friends, lovers or his fellow humans—is very great indeed. Sexual love outside marriage need not reduce the love dispensed within that relationship. Love is an unceasing fountain of tenderness, overflowing from inner springs of joy and, paradoxically, growing more abundant with the giving. Hence those involved in extramarital sex may well return to their spouse more loving than ever. Nena and George O'Neill state in their excellent book *Open Marriage:* "Despite our tradition of limited love, it is entirely possible to love your marital partner with an intensely rewarding and continually growing love and at the same time to love another or others with a deep and abiding affection. And this extra dimension of love feeds back into the love between the partners."[8] Amending the famous couplet by Richard Lovelace, one can say:

> I could not love thee, dear, so much,
> Loved I not others, too.

One of the most helpful practices for a happy marriage is for husband and wife to take occasional vacations from each other, through travel or otherwise, perhaps, but not necessarily, with a member of the opposite sex. Such vacations break the marital routine and the "together forever" syndrome to keep the married couple fresh for each other. As everyone in love knows, there is a special joy and delight in seeing your mate again after one of you has been absent for some reason.

A husband and wife need vacations, not only from each other, but from the whole family, especially when it includes several children. Such vacations are particularly needful for a housewife who is doing most of the cooking and also taking care of the children. In fact, everybody ought to have periods when he is entirely alone and able to meditate on the course of his life, reviewing his past and making resolutions for the future.

Clearly, the extramarital relationships I have been discussing, whether or not they involve intercourse, demand that both husband and wife have no part of the sexual jealousy that has traditionally tormented humankind in the West. Such jealousy reached dangerous extremes if wife or husband so much as exchanged affectionate glances with another member of the opposite sex. Historically, a primary reason for the enormous importance given to genital faithfulness and unfaithfulness was the lack of reliable birth-control techniques. Now that those techniques, including abortion, are generally available, this importance has more and more diminished.

Whatever the degree of extramarital sex, either married partner is justified in objecting if his spouse neglects him or her in favor of some third person. Actually, in a successful marriage that includes outside sex relations, the husband and wife are likely to spend most of their nonworking time, probably as much as 90 percent, with each other, or together with their family or friends. Also, when poor health or the aging process intervenes to affect one's physical condition, there may not be sufficient energy available for extramarital activity of a sexual nature.

The majority of men and women divorced in the United States remarry and thereby achieve variety in sex through "serial marriage." Yet, they too, in second or third marriages, may find that the variety principle is relevant. It is my position that general recognition of this principle would considerably reduce the number of divorces. In any case we must regard divorce as the worst possible way of obtaining sexual variety and as a step to be taken only when everything else has failed.

Obviously, the variety in love of which I speak has always been practiced to some extent, and is more prevalent than ever in the present era. Until recently, however, extramarital sex has seldom been openly acknowledged and has for the most part been a male pastime. We raise the whole thing to a higher level by frankly acknowledging it as a legitimate, life-enhancing activity and by abolishing the double standard so that women are able to participate on an equal basis with men. The ethics of Marriage with Freedom that I am describing demands complete honesty between wife and husband about the variety principle.

If a married couple accepts that principle—and many happy couples never feel the need—it is to be understood that the husband continues to give primary allegiance to his wife as his true mate; the wife ever looks upon her husband as her true mate, and treats any other sexual friendship as secondary. And both seek to maintain their marriage at the highest level as a union of two lovers devoted to each other's happiness and the well-being of their family.

NOTES:

1. Sir Julian Huxley, *Memories II* (London: Allen and Unwin, 1973), p. 246.

2. George Santayana, *Reason in Society* (New York: Scribners, 1927), p. 32.

3. Bertrand Russell, *Marriage and Morals* (New York: Liveright, 1929), pp. 123-24. This illuminating book anticipated more than forty years ago ideas on sex relations that are widely accepted today.

4. Rollo May, *Love and Will* (New York: Norton, 1969), p. 316.

5. Walter Lippmann, *A Preface to Morals* (New York: Macmillan, 1929), p. 308.

6. Corliss Lamont, *The Independent Mind* (New York: Horizon Press, 1951), p. 100, in "A Humanist View of Marriage." In that essay of more than twenty years ago I first suggested the variety principle in marriage.

7. From "Both Sides of the Medal," in David H. Lawrence, *Look! We Have Come Through* (New York: Huebsch, 1918), pp. 87-88.

8. Nena and George O'Neill, *Open Marriage: A New Life-Style for Couples* (New York: Evans, 1972), p. 250.

The Affirmation of Life

Except for the infinitesimal part of its career represented by a few countries during the last century or so, mankind has ever been confronted with the crushing hardships of an economy of scarcity and the ruinous blasts of a nature mighty and untamed. Influenced to a great extent by this forbidding background, man early proceeded to invent the stern superstitions of traditional religion and puritanical morality. And since the weight of history and tradition hangs so heavy, it has been extraordinarily difficult to convince men that they ought to enjoy wholeheartedly and without any sense of sin the natural goods of this world.

The major principle of any rational Humanism is that since we possess only this one life we should make the most of it in terms of an abundant and reasoned happiness, unmarred and unrestrained by the conscience-stricken suppressions of the past. Such a philosophy heartily welcomes all life-enhancing and healthy pleasures, from the rollicking joys of vigorous youth to the contemplative delights of mellowed age. This way of life draws no hard and fast line, sets up no confusing and corrupting dualism, between the personality or mind, on the one hand, and the body or physical organism on the other. For in whatever he does man is a living unity of personality and body, a functioning oneness of mental and emotional and physical qualities. Thus it should be perfectly clear that the so-called goods of the spirit—of culture and art and responsible citizenship—are, like all other natural goods, an integral and indispensable part of the ideal life, the higher hedonism, for which Humanism stands.

Source: Man Answers Death (*Freeport, N.Y.: Books for Libraries Press, 1969*).

Even if the general viewpoint of Humanism be accepted, there is still one danger. That is the widespread phenomenon of future-worship, a too great willingness to sacrifice the present welfare of people on behalf of some distant goal and too great a tendency on the part of the individual himself to think of personal happiness in terms of tomorrow rather than of today. As the poets make plain, the time to live and to be glad is now.

Often it is claimed that those who have given up supernatural religion have nothing positive to offer humanity in place of the old, hallowed myths. This is very far indeed from the actual truth. The humanist conception of life constitutes a profound and passionate affirmation of the joys and beauties, the braveries and idealisms, of existence on this earth. This philosophy, while it provides the most effective of all answers to death, has by no means been motivated primarily by the fact of mortality. It stands on its own feet as an independent and forthright expression of human living at its fullest and best.

The humanist attitude does not mean merely the happy acceptance and cultivation of the numberless goods of an abundant nature. It also means that, however desirable a long and rounded life may be, the *quality* of life counts above all. It means that, however rich and worthwhile may be the more pleasing human experiences, there may come a time when a man must forego personal contentment to stand up for the things which he holds dear. It means that, however wholesome may be the full-hearted enjoyment of the quickly passing present, there is always our obligation to the future and to the ideal of human progress. Particularly is this true in this extremely exciting but troubled period of world history, when mankind is beset on every side with the most momentous problems.

It remains to be said that no matter how bleak the fortunes of the world may appear at any particular moment, a certain philosophical optimism is always justified. Not only are the potentialities of man in energy and intelligence well-nigh inexhaustible, but in any case, *life goes on*. If death is inevitable, so is life, which gives to death its entire significance. Thus, through the veritable eternities of time left to this revolving earth, it is practically certain that life and the affirmation of life will endure.

II

CIVIL LIBERTIES

It All Began in the Yard

My first big battle for free speech occurred forty-five years ago when I was a senior at Harvard College. As chairman of the Undergraduate Committee of the Harvard Union, I initiated a campaign to have the Union enliven its lecture program by inviting Eugene V. Debs, William Z. Foster and Scott Nearing to speak. The Governing Board of the Union, controlled by faculty members and alumni, reacted with alarm to these proposals, and they were turned down *in toto*. But the controversy stirred up by these suggestions, and the accompanying newspaper publicity, did induce the Union to adopt a somewhat more liberal program of speakers.

After graduation from Harvard in 1924, civil liberties became a major interest for me. The defense of the Bill of Rights seemed to me one of the most important social functions for the concerned citizen, and working out the intricate problems involved in that defense proved a constant intellectual stimulus and challenge. In 1932 I was elected to the Board of Directors of the American Civil Liberties Union and remained a member for twenty-two years.

With the outbreak of World War II in 1939, I was among those who fought most vigorously against the Board's tendency to compromise basic ACLU principles. I stuck to my position as the nationwide witch-hunt against the communists gathered momentum, and my stand aroused increasing anger in the anticommunist bloc on the Board. This bloc finally forced me out in November 1953 by persuading the Board to rescind my renomination. Using a blackmail tactic, they threatened

Source: Bill of Rights Journal, *December 1969.*

to resign unless I was dropped. My doom at the ACLU was sealed two months earlier, in September 1953, when Senator Joseph McCarthy subpoenaed me to appear before his Senate Subcommittee on Government Operations. The ACLU, in theory, supported my refusal to answer, on First Amendment grounds, most of McCarthy's questions. In actuality the Board was extremely embarrassed by my stand and feared some kind of contamination by association.

In August 1954, McCarthy induced the United States Senate to cite me for contempt of Congress. My challenge to McCarthy was a high point in my long campaign for civil liberties. My lawyer, Philip Wittenberg, in a brilliant argument, pressed for dismissal of the indictment on the ground that the McCarthy committee had disregarded the First Amendment and had indeed gone beyond its Congressional scope in questioning me at all. Federal Judge Edward Weinfeld ruled in my favor on Mr. Wittenberg's second point. The Government dropped the case in September 1956 when a United States Appeals Court unanimously affirmed the Weinfeld decision. It was one of the great moments of my life when I heard the news of this victory over McCarthy.

Shortly after I left the ACLU Board, I began a close working association with the Emergency Civil Liberties Committee, which had been founded at the height of the postwar red scare and the McCarthy madness. I became Vice-Chairman of ECLC in 1955 and Chairman in 1965. The word "Emergency" has been retained, as the word "National" has been added to the name because the crisis in civil liberties obviously has continued and has reached another peak as a result of the Vietnam war.

I entered the courts again in 1963 with an action against the United States Postmaster General to prevent him from enforcing a Congressional statute that clearly violated the Bill of Rights. This law directed the United States Post Office to screen for "communist political propaganda" all second- and third-class mail from foreign countries and to destroy it unless the addressee returned a postcard saying he wanted it. Again, an outstanding lawyer, Leonard B. Boudin, handled my case. As general counsel of the ECLC, which sponsored the suit, he carried my appeal to the United States Supreme Court. In May 1965 the Supreme Court handed down a unanimous (8-0) decision in my favor and declared the statute in question unconstitutional because it violated the First Amendment. It was the first time in the history of the Court that it had struck down a federal law as unconstitutional on First Amendment grounds.

I had told my wife that if I ever won a civil liberties case in the United States Supreme Court, it would be time for me to retire from the fray. But in 1965 the struggle for freedom in the United States was still at a crucial stage—and as interesting and exciting as ever. Besides, I was Chairman of ECLC. So I decided to keep on with my civil liberties activities and, far from retiring, perhaps am going to find myself involved for the duration.

The most satisfying thing for me about working to preserve and extend the Bill of Rights is that all good causes, all vital movements, are served thereby. It is a dangerous folly to say that civil liberties is "old hat" or irrelevant. Whether the issue is international peace and disarmament, the ending of America's war of aggression in Vietnam, the establishment of racial equality in every sphere, population control and family planning, the conservation of nature, a greater voice for students in educational institutions or replacing capitalism with a socialist economy—whatever the issue, freedom of expression is an absolute necessity to get your message across. Yet while civil liberties helps everyone who seeks to participate in public affairs, in itself it is not a guarantee for the success of any project or cause. It simply gives individuals and groups of varying economic, political and social viewpoints their best opportunity to win over a majority of the people. And that is basic to any struggle.

The Assault on Academic Freedom

The defense of academic freedom has always been an important part of the defense of the Bill of Rights in America. This is truer today than ever before.

In the general onslaught on civil liberties in the United States no group has suffered more than the members of the teaching profession. We teachers are now being treated as second-class citizens whose loyalty to our country is considered so questionable that strict control of our ideas must be maintained and special legislation passed to guard the community against us. The governmental authorities are more and more taking the attitude: "Beware of the teacher! He is probably trying surreptitiously to lead your child astray with communist propaganda, and to corrupt his morals with ultramodern notions about sex relations."

Teachers all over the country are being punished for relying on the Bill of Rights and refusing to cooperate in the violation of the American Constitution. American college presidents and boards of trustees have in general given way to the outside pressures. Only a few educational institutions in this country have lived up to their obligations to defend academic freedom and resist the encroachments of tyranny. McCarthyism is in its essence an anti-intellectual movement, like any form of fascism. More than anything else, the demagogues fear reading and writing, teaching and, above all, thinking. Hence intellectuals—

Source: Address to the Teachers Union of New York City, November 21, 1954.

teachers, writers, actors, radio and television people—are the ones most persecuted.

But whether or not, as McCarthy and the rest say, intellectuals are properly to be called "eggheads," this is no time for the nation to depend on "blockheads." This is what General Telford Taylor said in his excellent article on Congressional investigations in *The New York Times Magazine*.

One of the worst aspects of the situation is that the American Government has been sending secret agents into the classroom posing as students. When I taught in 1943 at Cornell's Intensive Study of Contemporary Russian Civilization, the staff discovered that there were two U.S. agents sending full reports of the lectures and discussions to Washington.

In April 1953 Dean Carl W. Ackerman of the Columbia School of Journalism issued a strong public protest against the snooping of government agents in which he said in part: "The practical problem which confronts deans, professors, school teachers and students today is political freedom to discuss public affairs in classrooms or at lunch or at a 'bull' session without fear that someone may make a record which may be investigated secretly, upon which he may be tried secretly and also convicted secretly, either by a governmental official or a prospective employer."

But I believe the tide may be turning in this struggle for civil liberties. Look what is happening to McCarthy in the U.S. Senate. Also, the gradual improvement in the international situation makes for more calm and less fear in our behavior at home.

I found in my files the other day a little poem written by a friend of mine, Andrew McPherson, and printed in *The Daily Compass* of May 1, 1951, after President Truman had dismissed General MacArthur. Here is the jingle, "Chant for Progressives":

> MacArthur, McCarran, McCarthy and McGrath
> All richly deserve the people's wrath.
> Happy are we that one Mac was fired;
> Now let's make sure the others are retired.

In three years look what has happened to the persons mentioned! I have had a bit of trouble with McCarthy myself—as a writer. A book of mine he did not like caused him to come after me. So I have been indicted for contempt of Congress, and in fighting through that case I expect to spring several surprises on Senator McCarthy.

In conclusion, I want to read you a poem by George Abbe that might well have been written for this occasion.

ACADEMIC FREEDOM DENIED

Now wake, you people of a cloistered knowledge,
and on the keys of living strike a chord.
The time is now. The air is ripe for courage.
Burn on the strings of need a singing word.
What value is your learning, if in the hour
of mortal peril it can cry no power?
Here is the coin's refusal, the owner's thong
bound at your throat, and you emit no sound.
When you have walked from classroom to the grave,
What note will vibrate, showing what you gave?
What memory will lift the scholar's head?
Brave teacher, teach that boldness is not dead.

Sitting long hours at the instrument of truth,
you know its contour, its assembled plan;
now that oppression shouts, there is no truce.
Strike on the instrument the deeds of man.
Subdue the canny fear, the wise denial;
drown casuistry in fierce and flaring glory;
on academic forehead burn your trail,
from your stretched fingers stream tradition's story:
Greeley and Whitman, Paine and angry Shelley.
Yes, it is time again; and if you seek
to husband strength that you may later rally,
then in that fatal hour, your hands will be too weak.

—George Abbe
The Wide Plains Roar;
Verses of Protest and Prophecy

A Good Fight

Many people have asked me over the past year or so how it feels to tangle with the Senator from Wisconsin and how it is that I still remain in good health despite a few strains and stresses now and then. Well, there is a certain philosophy involved here, and I shall give you frankly my confession of faith.

In the great battle that is being waged today for America's freedom, our chief aim must not be to avoid trouble, to stay out of jail, or even to preserve our lives, but to keep on fighting for civil liberties, for constitutional rights and whatever else we believe in. Our central purpose is not a ripe old age—although that would be gratifying—but the generous expenditure of our energies for the good of our country and the welfare of humanity.

Since we do not fear death in the line of duty, we should not fear lesser evils, such as calumny, prosecution by the government or imprisonment for our beliefs. Fighters for freedom throughout history have had to face similar ordeals. In our time this is a necessary part of the struggle against repression. And we should remember that American liberals and radicals in general have suffered comparatively little compared with their counterparts in Europe and Asia during the past two decades.

As we grow older—and I myself am over fifty now—we ought to grow more militant rather than more timorous about the basic progressive issues. For we who have lived half a century or more have already

Source: Excerpt from a speech by Corliss Lamont at a meeting of the Teachers Union of New York City, New York, November 21, 1954; printed in Monthly Review, *January 1955.*

113

enjoyed a very interesting and varied existence, and probably a great deal of personal happiness. No dictator, no powerful demagogue, no tyrannical government can take away our past. True, they may interfere with our future, but the important thing is that we should continue to resist and combat evil men and evil institutions as long as our hearts go on beating.

Our permanent rebellion is not a matter of force and violence; it is the daily rebellion of our spirits against the injustices perpetrated by the cruel, the stupid, the selfish and the shortsighted. In our struggle for a better world, we find a constant challenge to our intelligence, our ability and our perseverance in the face of heavy odds. And we march forward with sensitive and courageous friends who are the salt of the earth. For my own part, I must admit that nothing gives me greater pleasure than a good fight in a good cause. If I can contribute something to the downfall of Joseph McCarthy and what he stands for, I shall be a happy man indeed.

The Unending Struggle for Civil Liberties

I accept this award with much gratitude and must say that I feel quite overwhelmed by it. You are placing a heavy responsibility on me to work harder and more effectively for intellectual freedom. I shall hang this beautiful scroll above my desk as a constant reminder of the job that needs to be done.

This citation I consider less as an individual award than as a symbol of the great battle for the Bill of Rights in which all of us here are engaged. And to you of the Teachers Union I apply these same words, "valiant and unswerving in defense of intellectual freedom."

I am proud to be a member of this union. For you are carrying on the great tradition of freedom of thought, which is not only the birthright of the American Republic as expressed in the Bill of Rights, but also Western culture's proudest heritage, reaching far back into the civilizations of the past. You and I live in the twentieth century, but man's fight for knowledge and the free use thereof was already a live issue in ancient Greece of the fifth century B.C.

We who support the unceasing liberty of the inquiring intellect can claim as ours the noblest of all freedom's martyrs, the Greek teacher of philosophy, Socrates. Whom does mankind honor and remember today—Socrates, who drank the hemlock rather than compromise on his beliefs, or those who brought about his death?

Let me mention some other thinkers who have taken part in the ages-long struggle of the human race towards democracy. In ancient Greece,

Source: This article was an address delivered April 2, 1955, on accepting an award from the Teachers Union of New York City for "Valiant and Unswerving Defense of Intellectual Freedom."

again, there was Protagoras who, because he was an agnostic, was accused of impiety, his writings publicly burned and himself banished from Athens. There was Anaxagoras, who fled from Athens after he was condemned to death for asserting that the sun was "a mass of red-hot metal" instead of a deity, as religion taught.

In my own field of philosophy we find yet another example: the Catholic Inquisition burned Giordano Bruno at the stake in 1600 for believing in pantheism. Bruno's words when he received judgment could aptly be quoted by many civil-liberties victims in America today: "Maybe you who condemn me are in greater fear than I who am condemned."

In the seventeenth century Spinoza was ostracized and hounded throughout his life because of his unorthodox ideas in philosophy. Spinoza's chief work, *Ethics*, did not appear until after his death because he kept postponing publication for fear of violent reprisals.

In the late eighteenth century the German philosopher and teacher Immanuel Kant, whose brilliant system had supposedly saved the day for the Christian religion, was severely rebuked by the King of Prussia as follows: "Our highest person has been greatly displeased to observe how you misuse your philosophy to undermine and destroy many of the most important and fundamental doctrines of the Holy Scripture and Christianity. We demand of you immediately an exact account, and expect that in the future you will give no such cause of offense. . . . If you continue to oppose this order, you may expect unpleasant consequences."

Kant, who was seventy years old at the time, replied that every scholar should have the right to freedom of opinion. He then compromised on the issue, however, saying: "Recantation would be abject, but silence, in a case like the present, is the duty of a subject." And he remained silent on religious philosophy until the death of the Prussian King three years later.

In twentieth-century America the College of the City of New York forced Bertrand Russell out of his professorship of philosophy in 1940. A group led by Bishop Manning had demanded that Russell be ousted on the grounds that he was "lecherous, salacious, libidinous, venereous, erotomaniac, aphrodisiac, atheistic, irreverent, narrow-minded, bigoted and untruthful." Incidentally, D. H. Lawrence had said in 1915: "Poor Bertie Russell. He's all disembodied mind."

Well, as you see, teachers and philosophers—not to mention scientists and writers—have had, from the beginnings of civilization, a perennial struggle to achieve and maintain freedom of expression. In the past some of mankind's greatest thinkers have been silenced—through imprisonment, execution, banishment or self-censorship.

Today we carry on that same struggle, and in so doing we implement our implicit pact of fellowship and understanding with the truth-seekers and dissenters of all history.

As New Yorkers we are proud in many ways of this splendid city, which perhaps deserves to be called the *first* city of the world. Yet the Russell case, in which academic freedom was so outrageously violated, indicated a trend here of which we cannot be proud.

In the last few years this trend towards the disregard of teachers' rights has become a disastrous plunge into the abyss of a modern inquisition. This city—our city—which should and could be an example for America and the world regarding academic freedom, has actually spearheaded the witch-hunt against teachers in the United States. Only a few weeks ago the Board of Education passed a resolution that attempts to compel teachers to become informers, on pain of losing their jobs.

Recently, too, we have discovered that this same Board of Education in 1952 employed a professional informer, Harvey Matusow, to help put the finger on alleged communist teachers. And now Matusow, in his book of confessions, *False Witness,* swears that the "information" provided was all a pack of lies.

Let's be frank about it: the burning shame of New York City for our generation has become the antifreedom policies of the Board of Education, the Board of Higher Education and the various educational authorities who cooperate with them.

It is time for this nation to end this racket in which lying ex-communists and ex-spies, through slander, perjury and frame-up, send innocent men to jail or ruin their reputations. It is time for Congressional committees, instead of utilizing these shameful characters for the violation of civil liberties and elevating them into heroes or heroines, to investigate and expose the entire sordid business. And I join many others in calling upon the Subcommittee on Constitutional Rights of the Senate Judiciary Committee to undertake immediately a thorough investigation of the informer racket. It would also be most salutary for the Department of Justice and Attorney General Herbert Brownell to do the same.

Because of the very nature of our work, we teachers are bound to be involved in these various battles. In a sense, the more laws and resolutions that are passed against us, the more we can congratulate ourselves on our importance. In fact, philosophers from Plato to John Dewey have kept repeating that education is the most important element in the molding of a person's mind.

Let me turn for a moment to some light verse that describes the situation:

> Congressmen and Senators have their little day,
> But in the end, you know, it's the teachers who hold sway;
> We're eggheads, dreamers and always troublemakers.
> Yet of the world, it seems, we are the movers and shakers.

The antidemocratic, anti-intellectual demagogues of today apparently realized this. That is why they make such mighty efforts to stimulate heresy-hunting and thought control in the schools, colleges and universities of the United States. They proceed on the assumption that what happens to American education will eventually happen to America.

But we teachers must not become too preoccupied with our own woes. I must remind you that one of the most significant signs of the gravity of the present civil liberties crisis is the extent to which free speech and the simple right to work are threatened throughout the whole sphere of our culture.

I do not recall that in the period of hysteria following the First World War, actors, for example, were in danger of losing their jobs for being dissenters. But recently, Congressional investigations and blacklists in the movies, the theatre and television have been very much the order of the day. One of the worst things about our current situation is that the penalization of political dissent has come so generally to include dismissing a person from employment, not only in government service, but also in most of the professions and private business.

In addition to teachers, actors and government employees, those who have lost their jobs in the great American purge include lawyers, ministers, doctors, engineers, businessmen, trade-union leaders, workers, journalists, singers, dancers, United Nations officials and liquor dealers. In California a bill was introduced into the legislature to revoke the license of any person coming under the Business and Profession Code who refuses to answer questions on political opinions and associations put by a Congressional or state investigating committee. Required to obtain licenses under this code are some 160 categories of business or professional people, including doctors, nurses, lawyers, druggists, beauticians, bartenders, barbers, plumbers, boxers, wrestlers and undertakers.

Meanwhile, the proud purgers of American literature scored one of their most resounding victories two months ago when they pressured the Girl Scouts of America into major revisions of the 1953 edition of the *Girl Scouts Handbook*. The American Legion, for instance, passed a resolution condemning the Girl Scouts on the ground that the handbook contained "un-American" literature. The Illinois commander especially criticized favorable references to the United Nations.

The Girl Scouts unfortunately yielded to these pressures and made some sixty changes in the handbook. The corrections eliminated the phrase "citizens of the world," all mention of the League of Women Voters, any reference to housing as an activity of the United States Government and much of the material on the United Nations, including any reference to the Declaration of Human Rights. The corrections also changed the phrase "one world" to "my world," struck out the word "world" entirely in more than twenty places, and substituted "Tea-India" for "Tea-China."

This ridiculous business of the *Girl Scouts Handbook* is less important in itself than for what it shows about the objectives of the American witch-hunters. Those who attacked the handbook did not make the familiar claim that it was spreading communist propaganda. Their main charge was that it gave space to facts and views which tended to support a liberal attitude in international relations. And this brings out the point that the antifreedom drive today is not just against communist ideas, but against all ideas that diverge from right-wing Republicanism.

Let us make no mistake about it. The ultimate purpose of the reactionary forces in this country is to bar all liberal, progressive and democratic ideas, enterprises and organizations. And the so-called liberal groups like Americans for Democratic Action that help to stir up the mad frenzy over the alleged communist menace will, through this unprincipled strategy, cut their own throats in the end. As Mr. I. F. Stone said of such people: "To prove that they are not soft on communism, they are ready to demonstrate that they are soft in the head."

The notion of an overriding communist menace in America has all along been a hoax, played up by rightist and fascist elements to camouflage their real antidemocratic aims; exploited by dangerous demagogues to advance their personal political fortunes; manipulated by yellow journalists and careerists of all types as a means of making money out of sensationalism; and utilized by government authorities to cloak a reckless foreign policy and to frighten the people into sanctioning tremendous expenditures on armaments and nuclear bombs.

Only in such terms as these can we explain how America, with the wealthiest and strongest capitalist economy in the world and possessing one of the smallest, weakest and most unsuccessful of all communist parties, has developed a deeper and more unreasoning dread of communism than any other country. Look across the Atlantic at England, 3,000 miles nearer to the supposed threat of Soviet aggression than we and infinitely more vulnerable in case of war. There is no hysteria there, no witch-hunt, hardly any of this pernicious nonsense about the communists. The British, cool and calm as ever, maintain the even tenor of their way and, without a written constitution, have come nearer than any other nation to actualizing the principles of the American Bill of Rights, now so flouted in our own land.

Yet surely in the long run we Americans are not going to let Britain or any other country establish a better record for freedom than we. But unless we are careful, this unhappy short run of the postwar period will indeed turn into a long run.

No professional group in the United States has a greater responsibility in this situation than the almost 2,000,000 school and college teachers. Yes, we teachers do have a central function in society. And our voice, our efforts, our perseverance may well be decisive in this struggle for civil liberties. That struggle, it seems to me, has already taken a turn for the better.

Upon its outcome depends the direction of American life for a long time to come. And because of America's influence in the world, what happens to democracy here will have an important effect on democracy everywhere else.

As long as human government and society remain in existence, indeed, as long as the race of man endures, complete civil liberties for all persons everywhere will remain a universally valid ideal. Today, then, we fight not only for full freedom of the mind as an ideal to be attained in this nation, but also as a world ideal to be securely established in every corner of the earth.

Dissent in the West

Humanists and civil libertarians have long needed, within the covers of a single book, a comprehensive and authoritative history of dissent in the Western world. Dr. Barrows Dunham provides just such a history in this notable volume, which starts with ancient Egypt, ancient Greece and Old Testament Palestine, and brings us down through the period of Senator Joseph McCarthy's ascendancy in the United States. It is a book, moreover, that is brilliantly written, interspersed with apt quotations and strewn with fascinating footnotes that reveal the corrosive wit of the author. *Heroes and Heretics* most certainly deserves a place on that much-discussed humanist bookshelf that contains the minimum volumes necessary for an understanding of the humanist way of life.

Early in his study Dr. Dunham defines heresies as those "ideas that disrupt an existing society in such a way as to change, or to threaten to change, the distribution of power within it." Carrying over this definition to the functioning of organizations—political, religious, academic or whatnot—the author states: "It is . . . part of the strategy of leadership and part of the politics of organizational life to regard doctrines not merely as true or false but as conducive to unity or disruptive of it. In this second pair of alternatives lies the distinction between orthodoxy and heresy. For a doctrine is orthodox if it helps unite the organization; it is heretical if it divides."

Dr. Dunham pursues this theme with great skill and erudition, giving an account and analysis in depth of practically all the chief heretics of

Source: This review of Heroes and Heretics (*New York: Knopf, 1964) was first published in* The Humanist, *September/October 1964.*

Western thought who challenged some aspect of the conventional wisdom and thereby collided (often losing their lives in the process) with the organization men of the Establishment. Because much of this struggle, especially after the onset of the Renaissance, centered around doctrines that completely discarded all ideas of supernatural gods and immortalities, Dr. Dunham's book has particular interest and significance for those who today believe in naturalistic Humanism. His survey gives to Humanists an inspiring sense of their historic roots.

Since governmental and other organizations are essential to the functioning and continuance of civilized societies, Dr. Dunham's sociopolitical history of dissent throws considerable light on contemporary controversies in America and throughout the world. We must admit that whatever heights of achievement and collective virtue a society may attain, there will always be some degree of antagonism between its ruling institutions and its heretics. But a truly democratic society, such as the American Constitution and Bill of Rights were supposed to guarantee, would not compel its heretics to become heroes by risking or undergoing death, imprisonment, ostracism or loss of employment.

Some readers will no doubt disagree with Dr. Dunham here and there, as when he claims that the historical Jesus was "the leader of an armed movement for national liberation," that Spinoza was a pantheist, that something vaguely called "dialectical logic" has become the key for solving human problems, and that "during the hundred years since our Civil War, heresy in the United States has narrowed to questions arising from the relationships between capital and labor." This last statement by the author overlooks the major conflict that is still raging between Humanism and the prevailing orthodoxies of supernaturalist religion and philosophy, as well as the continuing battle over the relation between church and state in America.

Despite the terrible ordeals of the truth-sayers, the Humanists, and the antiorganization fighters over the past 3,000 years, *Heroes and Heretics* is basically optimistic about the future. In Dr. Dunham's view, the oppressors in the West—the political and religious powers-that-be—have almost always been of the Right. Very hopeful, then, is his sweeping generalization: "It is interesting to observe, and I believe a moral can be drawn from it, that the whole of modern history . . . is a record of catastrophic defeat for right-wing politics. . . . Almost five hundred years of strife—stubborn, constant and decisive—proclaims the fact that, short of the maiming or annihilation of our race, the members of it are to be supreme upon the planet, with none to molest them and none to rule."

More on *Heroes and Heretics*

I am in general accord with Stephen H. Fritchman's enthusiastic review of Barrows Dunham's *Heroes and Heretics* (*Monthly Review*, May 1964). This book is a brilliant piece of work and stands out uniquely as a reliable and inclusive socio-political history of dissent in the West. To progressives, radicals, socialists, communists and anyone else who refuses to conform to the Establishment, this volume gives an invaluable understanding of their prototypes in the past and their own role and possibilities in the present.

At the same time this work gives rise to some important questions that were not covered in the Fritchman review. I refer especially to Dr. Dunham's chapter "Movement, Life and Dialectics" (pp. 392-422). Here he purports to show that modern man, in order to solve his problems, must adopt "dialectical logic—the view that things modify one another, 'opposites' acting upon 'opposites.'" (p. 405). This logic, "though it has not yet attained anything like the refinement of the logic that descends from Aristotle, does nevertheless describe the point of view, the expectations about reality, which enabled Darwin to produce his theory of evolution, Marx his theory of social development, and Einstein the physics which in doctrine and application has so much astonished us all." (p. 397).

Dunham admits that "in human discourse there undoubtedly is a need that every term shall maintain one identical meaning throughout any stretch of argument. . . ." (p. 406) and that "terms, no doubt, ought to have precise meanings—that is, 'clear and distinct' reference to the

Source: Monthly Review, April 1965.

world—and no term can, without perilous ambiguity, have two or more meanings at once." (p. 406). In these statements the author rather patronizingly concedes the pertinence of Aristotle's first basic law of thought, the Law of Identity, meaning that A is A, namely, that a definite thing is always that same thing.

The inescapable paradox is that Dunham, in trying to explain what he means by "dialectical logic" (never precisely defined), is compelled to utilize not only the Law of Identity, but also Aristotle's Law of Contradiction (A cannot be both B and not-B at the same time and in the same respect), and the Law of Excluded Middle (A is either B or not-B, meaning that an assertion is either true or false). The Soviet and Marxist philosophers who talk mystically about the dialectic fall into the same trap. If they tell you that *Aristotle's logic is false*, they have to rely on all of his laws in order to make sense. (In the italicized passage, "Aristotle's logic" is equivalent to A and "false" to B.)

Now Dunham is of course right in insisting that change and becoming go on everywhere all the time. But we do not need a new logic to bring us knowledge of these facts; all we require is careful observation and scientific deduction based on the old logic. Some relevant reading would likewise be helpful. Unquestionably, Hegel and Marx made twentieth-century thinkers and doers more aware of change as a fundamental trait in the very structure of things. However, Darwin completed his world-shaking biological discoveries before dialectical logic was formulated, and Einstein depended on no such logic in his great scientific achievements.

The three main principles of Marxist dialectics are: (1) the law of the interpenetration and unity of opposites, (2) the law of the transformation of quantity into quality and vice versa, and (3) the law of the negation of negation. The second law is universally acknowledged as true and was recognized by science long before Marx and Engels came upon the scene. But the first and third laws are, in my opinion, of doubtful validity, and their application to human life and society is vague.

But assuming for the moment that all three laws of dialectical logic are sound, my point is that they should be regarded as *supplementing* Aristotelian logic, not as *supplanting* it. For that traditional logic does make manifest the form, the frame, the structure in which human beings carry on all intelligible discourse, including discourse about dialectics.

My other chief criticism of *Heroes and Heretics* is occasioned by the following statement: "During the hundred years since our Civil War, heresy in the United States has narrowed to questions arising from the relationships between capital and labor. . . . To be sure, prosecutions for heresy have occurred within the churches, but these have had no importance except to the victims. . . . The Scopes trial of 1925, in which a young biologist was convicted of teaching Darwinism in a high school in Tennessee, was a pathetic comedy devoid of serious interest." (p. 450).

These generalizations seem to me far too sweeping. Philosophic and religious heresies, not to mention prosecutions centering around "obscenity," continue to be of immense importance in this country. Still on the current agenda is the ages-long conflict between the prevailing religious supernaturalism and the dissenting philosophies of Humanism, materialism and naturalism. In general, of course, witch-hunts no longer take place *within* the churches; but it is almost as difficult for a professed atheist as for a communist to obtain and hold a teaching position, or to get time on radio or TV.

Then also there is the major battle being waged over the First Amendment's guarantee of separation of church and state. Of great danger here is the amendment proposed to the Civil Rights Bill by Representative John Ashbrook, who wants the law to say that no employer need hire an atheist.

As for the trial of John T. Scopes for the teaching of evolution, that event was of enormous interest and importance to civil libertarians and progressives everywhere. Even today many American textbooks on biology play down or omit the central findings of Darwin; and as I write this comment, the press brings the news that a group of religious bigots in Arizona are attempting to put through an amendment to the state constitution that would ban as "atheism" the teaching of biological evolution.

Dunham's analysis is also faulty in that it overlooks entirely the sharpening struggle for educational integration and racial democracy in the United States and the fact that to support these aims openly and militantly is heresy in many parts of the country—heresy that is punishable by loss of employment, social ostracism, jail and sometimes death.

William O. Douglas's *A Living Bill of Rights*

Amid the flood of books on civil liberties published during the past decade, this brief summary of the Bill of Rights by Supreme Court Justice William O. Douglas stands out as one of the most valuable for the ordinary citizen untrained in the law. It is appropriately dedicated "To our high school students from Alaska to Puerto Rico, from Maine to Hawaii."

Justice Douglas points out at the start that the complete American Bill of Rights has come to mean not only the first ten amendments to the Constitution, but also "the guarantees of freedom contained in the body of the Constitution itself." It is so unusual for a book on civil liberties systematically to list these twelve important guarantees that I give them below in Justice Douglas's own words:

1. The prohibition of any religious test for public office.

2. The prohibition against the suspension of the writ of *habeas corpus*—the device used to test the legality of a person's confinement in a jail or penitentiary.

3. The requirement that a person be tried not in a distant place but in the state where the crime was committed.

4. The prohibition against *ex post facto* laws—which are passed today but made applicable to yesterday's conduct which was lawful when people engaged in it.

5. The provision against bills of attainder—legislative measures by which people are outlawed from the community and barred from enjoying any rights of citizenship.

Source: This review of A Living Bill of Rights *(New York: Doubleday, 1961) was first published in the* National Guardian, *May 22, 1961.*

6. The requirement that each act of treason be testified to by two witnesses.

7. The prohibition of slavery and involuntary servitude by the Thirteenth Amendment.

8. The guarantee that all persons born or naturalized in the United States are citizens regardless of their race or color by the Fourteenth Amendment.

9. The Fourteenth Amendment's command that no state shall deprive any person of life, liberty or property without due process of law.

10. The Equal Protection Clause of the Fourteenth Amendment barring any state from denying any person the equal protection of the laws.

11. The Fifteenth Amendment's guarantee that the right of citizens to vote shall not be denied or abridged either by the Federal Government or any state on account of race or color.

12. The Nineteenth Amendment that protects a woman's right to vote.

Justice Douglas goes on to discuss in plain and simple language the various provisions of the expanded Bill of Rights that he has outlined. In these critical times, when the Kennedy Administration has created throughout the United States a brink-of-war psychology with reference to Cuba, I find enlightening the author's four or five pages about "the principle of civilian ascendancy over the military" in the American system of government. This is revealed especially in the Second and Third Amendments, in the writ of *habeas corpus*, and in U.S. Supreme Court decisions ruling that the civil courts possess the power and duty to determine whether martial law is justified in some emergencies.

Towards the end of his book, Justice Douglas stresses the fact that the courts and the Constitution "can, at best, give only a minimum protection to our liberties. They can deal, for the most part, only with actions of government officials." What Professor Walter Gellhorn of Columbia calls the "power-aggregates of Private Government"—the vast conglomeration of business corporations, of radio and television stations, and of reactionary pressure groups such as the American Legion, the Daughters of the American Revolution and the John Birch Society—are a constant menace to freedom of speech in specific situations and, in general, help mightily to develop an atmosphere of conformity and fear.

This atmosphere is influential in determining the stand that the individual citizen takes concerning unorthodox opinions. Yet, as Justice Douglas says, "the reality of freedom in our daily lives is shown by the attitudes and policies of people towards each other in the very block or township where we live. There we will find the real measure of *A Living Bill of Rights.*"

While reading this book, we must remember that the uncompromising views on the Bill of Rights expressed here by Justice Douglas represent a minority position on the Supreme Court as presently constituted. This fact demonstrates that as regards civil liberties we are involved in a continuous seesaw battle which calls for the unrelenting efforts of all lovers of freedom during the years and decades to come. In this battle Justice Douglas's little book can serve as an important weapon.

The Right To Read

Paul Blanshard is author of the best-selling study, *American Freedom and Catholic Power*, which demonstrates the formidable extent to which the Catholic hierarchy opposes, in both principle and practice, the basic tenets of American democracy. In *The Right To Read* Mr. Blanshard has written what is likely to become another current classic on one of the most important aspects of civil liberties.

In this volume the author covers the whole field of literary censorship, from the suppression of books and other publications that voice unpopular political or economic opinions, to the suppression of material on the grounds of alleged obscenity or incitement to crime. And he fully identifies the chief agents of these repressive practices, from government officials such as the U.S. Postmaster General and the municipal police, to private organizations such as the early New England Watch and Ward Society, the American Legion and the National Organization of Decent Literature, founded in 1938 and controlled by Catholics.

In supplying the historical background, Mr. Blanshard shows how gradual has been the growth of tolerance in the form of the right to publish and to read. Even Milton in *Areopagitica* brushed aside freedom for "Popery and open superstition," and took the position that the law could not permit that "which is impious or evil absolutely against faith or manners." Thus he ruled out the free-speech rights of Catholics, atheists and social revolutionists. The American colonies, founded by religious dissidents emigrating from tyrannical England, unfortu-

Source: This review of The Right To Read (*Boston: Beacon Press, 1955*) *was first published in* Science and Society, *Summer 1956.*

nately adopted the main features of the English system of censorship.

The new American Republic's Bill of Rights, ratified in 1791, was an emancipation proclamation for civil liberties; but its concrete implementation has required ceaseless struggle from the day of its enactment to the present. As Mr. Blanshard points out, one of the worst setbacks to freedom of opinion in this country was the passage by Congress in 1872 of a general literary censorship law, commonly known as the Comstock Act, which barred so-called obscene literature from the mails. During and immediately after the First World War, government censorship of dissenting economic and political views vastly increased, and this trend has reached its apex during the past decade.

Mr. Blanshard is critical of the U.S. Supreme Court decision in the Dennis case because communist books played an indispensable part in the conviction of the eleven communist leaders. He writes: "When the use of a book may be part of a crime, the right to read that book is forever clouded. A guilty book is a little like a guilty man after he has been convicted. Thereafter he is tainted, and guilt by association becomes possible." (pp. 53-54).

The basic trouble behind the Dennis decision, Mr. Blanshard implies, is the clear-and-present-danger rule laid down by Justice Holmes in 1919. Quite rightly the author says: "A worried or reactionary or chauvinistic judge could sincerely interpret the present-danger theory in such a way as to justify a ban on virtually all pro-Communist literature." (p. 52).

In recent years the vague clear-and-present-danger test has also been used in an attempt to determine whether writings are obscene, and the American Civil Liberties Union, which ought to know better, has been advocating this extension of a legal standard which threatens all freedom of expression.

I suggest, as a rule far more concrete and susceptible of verification, that when the language or picture constitutes a clear, direct and deliberate incitement to the present commission of violence or some other serious overt and criminal act, then the government has the right to lay down restrictions and prosecute.

The application of this standard to the determination of obscenity would mean that no writing or picture could be censored unless it plainly had the intention of inciting, or would incite, to sexual crime. If such a legal test resulted in the reduction of obscenity prosecutions to a minimum, that would be all to the good. Prosecutions for blasphemy as a religious offense have virtually disappeared in the United States, and I for one shall welcome the day when the obscenity issue has faded away into the same obscurity.

Since the end of the Second World War civil libertarians in this country have quite understandably been preoccupied with the manifold violations of political freedom. Mr. Blanshard's book serves vividly to remind us that censorship on the grounds of obscenity establishes precedents and creates an atmosphere that facilitates suppression in other fields of opinion. Civil liberties are indivisible. And so liberals and radicals who uphold the Bill of Rights have the obligation to oppose unjustified prosecutions for obscenity and to defend the constitutional rights even of those who publish comic books featuring crime, violence, torture and sexual sadism.

Even now New York State has a law, passed in 1955 and aimed at comic books, which is so broad in its language that it puts in jeopardy many a literary classic. Mr. Blanshard is opposed to such laws and favors "voluntary reform" on the part of the comic book publishers under the pressure of public opinion. He does not, however, adequately explore the point that, insofar as comics may be a menace to the minds of children, parents have the responsibility of protecting their offspring by guiding their reading to a considerable degree.

Another valuable reminder implicit in the Blanshard study is that in the field of civil liberties the right of the audience to read, to listen or to see is just as important as the right of the individual to express himself in one way or another. During the last decade there has been an overemphasis on the constitutional rights of the *individual* to express himself, partly because it is usually an individual who is blasted by a Congressional committee, dismissed from his job, prosecuted in the courts or sent to jail. But the right of people to seek and acquire knowledge and to make choices on the basis of this right—or the privilege merely to enjoy literature and the arts—is coequal with any other right in the whole roster of freedoms.

O, Canada . . .

"Cut out this nonsense," said the Toronto Globe and Mail in an editorial castigating the strange behavior of Canada's Immigration Department. The comment came after local immigration officials at Windsor, Ontario, excluded me from Canada on Tuesday, May 8, as an "undesirable visitor," and then on Wednesday, May 9 (after I had lodged an appeal with the Minister of Immigration at Ottawa) suddenly reversed the decision and permitted me to enter the country.

The Globe and Mail criticism was typical of the Canadian press. Several other editorials, as well as cartoons, appeared, attacking the government, and news reports and columnists gave sympathetic accounts of my case and of my statements ridiculing the position of the Immigration Department. The American press also gave my case remarkably good coverage.

The "nonsense" started on May 8 on the morning train from Detroit to Toronto. One minute I was quietly reading The Readers Digest; the next minute immigration authorities at Windsor escorted me from the train and, after detaining me for two hours, sent me back to Detroit. I had planned my trip to Toronto to give two evening lectures at the First Unitarian Church under the auspices of the Toronto Humanist Association. My topics were "Humanism and Civil Liberties" and "Humanism versus the Traditional Religions." I was also to have appeared May 8 on CBC-TV, which is run by the Canadian Government. This broadcast had to be canceled. However, at the church meeting that night, the Reverend W. P. Jenkins of the Unitarian Church spoke in my stead, assailing

Source: National Guardian, July 2, 1956.

my deportation as a sign that Canada was suffering "a backlash of American McCarthyism."

The prospects of a quickly moving appeal seemed hopeless, since the officials at Windsor told me no action would be taken for weeks. However, after I consulted counsel and filed an appeal late Tuesday night, the Canadian Minister of Immigration, John W. Pickersgill, reversed the deportation within twelve hours. I got the news at the Hotel Statler in Detroit about noon on May 9.

My second lecture was due to be given in Toronto at 8 p.m. Could I make it? There were no afternoon trains from Detroit that would get me there in time, and I was reluctant to fly because it was raining pitchforks. Finally I hired a drive-your-own car. Starting about 1:30, I drove the 250 miles to Toronto, eating sandwiches for lunch and supper while steering with one hand. It was a tough, fast trip on an unfamiliar route through the rain, and I lost my way several times. At 7:45 p.m. I arrived at my hotel in Toronto, had two cups of coffee, was interviewed by a *New York Times* correspondent on the phone and got to my meeting at the Unitarian Church only twenty minutes late.

In spite of the heavy rain, there was a good attendance; perhaps because of the publicity, the audience was considerably larger than it otherwise would have been.

Meanwhile, furor had broken out in the press and in Parliament. M. J. Coldwell, leader of the socialist CCF (Cooperative Commonwealth Federation) and other M.P.s raised questions on the floor of Commons about my being barred from Canada. Mr. Pickersgill reacted like the typical bureaucrat on a hot tin roof. He said I myself was to blame for the entire incident because I had informed the press of my proposed lectures in Canada. This had led the United Press to ask embarrassing questions.

Actually my Toronto lectures had been well advertised by the humanist group; and since I was on a general speaking tour, including engagements in Los Angeles and San Francisco, I had released my itinerary to the press. This procedure is routine for me.

Mr. Pickersgill suggested that the whole affair "was a deliberate attempt on the part of a communist front organization to portray this country as a country in which we are afraid to allow free speech." He said the National Council of American-Soviet Friendship was the group responsible, in spite of the fact that the council had had nothing whatsoever to do with my tour. My reply to Mr. Pickersgill's canard of a communist conspiracy was that his own immigration inspectors must have been in on the plot, since they had made the original decision against me.

I do believe that my Canadian experience finally added up to a significant victory and precedent for civil liberties and the right to travel. The original decision to bar me quickly boomeranged against the Canadian Government under the pressure of public opinion. As an editorial in the Rochester *Democrat and Chronicle* put it, Canada quickly became "pink in its official ears."

For the first time in my memory New York's *Daily News* and *Daily Mirror* attacked me editorially. The best explanation I can give for this phenomenon is that these two newspapers thought the Canadian fiasco had redounded so much in my favor, and as a civil liberties victory, that they felt it necessary to try to discredit me. This explanation suggests itself because a decided majority of editorial and news accounts in both countries was either outspokenly sympathetic to me, or at least fair and neutral.

Paranoia on the Loose

After a three weeks' speaking tour to the Pacific Coast and Middle West, chiefly on civil liberties and philosophy, I can report that fanatical right-wing groups made a greater effort than ever before to disrupt my meetings and discredit me as a lecturer. My trip was made under the auspices of the American Humanist Association, an organization strictly nonpolitical and nonpartisan.

The first skirmish occurred in San Diego, where the John Birchers and their friends have set up the "Patriotic Information Bureau," with AT 1-1776 as its telephone number. If you dial 1776, you receive the "Message of the Day" on a special recording. The day before I was to appear at the Independent Forum of San Diego County, the "message" all day warned the citizenry that I was coming to town. It named all the allegedly subversive organizations to which I have belonged.

At the entrance to the lecture hall, four persons representing the rightist San Diego Speakers Information Bureau distributed two-page summaries of a report about my "sinister" associations—stale old material issued years ago by the California Senate Committee on Un-American Activities. Among the crimes: my inclusion of an introduction by John Dewey in my book *The Illusion of Immortality;* speaking at the Reverend Stephen Fritchman's First Unitarian Church in Los Angeles; opposition to William Randolph Hearst; and serving as a director of the American Civil Liberties Union, a position I have not held since 1954.

In my speech I said I was especially interested in the year 1776 be-

Source: National Guardian, *May 14, 1962.*

cause my ancestors had fought in the American Revolution, and one of them, Elihu Corliss, had taken part in the Battle of Bunker Hill.

Another San Diego area incident demonstrates more vividly the pitiful pathology of the pseudo-patriots behind the right-wing upsurge. On March 31, a few days before I arrived, Newton E. Armstrong, Jr., a resident of nearby Coronado and a sophomore at San Diego State College, was found hanged by a clothesline from a beam in his parents' bedroom. The coroner's verdict was suicide; but Armstrong's father, a retired Army major and a member of the John Birch Society, maintained that his son had been assassinated by "the communists" because he was active in Students for Freedom, a campus right-wing extremist group.

An uproar ensued. The local press ran big headlines and newspaper stories appeared throughout the country. San Diego County's district attorney, up for reelection in the fall, tried to cash in on the anticommunist angle. Students for Freedom members reported threatening phone calls, and one said he had found a hangman's noose in his car. Si Casady, editor of the *El Cajon Valley News,* wrote: "You got the impression that the entire student body of San Diego State College was threatened with extinction, if only the supply of clothesline held out." In the next two weeks Casady received more than thirty postcards from all over the U.S., all bearing the same message: "Dear Comrade: Did your communist friends murder Newton Armstrong, Jr.?"

The authorities finally called in crime expert Ray Pinker from the Los Angeles Police Department. After a thorough investigation Pinker declared categorically that Armstrong's death was a suicide. No one knows why he killed himself, but some weeks before his death West Point had rejected him as a cadet. Query: Is West Point controlled by the communists?

At my meeting in Sacramento an American Legionnaire started to read the same list of my "subversive" connections. When he noted committee citations of me, the audience clapped vigorously. I pointed out that the Legionnaire was pursuing Joe McCarthy's smear technique and was in fact a little McCarthy himself.

At a meeting a few nights later at the University of Wisconsin, the commander of a local American Legion post insisted that I had neglected the Ten Commandments. I replied that I accepted at least half of them and told him to watch his step in light of the Ninth Commandment: "Thou shalt not bear false witness against thy neighbor." It didn't deter him. The subject of the meeting was "A Humanist Ethics."

I was preceded in Indianapolis by an anonymous letter headed "Same Man?" in the *Indianapolis Star.* It called attention to the fact that I had been sympathetic to the Soviet Union and had recently been chairman of a memorial service for Albert Rhys Williams, author of several outstanding books about the USSR. On the day of my address the *Star* published a reply from the woman in charge of my meeting. Thus alerted, both the *Star* and the *Indianapolis Times* ran excellent stories about my meeting. Outside the hall several persons handed out mimeographed sheets with my dossier. The right-wingers dreamed up a new organization for this job: "The Ad Hoc Committee of the Stephen Decatur Society."

At Michigan State University at East Lansing, the student in charge told me that the faculty chairman of the meeting had been awakened that morning by a call from the chief of police asking my arrival time. The chairman mentioned the incident. In the question period, a benign-looking gentleman identified himself as the phone caller and as the head of the School of Police Administration and Public Safety at the university. He said he had merely wanted to come to hear about the philosophy of Humanism.

Almost without exception the attacks by ultra-rightists during my tour boomeranged. Like General Edwin A. Walker, they are bound to make idiots of themselves as soon as they ask or answer a question. They provide the audience with excitement and comic relief.

The John Birch Society and all its variants are making a lot of noise these days, but it is difficult for me to believe that these groups are making much progress in the realm of politics and public opinion.

The Bill of Rights Fund

The Bill of Rights Fund was founded in 1954 by a small group of citizens who believed that the struggle for civil liberties in the United States needed and ought to have more generous financial support than it had been receiving. This fund is strictly nonpartisan and is the only existing organization in America whose sole function is to raise and dispense money for the defense of the Bill of Rights. Its basic premise is that the civil liberties guarantees embodied in the original United States Constitution and its Amendments should apply impartially to all individuals and groups, regardless of their economic, political, religious or social viewpoint.

From the start, I have been president of the fund, while the counsel has been Philip Wittenberg, a New York attorney well-known for his civil liberties work. The present secretary is Mrs. Eleanor Jackson Piel, another New York lawyer, and the treasurer, Palmer Weber, a liberal stockbroker. Other members of the executive committee are Edna Ruth Johnson, managing editor of *The Churchman,* and Gifford Phillips, publisher of the California monthly, *Frontier.*

In the more than seven years since the fund began functioning, it has made grants—ranging from $100 to $3,000—totaling about $125,000 in over 125 outstanding civil liberties cases. Many of these have marked the first court tests of important constitutional issues. In scope our grants have covered practically the whole field of civil liberties: First Amendment rights, for example, arising from unconstitutional investigations by Congressional committees; Fifth Amendment pro-

Source. The Churchman, *April 1962.*

tection against self-incrimination; government prosecutions under the Smith Act and the Internal Security (McCarran) Act; deportation and denaturalization cases; the denial of passports by the U.S. State Department; illegal discharges from the U.S. Army for alleged subversive activities prior to induction; censorship of periodicals for "obscenity"; and issues involving religious freedom as guaranteed in the First Amendment.

The first action taken by the executive committee of the fund at its first meeting in November 1954 was to vote a $1,000 loan to the First Unitarian Church of Los Angeles for aid in its resistance to the California Levering Act, which required loyalty oaths from all religious, educational and charitable organizations as a condition for state tax exemption. Under the leadership of the Reverend Stephen H. Fritchman, the Church refused to sign the oath on the grounds that it violated the constitutional separation between church and state. In 1958 the Church won a smashing victory for itself and all other religious groups in California when the United States Supreme Court pronounced the Levering Act unconstitutional by a seven-to-one vote.

The Bill of Rights Fund also contributed substantially to the defense of the well-known religious and peace leader, Dr. Willard Uphaus, a Methodist cited for contempt for refusing to turn over to a New Hampshire State investigating committee the names of those who had attended the 1954 summer conference of World Fellowship, a group of which he is executive director. At his first hearing before the state's attorney general, Dr. Uphaus laid the Bible and Methodist Discipline on the former's desk to indicate the main sources of his inspiration. The U.S. Supreme Court decided against Dr. Uphaus's First Amendment appeal in June 1959, and he later served a year's term in jail.

Apart from individuals, our fund has given financial support to Americans United for Separation of Church and State; to the Religious Freedom Committee, which carries on extensive educational work on behalf of civil liberties; and to The Churchman to help in the distribution of its special Civil Liberties issue of February 1955. If I were able to present here a more complete account of what the Bill of Rights Fund has done, I would summarize scores of other cases in which we have made grants.

We have found that most civil liberties victims in America do not possess the means to finance their own defense. While public-spirited lawyers have often been willing to render services free of charge, there remain, apart from legal fees, expenses for the printing of briefs and other inescapable charges connected with court appeals. Hence, the fund's grants have provided assistance at the critical point of financial necessity. We make an annual appeal by letter for contributions, but have received little publicity and carry on our work in an unobtrusive way.

Meanwhile, the need for a fund of this sort remains as great as ever since the civil liberties crisis continues to be the most serious this nation has ever faced. McCarthyism did not end with the death of Senator Joseph McCarthy in 1957, and today antifreedom right-wing organizations are more numerous and better organized than in his day. Our courts of justice have in many instances ruled against violations of the Bill of Rights, but their decisions are often flouted by community sentiment, as in the South after the Supreme Court declared that racial segregation in public schools is unconstitutional.

The Supreme Court itself, however, is unreliable in sustaining the fundamentals of civil liberties and during the past two or three years has apparently become frozen into a five-to-four majority against the uncompromising application of the First Amendment. This is seen in the unfortunate decisions against teacher Lloyd Barenblatt and Willard Uphaus in 1959, against Carl Braden and Frank Wilkinson in February 1961, and the ruling in favor of the Internal Security Act in June 1961. The split in the Supreme Court reflects the closeness of the civil liberties struggle in the country at large and shows, in my opinion, that the battle will go on unabated far into the future.

Mission to Mexico

I first met David Alfaro Siqueiros a decade ago in 1951 on my first visit to Mexico, which came about after the U.S. State Department refused to renew my passport for a European trip I had planned. When I reached Mexico City, I set out to satisfy my long-standing interest in Mexico's renaissance of mural painting by studying the works of the great triumvirate, José Clemente Orozco, Diego Rivera and Siqueiros. Orozco had already died, but, by good fortune, I met both Rivera and Siqueiros, each hard at work on new government-commissioned jobs. I was able to interview both of them for the New York *Daily Compass*.

I first saw Siqueiros standing high up on a scaffolding in the Palace of Fine Arts, where he was finishing a fresco of heroic proportions. I waited around for more than an hour for him to come down, and then introduced myself. He was most cordial and invited me to have lunch the next day with him and his wife, where I interviewed him at length on the subject of art. An alert man with blue eyes and bushy black hair, Siqueiros impressed me by his intelligence, sincerity and strength of character.

Having met him personally and seen so many of his distinguished murals, it was natural for me to feel deep concern ten years later when I read that the Mexican Government had jailed him in apparent violation of civil liberties principles. Hence, last November I readily joined a three-man Committee of Inquiry into the Siqueiros case, representing the United States Friends of Mexico and other U.S. citizens interested in the matter. The other two members of the committee were Stanley J.

Source: New World Review, *January 1962.*

Faulkner, a prominent civil liberties lawyer, and Robert Gwathmey, a well-known painter, both of New York City.

Undoubtedly the high point of our trip to Mexico City was when we talked with Siqueiros himself one morning through a wire grill at Lecumberri Prison, where defendants accused of crimes involving possible sentences of more than five years are held without bail while awaiting trial. Having been arrested in August 1960, Siqueiros had been in this jail for fifteen months. Although sixty-four years old and seriously ill with a liver disorder, he seemed to me as vigorous and militant as ever. Standing beside Siqueiros behind the wire barrier was his fellow-prisoner Filomeno Mata, a journalist, who had been thrown into jail at the same time. We were able to shake hands with them through a narrow opening in the wire grill.

Siqueiros told us with a wry smile that he had been lodged in this same jail three times previously for various offenses. He said that though the prison fare is not bad, his wife is allowed to bring him food from home every day and that on Sundays five relatives are allowed to visit him. The prison authorities also permit him to do small paintings in his cell, which is about six feet wide and twelve long. The next day, at the Palace of Fine Arts, I saw on the wall an excellent self-portrait painted by Siqueiros in January 1961, while in prison.

Our committee talked about the Siqueiros case with a number of well-informed Mexicans, including his able defense lawyer, Ortega Arenas. We also had an informative conference with leading members of the recently formed National Committee for the Liberation of Political Prisoners, including the son of Lazaro Cardenas. Siqueiros was chairman of this committee when arrested. Then, at the Siqueiros home one evening Mrs. Angelica Arenal Siqueiros, the artist's indomitable wife, and Siqueiros's younger brother Jesús, a retired actor, introduced us to various liberals. We were also privileged to meet the beautiful young Siqueiros daughter, Adrienna, a professional ballet dancer.

Although we made repeated attempts to discuss the Siqueiros affair with responsible government officials, we were not able to make the necessary appointments. In fact, we got no closer to the Mexican Government than its secret service agents who were trailing us. When we held a press conference at our hotel, two of them attended and falsely registered themselves as representing two Mexican journals that did not send reporters. We hope that these agents gave our press release to high government authorities!

In our press conference and news release, the Committee of Inquiry made clear that in its opinion the arrest and imprisonment of Siqueiros constituted a serious violation of elementary civil liberties. Although five of the indictments against Siqueiros have been dismissed, the two most serious remain, including the one based on Article 145 of the Mexican Penal Code. This article is so vague and sweeping that on its face it infringes freedom of speech and association. Under this law a man is presumed guilty of "social dissolution" (another one of those catchall crimes) and may be imprisoned for up to twelve years if, "in written or oral form," he *may tend* to provoke rebellion, sedition, tumult or riot . . . or propagate disrespect on the part of the Mexican citizens for their civic duties." [Italics mine—C.L.] Like certain statutes in the United States, this law was originally passed with fascists in mind, but was never used against them.

The circumstances leading up to Siqueiros's arrest also point to the violation of democratic rights. First, he incurred official displeasure for helping to organize the Committee for the Liberation of Political Prisoners after 5,000 railroad workers were jailed in 1959 during a big strike. More than twenty of these workers are still languishing in Lecumberri Prison with Siqueiros and have now been there for over two and a half years without trial.

Second, early in 1960 Siqueiros bitterly attacked President López Mateos of Mexico in speeches made during visits to Cuba and Venezuela. This violated a sacrosanct Mexican tradition that, while one may criticize the Government and cabinet ministers at will, one does not attack the president himself. President López Mateos decided to take revenge and, according to Harvey O'Connor in his article "McCarthyism in Mexico," has vowed not to free Siqueiros during his term of office, which still has some three years to run.

Third, the arrest of Siqueiros followed immediately a series of student demonstrations in Mexico City that were perfectly legal but which police violence transformed into "riots." Government authorities claimed that he had "intellectual responsibility" for the demonstrations, though he was not present during them and no proof was offered that he had anything directly to do with them. But, argued the government prosecutor, since Siqueiros is a member of the Communist Party, he must have favored the student actions.

While our Committee of Inquiry has stressed the civil liberties aspects of the Siqueiros case, we are also urging his release so that he can once more resume his outstanding work as an artist. We went to Chapultepec Castle to see the splendid mural that Siqueiros was working on at the time of his arrest. Depicting the Revolution of 1910, this fresco is but half finished, and Siqueiros's paint brushes, pots and big spray gun remain in the hall just as he left them, ready to use again.

We viewed another uncompleted Siqueiros mural at the headquarters of the National Association of Actors. The main panel had been boarded up, owing to government pressure, because it showed a railroad strike in which helmeted police shot and killed a worker. Once again, as so often before, Mexican reactionaries had succeeded in canceling freedom of expression in art.

It is impossible to estimate precisely how much our mission to Mexico accomplished on behalf of Siqueiros. However, owing to our press interview, we did break through the news blackout, even though the stories in about half a dozen Mexico City newspapers tended to be hostile. *The New York Times* also printed a brief account of our trip.

Finally, after our return to New York, we sent the following telegram to Prime Minister Nehru of India, in care of the Indian embassies in both Washington and Mexico City: "In view of your trip to Mexico, we respectfully remind you that the great Mexican mural painter David Alfaro Siqueiros, for whose work you have expressed admiration, is still in jail after fifteen months imprisonment and that his prosecution by the Government violates elementary principles of civil liberties and free speech. This message comes to you from a special Committee of Inquiry into the Siqueiros Case representing many Americans."

We believe that the Siqueiros case has become nothing less than an international scandal. It is to be hoped that all Americans who are concerned over it will communicate their views to President López Mateos of Mexico with a request for clemency.

The Cassandras in America

The cry of calamity is contagious. Repeatedly in public print and in conversation, we have read and heard that fascism or neofascism is just around the corner for the United States. This shadow flung across the immediate future portends a police state with rigid censorship, suppression of all opposition, a one-party system and complete nullification of our democratic procedures.

It is true that during the last two or three years American democracy has been disgraced by a number of events: the wholesale jailing, for instance, of some 13,000 antiwar demonstrators—most of them illegally arrested—in Washington, D.C., in May 1971; the widespread brutality of city police; the killing of students at Kent State in Ohio, and Jackson State in Mississippi; the proliferation of lists of "subversives" by government agencies, both federal and local; and the passage of repressive new laws such as the antiriot provisions of the Civil Rights Act and the clearly unconstitutional provisions in the Crime Control Act and the Drug Control Act.

But are these the symptoms of a creeping or leaping fascism? I think not.

The Cassandras who respond to such dismal facts by crying "fascism is coming" are forgetful or ignorant of American history. Certainly the civil liberties crisis today is serious. But as a vigorous supporter of the Bill of Rights for some forty years, I am aware that some sort of civil liberties crisis is almost always with us. The current situation is not nearly so grim as after World War I and the Russian Revolution, when

Source: The New York Times, *July 25, 1971.*

the notorious Palmer raids took place, or during the fifties, when there was a spate of antifreedom legislation, and McCarthyism was blighting almost every area of our culture.

Those fearful of a fascist take-over also overemphasize the negative and consequently overlook the considerable gains American democracy has made in recent years. The witch-hunting investigating committees of Congress, typified by the House Un-American Activities Committee (now the House Internal Security Committee), are less of a menace today. Much progress has been made towards full constitutional rights for Negroes and other racial minorities, including the all but total disappearance of lynching. The courts, especially the U.S. Appeals Courts and the Supreme Court, have in general lent support to the Bill of Rights over the last decade.

It is possible that an Appeals Court or the Supreme Court, even with Mr. Nixon's appointees, will reverse the conviction of the Chicago Seven* and declare unconstitutional the antiriot statute under which they were held guilty. Indicative of the Supreme Court's stance on civil liberties was its recent decision that *The New York Times* and the *Washington Post* could not be restrained by the United States Government from publishing the Pentagon Papers on the Vietnam war.

In New York City in May 1971, a jury acquitted thirteen Black Panthers of conspiracy to murder policemen and to commit other violence, while in New Haven the same month the Government dropped its prosecution of Panther leader Bobby Seale for conspiracy to murder.

Those who are haunted by the specter of fascism also do not consider that certain rightist tendencies may well represent one of those temporary swings of the political pendulum typical of our history. Much of today's reactionary legislation is an overreaction to student riots and the seizure of college buildings, to the senseless bombings by the Weathermen and right-wing extremists, and to the murder of considerable numbers of policemen year after year.

Finally, the capitalist class in the United States does not need a fascist regime in order to maintain its dominance. The radical and revolutionary movements are weak and disunited. A large majority of the trade unions are conservative, and are actually part of the Establishment. We shall no doubt always have with us crackpot rightist and superpatriotic groups yelling about the "communist conspiracy," but I do not see in the offing any constellation of forces that could put fascism across here.

---

*In the fall of 1973 a U.S. Appeals Court reversed the conspiracy convictions of the Chicago Seven. The Government did not appeal.

All the factors in American life that violate or threaten democratic principles still do not add up to a clear-and-present danger of fascism. True, things could change drastically. But crying wolf meanwhile dangerously confuses the situation. If the conviction grows that fascism is here or almost here, unrealistic retreat may spread. The sound position for us is never to quail in fright of an alleged fascist threat, but always to stand fast and to do battle for freedom.

III

WORLD PEACE
AND
SOCIALISM

Ideas for Irreconcilables

The formation this spring of a College Division of the League of Nations Non-Partisan Association has been one of the most hopeful occurrences of the year in college circles. The Division was spontaneously started by college undergraduates who themselves originated the idea and later brought it before the Association's executives for ratification. The very fact that this Division has been organized should be encouraging to all thinking persons because it shows that college students are beginning to stir from their apathy towards American politics and towards foreign affairs, which are now inseparably linked up with our country's life. Even the most vehement irreconcilable must admit that an organization which tends to break down student indifference towards politics has some value. And, though the arousing of undergraduate opinion along general political lines is not the College Division's chief purpose, it is a most important consideration. For pro-Leaguers the formation of the Division is reassuring because it proves that there is strong sentiment among the most intelligent and enlightened group of young people in the country towards the United States entering the League.

The aims of the College Division can best be explained by first outlining the principles and purposes of the Non-Partisan Association itself. In simple terms, the Association is a group of men and women of different party affiliations who are seeking to cultivate "such a public opinion as will induce the present Administration, or if not this, the next one, to enter the League of Nations," either with or without reser-

Source: The Harvard Advocate, *June 1923.*

vations. The Association has already organized committees in every state, plans to do the same in every Congressional district in the Union, and proposes to secure the insertion in both Republican and Democratic party platforms in 1924 of a plank favoring entrance of the United States into the League. It is also an object of the Association to secure approval by the Senate of President Harding's World Court recommendation.

Most emphatically the Association does not accept the statement that the Republican majority in 1920 meant repudiation of the League by the voters of this country. As Samuel Colcord, a Republican, points out in "The Great Deception," the League was associated in the minds of a great mass of voters with other parts of the Treaty of Versailles that were particularly offensive to the foreign-born. This confusion sent many voters into the Republican ranks. To my mind, "anti-Wilsonism" and the natural reaction following the war played almost as important parts in the election as any other one thing. Then, also, it must be taken into consideration that millions voted for Mr. Harding following the advice of Taft, Hughes, Hoover, Root and the rest of the "31" who predicted that with the Republicans in power the United States would enter the League. In this group were included that large body of voters who went Republican, not because of hostility towards joining the League at all, but on account of opposition to going in without adequate safeguards. Finally, there were those reservationists who realized, in spite of the "31," that a Republican Administration would shelve the League and voted for Mr. Harding rather than give their approval to the nation's entering without suitable reservations. With these facts in mind it is difficult to see how any fairminded observer can say: "The League is a dead issue; it was settled in 1920." Suppose there had been a clearcut issue between the irreconcilables and the reservationists, aided by the nonreservationists. Suppose that the issue had been entering the League with the Lodge reservations or not at all. Would the people have rebuked the Senator from Massachusetts? Certainly not, for there is every reason to believe that a majority of the voters in 1920, all other issues disregarded, would have declared themselves in favor of this country's entering the League *with reservations*.

At the present time it seems plausible to go on the assumption that everyone who is not an irreconcilable is for the League, either with or without reservations, and that very few who desire reservations wish to go beyond the Lodge proposals of 1919. The Association aims to unite all those who are not irreconcilables and all who can be won over from the irreconcilables. When such a combination has been effected, it will, I believe, be plain to the administration in power that the irreconcilable element is in the minority. There can be little doubt, however, that the country as a whole is against the United States joining the League without reservations and that no administration within the next decade can bring about our entrance without reservations, unless there is an almost unbelievable reversal of popular feeling.

The part that the 618 colleges and professional schools of this country can play in carrying out the purposes outlined above is a great one. If the colleges line up solidly in favor of the United States entering the League, the effects will be far-reaching. The very fact that the colleges are behind the movement will, of course, carry weight throughout the country just as a united appeal of labor or any other group of public opinion would be influential. This will be a direct effect. The indirect effects will perhaps be more important. In 1924 practically all students now in college above the present Freshman Class will be old enough to vote; by 1928 four more college classes will have become eligible. Knowledge of this fact will cause party headquarters to look up sharply, not only because of the votes these students will cast, but on account of the influence they will exert on other voters in their communities and various fields of activity.

Although the Division is essentially an undergraduate affair, no opportunity will be lost in enlisting the support of members of the faculty and the graduate schools. In fact, in the branch recently established at Harvard the graduate schools are represented by two members on the Executive Council, while three faculty members are serving in an advisory capacity. The technical details of the scheme I do not intend to discuss here inasmuch as they have already been announced elsewhere.

It is not the purpose of this essay to go deeply into the arguments for and against the United States entering the League. Rather than trying to prove conclusively any specific points, let me make a few self-evident observations.

The great tragedy of 1919 and 1920 was that the League question became the plaything of party politics. It never had a fair hearing in the United States, misinterpreted and misrepresented as it was by the politicians. But this is 1923; and my plea is for all citizens of all parties to join now in repairing the mistakes of the past, whether Lodge or Wilson or both were in the wrong. Let the President, who as a Senator voted for the League with reservations in 1919, and the Republicans and Democrats of the Senate, many of whom did the same, reconsider. If they want reservations, let them make them—but go in! That the League will accept reservations from this country there can be little question. For instance, let us study what Lord Robert Cecil said recently in regard to Article X*: "Article X is an ill-drawn article and I never cared much for it. In practice it is doubtful if it could ever be brought into operation. Doubtless when the United States decides to enter the League, it will ask, reasonably and properly, that the article should be either struck out or redrafted, so as to make its real purpose unmistakable, and I do not imagine that there will be any serious opposition to that being done." But even with the Article X bogy eliminated and the "six votes to one" bogy answered in full by the President in his World Court defense, the irreconcilables can read into the League covenant numerous other objections.

Supporters of the League in this country have often been called impractical idealists. Let me simply call attention here to the present plight of the farmers in the Middle West. Why are they suffering so? The hard-headed businessmen of the country, to whom reasoning in facts is more familiar than to most of us, say that the primary cause is the lack of foreign markets. I can illustrate my point no better than by quoting from Mr. Bernard M. Baruch's address on "Agricultural Finance." He says in conclusion: "I affirm that there is nothing in the world that affects your credit so much as the shrinking of foreign markets for your products. There is nothing to which you can give your attention that is of greater moment to you in a practical way than the creation of the international relations that are a precedent to a re-establishment of those markets. I do not speak of our moral responsibility in the matter, nor of the great opportunity that America has to lead a stricken world into a finer and better order of things—an opportunity toward which the noble thoughts of all men urge them, though I do think this consideration the most compelling of all. . . . Rather, I dwell merely upon what enlightened selfishness or even just plain greedy selfishness demands—the necessity of keeping open and enlarging an ever-increasing market for the products of your hands and minds."

Of course there are those who wish to see the United States enter the League, not merely because such a step will aid our country materially, but also because it will help Europe, further the interests of world peace and make this country greater in the eyes of its own and other peoples. Such sentiments may indeed be termed idealism, but combined as they are with common sense and practicability, they express a kind of idealism of which we should be most proud. Impracticable idealism I decry—and it is just that sort of idealism that I believe the bitter-enders uphold. They demand a perfect League, a perfect treaty,

*Article X of the League Charter established the principle of collective security, which opponents of the League argued would threaten our national sovereignty and violate the exclusive constitutional right of Congress to declare war.

and they will never obtain either. Of course the League has grave faults, but what human document of its kind has not? I call it impracticable idealism of the plainest sort to oppose the United States joining the League or the World Court because these organizations are imperfect. Yet that is a fundamental part of the irreconcilables' doctrine. (Their other cry, for out-of-date "isolationism," is based on an utter disregard of fact and is not worthy of discussion.) And yet they have the effrontery—they who have grown morbidly sentimental over sentimentalism—to call their opponents political sentimentalists or impractical idealists.

It does not seem probable that these pages will be read by those whom I most wish to reach. They are sitting back in contentment timorously meditating—if they meditate at all—on worn-out commonplaces—certainly least of all things on politics. This is not Harvard indifference. It is the same throughout all the colleges of the country. Most of the students will live prosperous lives as bankers, lawyers, doctors or whatnot. A courageous few will enter politics to struggle in an uphill battle against the sort of loose, timid or wilfully perverted thinking that we now see on every hand in our government. I repeat the well-known statement that more college men must enter politics and that those who do not must take a keener interest from the outside. This is necessary if the United States is to attain the greatness of which it is capable. But that is for the future. For the present, every college student has an immediate opportunity to use his influence in politics, to help make this America a greater nation at home and abroad—the opportunity of fighting, preferably but not necessarily as a member of the Non-Partisan Association, for the entrance of the United States into the League of Nations.

Why I Believe in Socialism

I became a convinced believer in socialism as the best way out for America and the world almost twenty years ago, about 1931 or 1932. Since that time, the rise of fascism, the undoubted economic success of socialism in the Soviet Union, the coming of the Second World War, the defeat of international fascism and the postwar developments of 1945-49 in America, Europe and Asia have all deepened and strengthened my socialist convictions.

Unquestionably, the Great Depression that started in 1929 was the immediate stimulus that caused me to become skeptical of the capitalist system and to explore systematically the possibilities of the socialist alternative. My upbringing in a prominent capitalist and banking family certainly had not instilled in me any initial bias in favor of socialism. But my parents early made me see that consideration for others was a high ethical value and gave me a liberal slant on many questions; the Phillips Exeter Academy imbued in me a strong feeling for the American tradition of democracy and equality of opportunity; and Harvard and Columbia taught me that reliance on reason is the best method of solving human problems. In my late twenties I developed an affirmative humanist philosophy of life that holds as its chief ethical goal the happiness, freedom and progress of all humanity—irrespective of nation, race and social origin—upon this earth, where it has its only existence. If we are really serious about achieving this end, I think that intelligence then leads us to work for a planned and democratic socialism on a world scale.

Source: Monthly Review, *October 1949.*

My own path to socialism, therefore, was that of analysis through reason, combined with belief in a humanist ethics and a deep attachment to democracy in its broadest sense. However, half-baked Freudians and capitalist critics who use amateur psychoanalysis as a political weapon are always claiming that well-to-do radicals like myself must be primarily impelled by personal neuroses. We have either a publicity complex, an Oedipus complex, a martyr complex, a romantic-revolt complex or a special complex due to neglect or abuse as a child. Yet, relatively few of those who have come over to socialism from the capitalist class seem to have been afflicted with psychological complexes; indeed, most of those who have severe psychoses or suffer nervous breakdowns or commit suicide are members of the bourgeoisie who are faithful to the capitalist system but who cannot stand the gruelling strains it imposes, or their own nightmares of Reds and Russians under every bed.

Apologists for the status quo cannot, of course, admit for a moment that intelligence supports the socialist case, and so they resort to fantastic fables to discredit those who use their brains and go Left. At the same time, these capitalist apologists have been so blinded by the long-cultivated myth that the profit motive and brute selfishness are the main driving force in men that they consider it dangerously abnormal for people to be motivated by the vision of a just and generous social order and by the desire to serve mankind or the working class.

I like the old phrase "public service." Many honest liberals and conservatives have tried hard to serve the public interest, and I am not implying that only radicals are public-spirited. What I am saying is that the ideal of public service in this era ought to bring more and more people over to the cause of socialism.

Another charge with which I have had to contend is that I am insincere because, while proclaiming the goal of a socialist society, I do not at once reduce my standard of living to that of the most poverty-stricken group in the United States. Many years ago I had an encounter with that picturesque blusterer, former general, banker and Vice-President, Charles G. Dawes, who leapt up from an excellent Sunday dinner at the home of the late Dwight W. Morrow, and paced around the table chewing angrily on his pipe, charging that I had no right to believe in socialism until I gave away my last penny. I reminded the Christian multimillionaire that it was not Marx but Jesus who had advised selling all one's goods and giving the proceeds to the poor. Mr. Morrow, a brilliant and sensitive person, remarked that I still seemed to enjoy heartily the fine facilities of my father's country estate on the Palisades. To this I replied that I liked my parents very much and that I would continue to visit them whether they lived in a palace or a hovel.

The point is that there are far more significant things to do for socialism than to make dramatic gestures such as giving away all one's money or breaking off family relations. It takes all kinds of people from many different walks of life to create a successful radical movement. Workers for socialism like myself do not pretend to be either angels or martyrs; it is our unfriendly critics who concoct that myth and then accuse us of hypocrisy because we do not live up to it. It would be folly for us, as for anyone else in capitalist America, to attempt to act *now* as if full-fledged socialism already existed here. And we cannot help feeling that it is more important for us to be effective on behalf of the socialist goal than to satisfy the preconceived whims and malicious criticisms of upper-class folk who are dedicated to the eternal preservation of capitalism.

I have said enough to indicate that in the particular environment in which I grew up and with which I still have many close connections there were plenty of pressures against my becoming a socialist. I first gave some attention to the merits of socialism when I was a senior at Harvard in 1924. And although at that time I fought, unsuccessfully, for the right of a student organization to invite Eugene V. Debs to speak at the Harvard Union, I personally rejected socialism as undesirable and impracticable. That some years later I reversed my opinion was primarily attributable, I believe, to a more profound study of economics and to a better grasp of the method of reason, which, when most accurate, conforms to modern science's method of experimentation and verification.

My capitalist friends are always accusing me of being biased, but in truth I overcame the antisocialist biases natural to my upbringing and have resisted the unremitting pressures to return to the fold of the capitalist faithful. While emotions have their proper and important place in the life of a radical, as in the life of everyone else, I am convinced that the deciding factor in winning me to socialism was not some sort of emotional urge or reaction, but the voice of reason. Ultimately, the socialist case rests on the mind's objective consideration of the relevant facts and theories. And I find at least eight good reasons why the socialist solution is the best answer to our pressing contemporary social-economic problems in the United States and the world at large.

First, while capitalism has enormously increased the productive capacities of mankind, especially through the development of science and the machine, it has not been able, and never will be able, to overcome the fundamental difficulties and contradictions that beset it. Reforms within the structure of the capitalist system can result in genuine amelioration, but I do not think that they can resolve its major dilemmas of recurring overproduction, economic depression and mass un-employment. The basic cause of these phenomena is that in an economy in which profit is both the chief regulator of business and the main motive of businessmen, the capitalists strive to make as much money as they can and to reinvest the greater part in expanding their profit-yielding enterprises. The result is that the capacity to produce grows much faster than the ability to consume, as determined by the people's purchasing power; and it happens again and again that the disproportion can be "solved" only by a costly crisis and depression. The crisis of overproduction is at the same time a crisis of undercon-sumption; both are the reflection of the accumulation of wealth at one end of the social scale and of poverty at the other.

Various superficial devices, such as fancy currency schemes and share-the-wealth measures, have been suggested or tried as the cure for this central contradiction of capitalism. The most common and sub-stantial remedy attempted has been government spending on public works, as under the New Deal, or on armaments and Marshall Plans, as under the present Administration. Needless to say, war and war prepa-rations constitute a cure that is worse than the disease, and experience shows that so long as capitalism exists, no program of large-scale public works will be permitted to transcend the character of a tempo-rary emergency program, to be discarded as soon as the economy shows signs of returning to prosperity.

Second, there is the tremendous waste inherent in the capitalist system and its wanton exploitation of men and natural resources. In the United States the drive for big, quick profits has brought about the irredeemable spoilage of billions of dollars worth of oil and gas, coal and timber; and reckless deforestation has led to chronic floods, life-devouring dust bowls, and the ruination of huge tracts of fertile land. Throughout the capitalist world, money-minded businessmen, without regard for the consequences to future generations, have been speedily exhausting the natural abundance of our good earth, creating a situa-tion aptly described as *Our Plundered Planet*, to cite the title of a re-cent book by Mr. Fairfield Osborn. Also, consider the untold loss of wealth through millions upon millions of men and machines standing idle in depression after depression since the Industrial Revolution; through the deprivation of potential production in "normal" times owing to the competitive, chaotic, unplanned nature of capitalism; and above all, through the colossal squandering of human beings and goods in capitalist-caused wars.

My third point is that a planned socialist society, operating for use instead of profit, can put an end to most of the economic waste that occurs under capitalism and prevent the tragic paradox of poverty amid potential plenty. Socialism does not automatically solve all economic problems, but it will do away with the general crises and mass unemployment so characteristic of the capitalist era. And it will unlock to the fullest extent the economic potentialities of the machine age with its scientific techniques. Because it has no fear of overproduction and technological unemployment, a socialist economy heartily welcomes new industrial inventions and labor-saving devices. Today we all know that in the industrially developed nations there is enough goods-producing machinery to ensure a high standard of living for all of the people in such countries. In the United States, an intelligently run economy such as socialism proposes could promptly guarantee to every American family an annual return of goods and services equivalent in value to more than $5,000.

Fourth, it seems to me that if we follow through the logical implications of the idea of public planning, which has been gaining more and more weight in present-day society, we arrive at the key concept of overall *socialist planning* functioning in conjunction with *public ownership of the main means of production and distribution*. Socialist planning for abundance, democratically administered throughout, permanently overcomes the contradictions of capitalism. The government planning organizations, with control over output, prices, wages, hours of work and currency, are able to keep the purchasing power of the population in close equilibrium with the total production of goods. Under capitalism, countless fine individual intelligences and abilities continually work against one another and cancel one another out. Socialist planning would release and coordinate these frustrated intelligences and abilities, bringing into action a great community mind operating on behalf of the common good and embodying the life of reason in social-economic affairs.

Fifth, I see in the very considerable achievements of the Soviet Union a concrete example of what socialism and socialist planning can do. From an economically backward, chiefly agricultural, 70 percent illiterate country under the Tsars, the Soviet Five-Year Plans have transformed Russia into a dynamic, forward-moving economy with highly developed industry and collectivized agriculture. At the same time the people of the USSR have become 90 percent literate, well educated by twentieth-century standards and excellently trained in modern machine techniques. During the Nazi invasion and four years of all-out warfare, the planned economy of the USSR made an impressive showing, utterly refuting foreign observers who had predicted its speedy collapse. Although American and British Lend-Lease was extremely helpful, the Soviet factories themselves turned out more than 90 percent of the guns, airplanes and tanks that swept Hitler back all the way to Berlin; and the Soviets had the trained manpower to handle efficiently the most up-to-date and complicated engines of war. In its supreme test Soviet socialism worked most successfully.

Since the end of World War II in 1945, a new Soviet Five-Year Plan has been performing a Herculean job of economic reconstruction, and the general standard of living is resuming the advance which was interrupted by the fascist onslaught. The Soviet Union is certainly no Utopia and it still has many defects. It has, for example, shown a definite lag in respect to political democracy and civil liberties, despite forging ahead of any other country in the realm of racial democracy and equality. As a radical who has long been sympathetic to Soviet accomplishments, I think we should guard against being uncritical of Soviet Russia; we must frankly criticize that country for its shortcomings and learn from its mistakes. Other nations that are making progress towards socialism also have much to teach us.

I believe, sixth, that socialism not only lays the basis for a rational and just economic system but also gives promise of bringing about a far-reaching cultural revolution. By creating an economy of abundance, socialist planning is able to multiply the production of cultural goods such as books, school and college buildings, radio sets, musical instruments, theatres and the like. It greatly increases the number of teachers and pays them decent salaries. By replacing production for profit with production for use, socialism ends the capitalist method of judging artistic and cultural products primarily in terms of the money they may make and fosters their evaluation in terms of true merit. The socialist economic system together with socialist teaching effects a transformation in human motives, coordinating the altruistic and egoistic impulses so that people find their welfare and happiness in working for the general good instead of always putting their economic self-interest first, as in capitalist theory. This aspect of socialism entails a far higher ethical philosophy than that of capitalism and one that is decidedly more in harmony with the most enlightened social ideals of Christianity.

My seventh point on the advantages of socialism is perhaps the most important of all because it deals with the elimination of international war—the most terrible scourge that has ever afflicted mankind and so dangerous today, in light of the new weapons of the atom bomb and germ warfare, that it could set back for centuries all civilization, socialist and capitalist. My thesis is that, while economics is not the whole story, economic dilemmas and drives are the primary causes of war and that in our modern era the capitalist system itself has been responsible for almost all international conflict, notably the two world wars of the twentieth century. Imperialist rivalries between the European capitalist powers brought on World War I. Capitalism in its last, most brutal stage—fascism, as exemplified in Germany, Italy and Japan—started World War II, aided by the Munich appeasers. It attacked both the Western democracies and the Soviet Union, a nation that had made every effort to preserve peace through a genuine system of collective security.

A socialist society cuts away the economic roots of war. Public ownership of the instrumentalities of production means that no individuals or groups can make money from manufacturing armaments. Central planning, by establishing a coordinated economy at home, makes it unnecessary for a socialist country to extricate itself from domestic economic troubles through military adventures abroad, or by striving desperately to get rid of surplus goods on the foreign market. As it unfolds internationally, socialism puts a finish once and for all to the fierce struggle, with the whole earth as the arena, among the capitalist imperialisms, to survive and expand at the expense of one another and of exploited colonial peoples. It brings into being the essential economic conditions for permanent peace and for that enduring fraternity of peoples that has always been one of its highest aims. When the socialist principle has gained enough strength throughout the world, we can be confident that the United Nations will be a success.

Eighth and finally, I am convinced that socialism offers the best way of fulfilling the promise of modern democracy, both in America and elsewhere, and of preventing the resurgence of fascism. Since fascism is simply capitalism stripped of all democratic pretenses and other unessentials—capitalism in the nude, as it were—the danger of fascism remains as long as the capitalist system is with us. A socialist society builds the necessary foundations of a broad and lasting democracy by establishing a stable economy and giving to the workers and the masses of the people the economic and cultural prerequisites for their democratic liberties. And it insists on extending full democratic rights to all racial groups and to the approximately one-half of the population that is female.

Furthermore, I am of the opinion that in countries like the United States and Great Britain, which have long and strong traditions of political democracy and civil liberties, we can accomplish the transition to socialism through peaceful and democratic procedures. In nations like Russia and China, however, where under the old regimes democratic institutions were extremely weak or practically nonexistent, violent revolution was in all probability the only way out. So far as the United States is concerned, in order to smooth the path to socialism and maintain our constitutional guarantees for *everyone*, I am in favor of the government's buying out the capitalists when it receives the voters' mandate to socialize the natural resources, the factories, the banks, transportation and communication facilities, and so on. This would be in accordance with that section of the Bill of Rights which reads: ". . . nor shall private property be taken for public use without just compensation." America is wealthy enough to adopt this procedure, and it would go far in staving off counterrevolutionary violence on the part of the capitalist class.

With the coming of Hitler to power in 1933 and the onset of World War II in 1939, American radicals naturally became largely preoccupied with stopping fascism as the best method of furthering socialism. Since the end of the war we have continued to concentrate on immediate problems of both a domestic and international character. The day has arrived, I think, to renew our direct educational and political work on behalf of a socialist America, while in no way neglecting day-to-day problems. Capitalism has failed America and mankind, and the most fundamental need of our country is to institute a socialist economy. The various types of socialists in the United States have too long been on the defensive; now is the time to militantly take the offensive in order to make American socialism a reality.

Dangers of American Foreign Policy

In his speech of November 1945, Undersecretary of State Dean Acheson, referring to American-Russian relations, said: "For nearly a century and a half we have gotten along well—remarkably well when you consider that our forms of government, our economic systems and our special habits have never been similar. . . . Never, in the past, has there been any place on the globe where the vital interests of the American and Russian people have clashed or even been antagonistic—and there is no objective reason to suppose that there should, now or in the future, ever be such a place. There is an obvious reason for this. We are both continental peoples with adequate living space—interested in developing and enjoying the living space we have. Our ambition is to achieve the highest possible standards of living among our own peoples, and we have the wherewithal to achieve high standards of living without conquest, through peaceful development and trade. We have that opportunity, moreover, only to the extent that we can create conditions of peace and prevent war. Thus the paramount interest, the only conceivable hope of both nations, lies in the cooperative enterprise of peace."

Mr. Acheson's words are as applicable today as in 1945. But Mr. Acheson as Secretary of State has, I submit, followed policies inconsistent with his earlier opinions. As the member of President Truman's Cabinet primarily responsible for the foreign policy of the United States, he has taken the lead in curtly turning down the repeated proposals of the Soviet Government over the past few years for a top-level

Source: Basic Pamphlet, 1952.

conference between the USA and the USSR for the purpose of coming to an overall settlement. Mr. Acheson and Mr. Truman have fallen into the bad habit of stigmatizing all such offers as mere propaganda on the part of the Soviet Union. The trouble is, of course, that the American Government cannot admit the sincerity of Soviet peace campaigns without undermining its favorite thesis that Soviet aggression is the great menace facing the United States and the world at large. The underlying premise of the Truman Doctrine, of the Cold War, of the North Atlantic Pact and of the stupendous American armaments program is that Soviet armies will invade and overrun Western Europe if they have the opportunity.

Undoubtedly many high-ranking officials of the U.S. Government, as well as members of Congress and party leaders in the country at large, do not themselves really take stock in the fearful Soviet military threat which they keep talking about. But the originators of our bipartisan foreign policy have succeeded in creating a situation in the United States in which loud cries about Soviet aggression and communist conspiracy have become fundamental to orthodox political ritual both during and between elections. The high priests of the Democratic and Republican Parties have become the prisoners of their own myth-making and must maintain the pretense of absolute Soviet wickedness lest the foundations of their ideology melt away in the light of the simple truth.

A lamentable consequence of all this is that a powerful public opinion has grown up in America that regards as appeasement any attempts to work out a peaceful accord with the Soviets. So it is that in various quarters the whole notion of peace has become suspect, and peace committees, peace meetings, peace addresses, peace articles are all regarded as most likely originating in a Soviet plot to undermine the strength of the United States and its allies. In 1950 a Hollywood studio went so far as to suppress a movie on the story of Hiawatha because it was felt that the Indian chief's constant smoking of the peace pipe and general opposition to war might be interpreted as un-American. The continuing Red hunt on the part of such agencies as the House Committee on Un-American Activities and the Senate Committee on Internal Security, and by such demagogues as Senators Joseph McCarthy and Pat McCarran, has made most members of Congress and most citizens afraid to agree publicly with any part of the Soviet peace program, lest they then be smeared as communists.

Today most Americans tend to reject almost automatically any idea in the controversial realms of economics, politics and international relations that originated in Soviet Russia or is generally approved there. In fact, this trend has gone so far that the relatively few dissenters who do express agreement with some Soviet doctrines may be indicted or jailed as foreign agents on the grounds of "parallelism" between their views and those of the Soviet Government. Yet if Americans for one reason or another feel unable ever to agree with Soviet opinions, then the Soviets are actually controlling them in reverse by forcing them always to support contrary conclusions. The truly independent mind cannot permit itself to be placed in such a senseless position.

I wonder how many millions of Americans, during the steady deterioration of American-Soviet relations since the end of World War II, have asked themselves the question I have so often put to myself: Would the present American-Soviet impasse have developed if President Franklin D. Roosevelt had lived out his last term in office through 1948? My answer has always been that, while these postwar years would have been difficult in any case, President Roosevelt, with his wide experience in foreign affairs, his political sagacity, his liberalism and wisdom, would have been able to lay the basis for continuing American-Soviet cooperation. Assuredly he would have had the moral strength and the basic statesmanship to resist Winston Churchill's suggestion in his famous Fulton, Missouri, speech of March 1946, for an Anglo-American military alliance against the Soviet Union.

President Truman, however, never noted for his forcefulness of personality or independence of mind, fell in readily with Churchill's anti-Soviet rhetoric and apologia for a Cold War. Moreover, being unsure of himself on international issues, Mr. Truman has consistently leaned on others in the formulation of American policy rather than assuming leadership himself. And he has often taken very bad advice, as in accepting the "containment" thesis put forward in the magazine *Foreign Affairs* in 1947 by Mr. X, now universally recognized as Mr. George Kennan, present Ambassador to the Soviet Union. Also, President Truman, despite his dismissal of General MacArthur for sabotaging American policy in Korea, has on the whole relied heavily upon the military mind.

Writing in the *New York Herald Tribune* about the powers of the National Security Council, composed chiefly of military men and defense secretaries, Mr. Sumner Welles, former Undersecretary of State, asserts: "No President since General Grant has had such childlike faith in the omniscience of the high brass as the present occupant of the White House. It is no surprise to learn that President Truman invariably approves every decision of the Council. . . . The Council passes on all important questions in this country's international relations and decides the policy to be adopted. It has now been given authority by the President to determine our political objectives in every part of the world. . . . But no emergency can justify the control of this country's foreign policy by a Council which reaches its decisions from a military standpoint."

Generals and admirals, secretaries of the army, navy and air force, have traditionally been in favor of continued expansion of the services in which they function. Such expansion increases their power, prestige and sense of mission. Furthermore, they tend to look for the solution of international tensions in terms of war rather than of diplomacy. These are some of the reasons why civilian control over the U.S. defense departments is of such great importance. But there are many indications that the White House generally bows to the Pentagon. One unhappy sign of this is President Truman's willingness to spur on a dangerous armaments race, to foist universal military training on America and to encourage wild war scares as the occasion demands. Even an anti-Soviet stalwart like Congressmen Joseph W. Martin, Jr., leader of the Republican minority in the House of Representatives, has stated: "Down through the years the high officials of this Government uttered time and again the direst warnings of bloodshed when a particular piece of legislation they wanted was before Congress."

In September 1951, as reported in *The New York Times*, President Truman signed a "measure authorizing a $5,864,301,178 global military construction program, including a ring of secret overseas bases close enough to the Soviet Union so that the Air Force could retaliate against attack and neutralize the enemy's war potential. It was the largest amount ever voted for military construction during peacetime." Although the stated reason for this vast appropriation was that it was essential for defense, it is obvious that the air bases alluded to could also be used for a sudden A-bomb onslaught against the USSR. The acknowledged U.S. policy of building a round-the-world network of air bases, now several hundred in number, as near as possible to the frontiers of Soviet Russia and its allies, makes the Soviets understandably nervous.

There are grounds for believing that Harry Truman hopes to go down in history as one of America's greatest Presidents because of his militant crusade against communism. Be that as it may, he will certainly be remembered as the Chief Executive who engineered through Congress the largest peacetime budgets on record up till his second term of office. For the fiscal year 1952 he obtained Congressional approval for a budget of almost 71 billion dollars, with 49.7 billion earmarked for military purposes, exclusive of payments to veterans. For the fiscal year 1953, running from July 1, 1952, to July 1, 1953, the President demanded, shortly after new Soviet peace overtures, a budget of over 85 billion dollars.

Of this budget, which the *Wall Street Journal* terms "so monstrous as to defy reasoned comment," approximately 76 percent, or 65.1 billion dollars, is for national security, including 52.4 billion for the armed forces and 10.5 billion for international security (aid to U.S. allies). This does not include 4.2 billion for veterans and 6.2 billion for interest, chiefly on loans which financed past wars. Fourteen billion of the new budget is to go to the building of airplanes, while 1.7 billion is for speeding up the stockpiling of atom bombs as part of a 5- to 6-billion dollar program over the next few years for mass production of America's "fantastic new weapons." The 1952 Soviet budget allocates to defense 24 percent, or 113.8 billion rubles, equal to 28.4 billion dollars at the official exchange rate. (The Soviet budget, however, covers a much larger proportion of the national economy than does the American budget.)

The astronomical U.S. totals mean that President Truman is asking the United States to spend approximately 180 million dollars a day on defense, or about 3.7 times the entire 48-million-dollar budget of the United Nations for 1952. Let that sink in: In a single day the U.S. is to expend for military purposes over three and a half times what the U.N. can devote to international peace during a full year. These colossal armaments figures seem alarming, not only to the Russians, but also to some of America's own allies.

The skyrocketing U.S. armaments outlays of the past few years have kept the American economy booming and headed off a depression that many competent economists think would have otherwise taken place. A brink-of-war economy, with government spending on a huge scale stimulating business and bringing enormous profits, is one way of temporarily overcoming fundamental economic difficulties in a capitalist economy. Government expenditure on weapons of war is the favorite form of public works for capitalist businessmen, since it results in very profitable contracts and since the end product is something that does not compete, like public hydroelectric developments or public housing, with private capitalist enterprise.

As a larger and larger proportion of American business becomes geared to the manufacture of arms and the servicing of armies, it grows harder and harder to turn back from a brink-of-war economy to a peace economy. It is for the time being more expedient, especially from a political viewpoint, to accelerate the armaments boom than to put the brakes on it. And the terrible communist blunder in Korea played directly into the hands of those powerful groups in America that had been agitating for an expanded armaments program.

That program has become so prodigiously enlarged over the past few years, and so interwoven with the basic fabric of the economy, that government officials, private businessmen and even trade union leaders are anxious lest the general Cold War and the little hot war be concluded too quickly and peace break out. Typical was the reaction to talk of peace in Korea as reported in the *Wall Street Journal* of May 16, 1951: "Stock prices experienced the sharpest decline since March 13. Brokers ascribed the break to widespread peace rumors. . . . Traders are fearful that the end of hostilities might also halt rearmament and catch leading companies with swollen inventories unbalanced for peacetime production."

As Mr. Norman Thomas, an outspoken anti-Soviet crusader, has said: "Millions of Americans, despite their best hopes, have acquired a vested interest in the economic waste of the arms race. Its sudden end would be greeted with an outpouring of joy, but it would be followed by economic panic—unless we were ready with constructive plans for a cooperative war on hunger, illiteracy and disease." Such plans the powers-that-be do not have, although vastly expanded government spending for great economic projects at home and Point 4 abroad (assigned only $600,000,000 in the $85-billion Truman budget), could obviously be just as much of a business stimulus as shoveling unending billions of dollars into the maw of Mars.

Resilient as it is, even the American economy will not be able to stand indefinitely the strain of such enormous arms budgets and staggering government deficits as those imposed by the Truman Administration. And if the people as a whole finally start to offer serious objection to the armaments burden, reckless political leaders may be tempted to overcome popular opposition by actually plunging America into a world war. When war preparations seem to the rulers of a country the easiest way to maintain prosperity and full employment, the danger is that they will choose the path of international conflict in preference to facing an immediate economic crisis and running the risk of becoming discredited.

The disturbing distension of armaments has already inflicted on the American people a spiral of inflation, with rising prices and rising taxes cutting drastically into the consumer's income. As former President Herbert Hoover stated in his address of January 27, 1952:

> The outstanding phenomenon in the United States is the dangerous overstraining of our economy by our gigantic expenditures. The American people have not yet felt the full impact of the gigantic increase in government spending and taxes. Yet we already suffer from the blight of inflation and confiscatory taxes. We are actually in a war economy except for world-wide shooting. We are diverting more and more civilian production to war materials. . . .
>
> Since the end of the Second World War the purchasing power of

our money, measured in wholesale price indexes, has decreased 40 percent. . . . It is the average family who pays the bulk of taxes, both income and hidden. Among them are corporation taxes. These are ultimately passed on to their customers or the corporation would quickly go bankrupt. . . . These huge taxes are also overstraining our economy.

In addition, President Truman's reckless program is using up America's limited natural resources, such as iron ore and oil, at such a furious rate that coming generations, under whatever form of economy, will be seriously handicapped. The Washington spendthrifts are robbing future Americans of their birthright for a wasteful mess of bombs and battleships, guns, tanks and warplanes.

The burgeoning American armaments economy has brought the United States to a condition, as described by Walter Lippmann, "of gigantic, almost explosive, industrial expansion which draws tremendously and competitively on the available supplies." America's accelerating need for raw materials, scrap metal and finished goods to meet the insatiable demands of a defense policy run wild has made it increasingly difficult for Britain, France, Italy and the Benelux countries to find the necessary imports for their own needs; to pay the inflated prices asked, most frequently by American manufacturers; and to put across their vast rearmament programs, in conformance with American foreign policy, without more and more depressing their own standards of living through domestic inflation, crushing taxation and a sheer lack of consumer goods.

Mr. Aneurin Bevan commented most persuasively on the situation in his speech of April 23, 1951, when he resigned in protest as Minister of Labor in the British Labor Government:

It is now perfectly clear to anyone who examines the matter objectively—the lurchings of the American economy, the extravagance and unpredictable behavior of the production machine, the failure of the American Government to inject the arms program into the economy slowly enough has already caused a vast inflation of prices all over the world. It has disturbed the economy of the Western World to such an extent that if it goes on more damage will be done by this unrestrained behavior than by the behavior of the nation the arms are intended to restrain. . . .

I say, therefore, with full solemnity of the seriousness of what I am saying, that the £4,700,000,000 arms program is already dead. It cannot be achieved without irreparable damage to the economy of Great Britain and the world. . . . The fact is that the Western World has embarked upon a campaign of arms production and upon a scale of arms production so quickly and of such extent that the foundations of political liberty and parliamentary democracy will not be able to sustain the shock.

In December 1951 Winston Churchill, soon after he became Prime Minister for the second time, declared frankly in the House of Commons that Britain would be unable to complete on schedule its three-year $13-billion rearmament program. He said that he was giving Aneurin Bevan "honorable mention" for having—"it appears by accident—perhaps not from the best of motives—happened to be right." Early in 1952 Churchill's Conservative Government launched a new austerity program "to avert national bankruptcy." Measures included a drastic curtailment of the social services, cuts in the civil service staff, a sharp reduction in manufactured goods for the home market and a record low European travel allowance of approximately $70 per year for each Englishman.

The remarks of Bevan and Churchill raise the portentous question of whether the long-range effect of American policy will not be to force Western Europe further and further to the Left instead of rescuing it from the communists. A most significant report issued in March 1952 by the ultraconservative U.S. Chamber of Commerce puts the issue squarely: "There is little surplus fat in Western Europe to permit the luxury of large armies. It will take decades fully to repair the destruction of the recent war. . . . Further sacrifices would inevitably drive many into the already large Communist and Socialist Parties. It would seem the part of wisdom, given these trends, not to overlook the political and economic problems of Europe. Heavy emphasis upon the military may well backfire."

The only sound way, of course, to prevent the spread of communist regimes is to institute far-reaching social and economic reforms that will do away with poverty, unemployment, depression, currency crises and the other ills that have afflicted Europe over the past few decades. But the heavy-handed Truman Administration, insisting everywhere on the *warfare* state in place of the *welfare* state, has offered no effective plan for permanent economic well-being and is, on the contrary, depressing living standards in the nations it purports to be aiding.

The careening American economic juggernaut has affected for the worse not only England, France and Western Europe in general, but the entire world. Wholesale price increases since the start of the Korean war amounted, as of July 1951, to more than 30 percent in Mexico, more than 33 percent in Brazil, more than 42 percent in Finland and more than 51 percent in Japan. If President Truman would study his own reports more carefully, he would be more conscious of the unhappy consequences of his policies. For example, his midyear economic report of 1951 stated: "The enormous price increases which have occurred constitute in some countries a danger to political and social stability, and to the security program of the free world. . . . Because the economies of these countries have been under great strain and because in some of them the political and social situation is tense, inflation raises not only the question of equitable distribution of the economic burden of defense; it also raises the grave question of the ability of their governments to carry through the needed defense programs and maintain economic stability."

With the economic situation steadily deteriorating in the very nations the American Government proclaims it is saving from the Soviet menace, the Truman Administration has all along insisted that its allies follow its own policy of curtailing trade with members of the Soviet-led bloc for the purpose of weakening communist military potential. This has meant a severe decline in commerce between Western and Eastern Europe and the cutting off of Japan from China, which has traditionally been both its best customer and its main source of raw materials. The lack of normal trade relations with Western Europe has indeed been some handicap to the Soviet Union and the smaller Eastern European countries in their postwar economic reconstruction, but it has been considerably more of a handicap to the Western European economies.

This is because Soviet Russia and its allies, with their far-reaching economic planning, have been better able to adjust to the falling off of trade than the West. Furthermore, the American-imposed barriers against economic relations with the East have forced the North Atlantic Pact countries to attempt to fill the vacuum through trade with the U.S. This endeavor is impossible of fulfilment because European exports run into the barrier of America's high tariffs and because European imports must be paid for in dollars. These difficulties have combined to create throughout Western Europe a critical and continuing dollar deficit. The U.S. "get-tough" policy towards the USSR is toughest of all on the Western European peoples.

In July 1951 the American Government took the extreme step of breaking off its formal trade and commercial agreements with Soviet Russia and its allies in Eastern Europe, despite the fact that these nations have been most desirous of maintaining trade relations with the West. American business of course loses out economically from this short-sighted policy. The total value of exports from the U.S. to the USSR fell from $149,504,000 (including $50,540,000 in aid and relief) in 1947 to $27,879,000 in 1948, to $6,617,000 in 1949, to a trickle of

$621,407 in 1950 and an estimated $70,000 in 1951.

Walter Lippmann makes some pertinent and penetrating remarks about the all too successful American campaign to cripple international trade. "A dominating part of Congress," he writes, "which Mr. Truman and Mr. Acheson have felt it necessary to appease, is demanding a virtual embargo and blockade of the whole Communist orbit. The reasoning of these Congressmen is that an embargo and blockade of this kind would hurt the Communists more than it hurts the United States. That, considering our immense self-sufficiency and enormous financial power, is no doubt true. But from this truth they have jumped to the quite unwarranted conclusion that the embargo hurts the Communists more than it hurts our weak and stricken allies. That is not true, and we shall be learning more and more, but in the hard way, how untrue it is."

Mr. Lippmann analyzes the situation further: "The great problem looming on the horizon is how to keep the large, congested, industrial populations of Britain, West Germany and Japan at work and at a standard of living which they will accept as reasonable for themselves. To deal with this problem we are compelled—as things stand now—to replace the markets and sources of supply which they have lost by finding markets and sources of supply within the world which is dependably in the Western political orbit. This is perhaps the most radical reconstruction and re-routing of the trade of the world which men have ever dreamed of trying to bring about." Although Mr. Lippmann does not say it, the chances are slim that this drastic and unnatural alteration in long-established trade patterns will succeed.

The reference by Mr. Lippmann to appeasement on the part of the Truman Administration brings out the extent to which American foreign policy is being formulated, not for the benefit of the American people or the world, but to enable the Democratic Party to stay in power by outdoing the Republican Party in anti-Soviet and anticommunist declarations and deeds. President Truman's announced determination to "contain" communism has been far more successful in containing the Republicans than in its original goal. And the Russians cannot help wondering whether this perpetual merry-go-ground of American political maneuvering might not lead one party or the other to precipitate a world war as the culmination of the great contest in denouncing, hating and combating the alleged communist menace.

Furthermore, current in Administration and Congressional circles is a strong feeling that an armed conflict with the Soviet Union is inevitable: Mr. Demaree Bess corroborates this fact in the *Saturday Evening Post:* "A fatalistic feeling has pervaded both major political parties that we can solve our own and the world's problems only by overthrowing the expanding Soviet Empire by force of arms. This fatalism has spread so widely that we no longer pay much attention to the most belligerent statements by our representatives in Washington."

One of the most disturbing—and threatening—features of American foreign policy is that the U.S. has lined up as allies an incredible assortment of fascist or semifascist governments dedicated to violence, terror and tyranny. The so-called "free world," supposedly banded together to extend the blessings of intellectual liberty and political democracy, includes sixteen Latin American dictatorships or quasi-dictatorships (I exclude here Cuba, Guatemala, Mexico and Uruguay); the royal fascist regime of Greece; the cruel police state of Turkey; the Formosan remnants of Chiang Kai-shek's bloody and primitive fascism; the Union of South Africa with its horrible racist laws; Franco's Falangist Spain, established with the help of Hitler and Mussolini and perpetuated in their image; the reactionary republic of West Germany; and still semifeudal Japan with its thin veneer of democracy. This roll call obviously shows that "the free world" is a propaganda myth.

Mrs. Vera M. Dean of the moderate Foreign Policy Association makes clear in the weekly *Bulletin* of that organization the strange double standard characteristic of American policy: "In Eastern Europe Washington has urged free and unfettered elections and has denounced the establishment of dictatorial governments dominated by Communists. Yet at the Bogotá conference of 1948 the United States proposed recognition of governments in Latin America without inquiry into their character and without the requirement of prior elections. In the opinion of many observers, this doctrine has encouraged seizure of power by military juntas in Peru, Venezuela and El Salvador at the expense of the kind of middle-of-the-road regimes we have urged for Eastern Europe and the Balkans."

The efficient manner in which the United States Government has enlisted in its coalition well-nigh every reactionary force and gangster government throughout the world indicates the possible use of such elements in the unscrupulous rough-and-tumble of aggressive warfare. Certainly the makeup of the American-led bloc must in itself awaken grave apprehensions in the Soviet mind. And when in addition the Truman Administration insists on the provocative rearmament of West Germany and Japan, both the Russians and all other peace-loving peoples have a right to be anxious. Let us remember that already coming to the fore in postwar West Germany and Japan are the same sort of economic and political groupings that so ruthlessly unleashed the Second World War.

The Japanese Peace Treaty, forced upon the world by the United States at San Francisco in September 1951, summarily violated the

1943 Cairo Agreement, which promised the return of Formosa to China, and also the 1945 Potsdam Declaration, which guaranteed that there should be no revival of Japanese militarism. The treaty provided for continuing American military occupation of Japan and for numerous U.S. bases for land, sea and air forces. With India and Burma refusing to attend the San Francisco conference because of their opposition to the treaty and with the People's Republic of China deliberately excluded, representatives of two-thirds of the people of Asia took no part in this settlement directly affecting that half of the earth's population living in the Orient.

Closely related to the Truman Administration's collaboration with and support of reactionary regimes is its reversal of America's traditional attitude of sympathy towards the aspirations of colonial peoples for self-determination and independence. Americans are themselves a proud and freedom-loving people who threw off the yoke of empire through revolution. But today the United States has become the great champion of Western imperialism, resorting to dollar diplomacy, political intimidation and military violence in taking over the suppressive functions of faltering empires.

The effects, then, of American foreign policy since Mr. Truman took over the White House have been such as to cause deepest misgivings throughout the globe. The apparent readiness of leaders in the United States Government to risk blowing civilization to smithereens for the sake of political advantage, the bellicose attitude of many American journalists, radio commentators and other prominent citizens, the stratospheric sums spent on atom bombs and other weapons, the expanding global ring of U.S. air and military bases, America's alliance with outright fascist or old-fashioned military dictatorships—all these things raise the question of whether American policy is not directed towards war rather than peace-through-preparedness. Even the conservative London *Economist* states: "In large measure the present American program is designed for fighting Russia, not for staying at peace by deterring a Russian aggression." And some of the missteps that Soviet Russia and other members of the communist bloc have taken in foreign policy are attributable in no small degree to fear of American intentions and a sharp defensive reaction to them.

Most of these deplorable developments flow from a policy that has been worked out and put through as the answer to the danger of "Soviet aggression." Returning to this theme for a moment, let us cite a man who, in the American community, is as respectable as the Washington Monument and who was denouncing the Soviet Union and all its works for years before Harry Truman even became a Senator. I refer to Mr. Herbert Hoover, who, in a speech in January 1952, noted that

Western Europe, in its judgment as to the risk of a communist invasion, takes a view "profoundly different from the attitude of Washington."

"There is in Europe today," asserted Mr. Hoover, "no such public alarm as has been fanned up in the United States. None of those nations has declared emergencies or taken measures comparable with ours. They do not propagandize war fears or war psychosis such as we get out of Washington. Not one European country conducts such exercises in protection from bombs as we have had in New York." Mr. Hoover then cited eight major reasons why public opinion in Western Europe estimates the "risk of invasion as so much less than does Washington." "I cannot say," he added, "whether these eight assumptions are correct or not. But they do contribute to Western Europe's lack of hysteria and their calculation of low risk and, therefore, their lack of hurry to arm. In any event this whole European situation requires that the United States recalculate our own risks and reconsider the possible alternatives."

I have quoted former President Hoover at some length, not only because of the intrinsic soundness of the statements cited, but also in order to show that conservative defenders of the capitalist system, opponents of socialism and enemies of the Soviet Union are also critical of American foreign policy and agree with liberals and radicals on important international issues. The point is that the U.S. drift towards war and a garrison state is likely to prove catastrophic for the well-being of all Americans, regardless of their political and economic viewpoints.

Another conservative gravely troubled by the international situation is Pope Pius XII. In a Christmas message broadcast to the world on December 23, 1950, the Supreme Pontiff of the Roman Catholic Church appealed to Soviet Russia and the Western Powers to enter into direct negotiations before their deepening cleavage degenerated into war. "How earnestly," he pleaded, "the Church desires to smooth the way for these friendly relations between peoples! For her, East and West do not represent opposite ideals, but share a common heritage to which both have generously contributed and to which both are called to contribute in the future also."

Now it is precisely "direct negotiations," especially with the United States, that the Soviet Government has been suggesting over the past few years and to which the Truman Administration has turned a cold— very cold—shoulder. The U.S. Government argues that diplomatic negotiations for the settlement of the Cold War and the easing of American-Soviet tensions should take place within the framework of the United Nations. Yet the United States has itself bypassed the U.N. whenever it seemed convenient, as in the drawing up and effectuation of the Truman Doctrine regarding Greece and Turkey, the institution of the North Atlantic Treaty and NATO, and the negotiations with West Germany and Japan.

Certainly the founders of the United Nations never intended that its establishment was to rule out special conversations and confidential negotiations between two or more of its members. Indeed, the first article in the U.N. Charter's chapter on the Pacific Settlement of Disputes reads: "The parties to any dispute, the continuance of which is likely to endanger the maintenance of international peace and security, shall, first of all, seek a solution by negotiation, enquiry, mediation, conciliation, arbitration, judicial settlement, resort to regional agencies or arrangements *or other peaceful means of their own choice.*" [Italics mine—C.L.]

The negative American attitude towards Soviet overtures has brought forth from the conservative David Lawrence, writing in the conservative *New York Herald Tribune,* the following comment: "The biggest barrier to world peace today has been erected by persons inside and outside Washington who have closed their minds to any further discussion with the Russians. This school of thought says conferences are no good, that Russians can't be trusted, that sooner or later there will be war and that America must stay on a war footing every day and night, borrow unearned billions from tomorrow's generations and even perhaps fight a 'preventive war,' striking before the enemy can. The exponents of that doctrine have nothing to offer but physical force and threats."

Soviet foreign policy does not and cannot function within a vacuum; to be realistic it must take into consideration the fundamental forces operating in international affairs, including the actions and policies of the United States, world capitalism's acknowledged leader. Hence, the Soviet Government shapes and reshapes its own policies with the particular attitude of America always in mind. As we have seen, you do not have to be a Soviet diplomat to feel that the effects of current American policy are not conducive to world peace and economic stability. If I am correct in my analysis, then the economic, trade, armament and Cold War policies of the Truman Administration, while certainly not helpful to the Soviet-led coalition, will not in the long run be helpful to U.S. capitalism and democracy either. And these policies may well prove fatal for Western Europe.

The all-out anti-Soviet atmosphere in the United States so stifles objective thinking that there is a tendency here among many leaders in government, business and public opinion to discard summarily as bad any move that would be good for the Soviet Union or the other communist countries. Now indubitably international peace, disarmament and a normal exchange of goods on the world market would be beneficial for the communist nations. But to reject these aims on this account is to negate the processes of reason. For plainly the fulfilment of such goals would also be immensely beneficial to America and the rest of the noncommunist world. *Mutual self-interest is the key to ending the present American-Soviet impasse.*

There is much in Soviet international proposals that is valid not only for the USSR, but also for the USA. A sound American peace policy is bound to have a number of basic points in common with Soviet policies. During the war against the Axis, Soviet Russia and the United States drew up and faithfully carried out many joint military agreements that were in the obvious interests of both countries. In those years high officials in the Roosevelt or Truman Administrations did not turn down suggestions merely because they were initiated or advocated by the Soviets. It is not sensible to do so today.

War and violence have always been the worst ways to deal with problems between countries. There is a far, far better method for the solution of current dilemmas—better for nations, for peoples, for governments, for capitalists, for communists, for conservatives, for radicals, for politicians, for businessmen, for this alliance and that bloc, for East and West. That is the method of reason, understanding, negotiation and compromise. I believe that this method now demands that the American Government give more serious and reasonable consideration to Soviet proposals for disarmament, international control of atomic energy, the reestablishment of East-West trade, the unification of Germany and a Five-Power peace pact.

Above all, it is time for Washington to accept the invitation of the Soviet Government to have the highest-ranking officials from each side sit down and talk things over calmly, with the aim of coming to a general agreement on peaceful coexistence and settling the chief issues in dispute on terms advantageous to both the USA and the USSR.

Why the Bomb Was Dropped

The twentieth anniversary of the dropping of the atomic bomb on Hiroshima and Nagasaki has inspired a spate of books on the subject. Len Giovannitti and Fred Freed, able producers of television documentaries, have written, after two years of research, a first-rate, exciting and carefully documented study of the political aspects of the United States' decision to bomb Japan.

As to their own opinion about whether the decision was justified, the authors keep the reader in suspense until the very last sentence of their narrative. That sentence reads: "Until and unless new evidence is uncovered to prove otherwise, it is our belief that the decision to use the bomb was taken in good faith not to unleash a weapon in vengeance against a ruthless enemy, but primarily to bring a quick end to a barbaric war and secondarily to derive the benefits of a timely victory."

Yet throughout this volume there runs a pattern of statements by the authors and quotations from leading American officials that strongly suggests quite another thesis. That thesis is that the A-bombs were unleashed on two Japanese cities, not because Japan's surrender was in doubt, but to bring it about *before* the USSR entered the Asian theatre of war and to stage the mightiest military demonstration in history for the purpose of making the Soviets more amenable to U.S. pressure. In fact, Giovannitti and Freed themselves concede that the bombs were used partly "as a political weapon against the Russians."

Although President Roosevelt never said a word to Vice-President Truman about the Manhattan Project that was to produce the atom

Source: This review of The Decision To Drop the Bomb (New York: Coward-McCann, 1965) was first published in New World Review, November 1965.

bomb, he did confide the details of this portentous enterprise to James F. Byrnes, who was Director of the Office of War Mobilization. After Truman became President, he appointed Byrnes Secretary of State at the beginning of July 1945. Byrnes had already stated that Russia might be more manageable if impressed by American military might and that a demonstration of the bomb might serve this purpose. Later, in high-level talks about the bomb in April, Byrnes told Truman, "It might well put us in a position to dictate our own terms at the end of the war."

In discussing these talks Giovannitti and Freed write: "The policy makers were thinking beyond the end of the war, to the use of the bomb as a political and diplomatic weapon in the peace that would follow, in particular in the relations of the United States to the Soviet Union. And if they still regarded the bomb primarily as a means to end the war, to avoid the invasion of the Japanese home islands, to save thousands of American lives, they nevertheless more and more turned their attention to those secondary benefits they foresaw growing out of its use against Japan."

President Truman twice postponed his meeting with Churchill and Stalin in Germany because he hoped to go there with the trump card of knowing that the Manhattan Project had attained its end. Finally, the Potsdam Conference was scheduled to open on July 16, but was put off one day because Stalin was delayed. Truman had timed the conference perfectly, for the amazingly successful explosion of the first atomic bomb took place early on the morning of July 16 in a desert area of New Mexico designated by the code name Trinity. Recalling the psychology of the scientists in charge of the test, J. Robert Oppenheimer, director of the laboratory that built the bomb, asserted: "It was certainly very true that we felt very earnest about doing it in time for the Potsdam Conference . . . and we did it under weather conditions which were not ideal because we saw there was danger in postponement."

The authors show that very soon after Truman appointed Byrnes Secretary of State, he began to rely on the new cabinet member rather than on Secretary of War Henry L. Stimson for advice on how to end the war with Japan. Truman invited Byrnes, not Stimson, to sail with him on the U.S. cruiser *Augusta* for the Potsdam Conference. And on that trip across the Atlantic the new Secretary of State had plenty of opportunity to win the President to his views. Writing later about the conversations on the *Augusta*, Byrnes noted: "I cannot speak for others but it was ever present in my mind that it was important that we should have an end to the war before the Russians came in." Both Byrnes and Truman, of course, were aware that by the terms of the Yalta

Agreement drawn up by Roosevelt, Stalin and Churchill in February, the Soviet Union was scheduled to launch an offensive against the Japanese forces in Manchuria ninety days after V-E Day. That meant that the Soviet attack would begin August 8.

On the evening of July 16 Truman, Byrnes and Stimson learned by cable from Washington that the A-bomb was a fearsome reality. This news brought about a drastic change in Truman's attitude on the Russians entering the Japanese war and reinforced Byrnes's earlier position. Byrnes later recalled: "Neither the President nor I were anxious to have them enter the war after we had learned of the successful test. . . . Personally, I was praying that the Japanese would see the wisdom of surrendering and we could bring the war to an end before the Russians got in." Secretary Stimson and Army Chief of Staff Marshall agreed in general with Byrnes.

Prime Minister Churchill reported to Foreign Minister Eden: "It is quite clear that the United States do not at the present time desire Russian participation in the war against Japan." After both Truman and Churchill had received a more detailed report of the Trinity blast, Churchill wrote: "Now I know what happened to Truman yesterday [at the July 21 plenary session of the Conference]. I couldn't understand it. When he got to this meeting after having read this report, he was a changed man. He told the Russians just where they got on and off and generally bossed the whole meeting."

Beginning late in 1944, the Japanese Government had been making peace overtures to the United States through one channel or another. Early in 1945 General Douglas MacArthur forwarded to the White House surrender terms suggested unofficially by the Japanese and almost identical with those finally accepted. In the spring of 1945 the Japanese were reeling from the effects of firebomb air raids on Tokyo and other cities and from the blockade of the country by the United States Navy. On June 22 Japanese realization of their desperate situation was intensified by the American capture of Okinawa after a fierce and bloody campaign. But even then, according to Eugene Dooman, Far Eastern expert in the U.S. State Department, Secretary Stimson "wanted no call for surrender until or unless the A-bomb was a reality."

As early as May 10 the Joint Chiefs of Staff, meeting in Washington, had concluded that "the 'threat' of a Soviet invasion of Manchuria might, in itself, be enough to 'shock' Japan into surrender before the American invasion was launched." And in June General Marshall was of the opinion that "the entry of Russia on the already hopeless Japanese may well be the decisive action levering them into capitulation."

However, in this book of many merits, the authors unfortunately make no attempt to explore this theme. President Truman has never answered the question as to why he allowed the two A-bombs to be dropped on August 6 and August 9 without awaiting the results of the Soviet offensive starting August 8. As the Joint Chiefs of Staff and General Marshall suggested, the Japanese Government might have quickly surrendered after the Soviet onslaught, and there would then have been no further loss of either American or Japanese lives.

To the unanswered question my own reply, buttressed heavily by evidence from *The Decision To Drop the Bomb,* is twofold: first, Truman and other top American officials were most eager to obtain the capitulation of Japan before the Soviet Union came into the war, or could mount more than a symbolic involvement, because they wished to avoid Soviet participation in the Far Eastern peace negotiations; second, they wanted to make a tremendous demonstration in weaponry that would impress the entire world, especially the Russians, and which would thereby, as Byrnes had put it, enable the United States "to dictate our own terms at the end of the war," in Europe as well as Asia.

I do not deny that other motivations played a role in the decision to drop the bomb, but I think they were *secondary.* My basic disagreement, then, with Giovannitti and Freed is that they evaluate as *secondary* the political, anti-Soviet reasons for the atomic massacre of some 140,000 Japanese, mostly civilians. Their own book, I contend, gives much more support to my interpretation than to theirs. I must add that my position is in general the same as that adopted by many scientists, historians and writers more competent in this field than I.

Our two authors go deeply into the question of whether a warning demonstration of the power of the A-bomb should have been given the Japanese people and the Japanese Government. They agree with a host of other students of the subject that some such warning should have been arranged. Curiously enough, however, they do not cite the important article in *Look* magazine of March 14, 1950, in which Dr. Alexander Sachs, a New York economist and close associate of President Roosevelt, tells how the latter, a few months before he died, approved a complex plan for a warning demonstration of the A-bomb to both the Japanese and the Germans.

The book under review quotes a number of eminent persons who opposed the detonation of the A-bomb over Japan. For instance, Rear Admiral Lewis Strauss, who later became Chairman of the Atomic Energy Commission, said: "It seemed to me that such a weapon was not necessary to bring the war to a successful conclusion, that once used it would find its way into the armaments of the world." Leo Szilard, a physicist who helped initiate the development of the A-bomb, drew up a petition to be presented to President Truman, who

never saw it. Szilard argued: "Once they were introduced as an instrument of war it would be very difficult to resist the temptation of putting them to such use. Thus a nation which sets the precedent of using
these newly liberated forces of nature for purposes of destruction may
have to bear the responsiblity of opening the door to an era of devastation on an unimaginable scale."

That the statements of Strauss and Szilard were prophetic can easily
be verified by noting the proliferation of nuclear weapons and
particularly the policies and plans of the United States. It has been
common knowledge that Secretary of State John Foster Dulles, the
brink-of-war apostle, and President Eisenhower offered nuclear bombs
to France in 1954 when the French forces were on the verge of decisive
defeat in Vietnam. Fortunately the American plan did not go through
because of the vacillation of the French and the opposition, at the last
moment, of Prime Minister Churchill and the British Cabinet.

As part of a preview of Eisenhower's new book, *Waging Peace,
1955-60, The New York Times* of September 12, 1965, disclosed that in
1953 President Eisenhower "let word leak out that unless a satisfactory
armistice could be arranged in Korea, the United States would use its
nuclear power to gain full victory. Shortly thereafter the Communists
agreed to armistice terms." In the same article the *Times* revealed that
in order to successfully defend the Chinese offshore islands of Matsu
and Quemoy (less than seven miles from the mainland) against the
communists, Eisenhower and Dulles drafted a memorandum in 1958 on
how the United States might "face the necessity of using small-yield
atomic weapons against hostile airfields."

In view of Eisenhower's willingness on three separate occasions to
bring into play atomic weapons, it is small wonder that the United
States Government has refrained from following the example of the
Soviet Union and Communist China in pledging not to be the first to
utilize nuclear weapons in the future.

Evaluating finally the U.S. destruction of Hiroshima and Nagasaki by
means of nuclear bombs, with no warning demonstration and no
serious effort to follow up the Japanese peace overtures, I am compelled to agree with that large segment of public opinion throughout
America and the world that has found the explosion of the atomic
infernal machine unjustified from both the military and moral viewpoints.

The Truman decision to make use of the A-bomb against Japan, his
later insistence on the manufacture of the far more powerful H-bomb
(first tested by the United States in 1952), and the Dulles-Eisenhower
blueprints for using atom bombs against the Chinese communists—all
this in my judgment adds up to a callous disregard for human life and

191

for elementary ethical standards in international conduct. The cruel precedents established have brutalized a considerable proportion of the American people and have helped pave the way for the wanton military bombing and indiscriminate slaughter of noncombatants in President Johnson's war of aggression against Vietnam. The United States Government has truly become a past master in the practice of international immorality.

In view of the steady U.S. escalation of the Vietnam conflict and the plentiful supply of nuclear warheads in Guam, from which B-52s frequently fly to bomb the Vietnamese, there is no guarantee that the President and the Pentagon will not resort eventually to nuclear weapons in Southeast Asia. In fact *The New York Times* on April 27, 1965, reported that high officials from President Johnson down have stated, in reference to Vietnam, that "they do not rule out the possibility that circumstances might arise in which nuclear weapons would have to be used."

This terrible danger today is our legacy from Hiroshima.

Juggernaut: The Warfare State

Fred J. Cook, the crack journalist who wrote *The Nation*'s special issues on the Federal Bureau of Investigation, the Central Intelligence Agency, gambling and the Hiss case, has now done another brilliant job in "Juggernaut: The Warfare State" (*The Nation*, October 28, 1961).

Mr. Cook takes his cue from an unexpected source, Dwight D. Eisenhower's farewell address to the American people last January, when the retiring President stated: "This conjunction of an immense military establishment and a large armaments industry is new in the American experience. The total influence—economic, political, even spiritual—is felt in every city, every state house, every office of the Federal Government. . . . We must guard against the acquisition of un- warranted influence, whether sought or unsought, by the military- industrial complex."

Following the President's lead, Mr. Cook traces the growing eco- nomic, political and propaganda power of "the military-industrial octopus" throughout many different sectors of American life. He points out that the U.S. Defense Department owns 32 million acres of land in the United States and 2.6 million abroad, that it employs 3,500,000 persons, and that its annual payroll is $11 billion (more than twice that of the automobile industry).

"In addition, an estimated 4 million persons are employed directly in defense industries. This means that a total of some 7.5 million Ameri- cans depend for their jobs directly on the Military—almost precisely one-tenth of the nation's entire labor force. . . . In Los Angeles, it has

Source: National Guardian, *December 20, 1961.*

been estimated that fully half of the jobs are dependent, either directly or indirectly, on the continuance of the arms race—and arms spending. Under such circumstances every food store, every gas station feels it has a stake in keeping the war plants going. Under such circumstances, any cutback, even any threat of cutback, elicits screams of protest from workers who have jobs at stake, from a wide variety of businesses that have profits at stake, from politicians who have votes at stake."

These considerations, together with the fact that the Federal Government is spending more than $50 billion a year for current military purposes, show how closely geared is the American economy to vast armaments expenditures and to the Cold War, threatening periodically, as now, to become a shooting war. A Republican or Democratic Administration, fearful of increased unemployment on a national scale and faced with widespread corporate opposition to reduced profits resulting from reduced military spending, is not likely to be enthusiastic over greatly reduced armaments budgets. This is one powerful reason why the American Government year after year has dragged its feet at disarmament conferences, especially since it has had no rational plans in view for conversion to a peace economy. An economic system that permits its functioning to depend in a large degree on the stimulus of war and war preparations, on the manufacture of weapons, both conventional and nuclear, of mass terror and mass slaughter, seems to me to have reached the apex of immorality.

Naturally the military-industrial Juggernaut, in order to obtain political and popular support, must maintain in the country a psychology of tension. Thus for Mr. Cook "the double-edged propaganda of the postwar era becomes self-evident. One purpose, as General MacArthur said, is to keep us 'in a perpetual state of fear . . . a continuous stampede of patriotic fervor,' so that we shall support without question a munitions budget of ever-expanding billions. At the same time the other edge of the propaganda sword brands with the label of 'radicalism' any proposal that might conceivably siphon off some of those munitions billions—and possibly interfere with the prerequisites of industry—to benefit the people." The Warfare State has no use for the Welfare State.

One of the most significant sections in Mr. Cook's tract tells how the military has all along lined up with the radical Right in fostering a fanatical anticommunist hysteria, in advancing the doctrine that communism can and must be destroyed in the practically inevitable war with Soviet Russia, and in organizing witch-hunts against civil liberties. The author gives a step-by-step account of how the military, after General Leslie R. Groves had indiscreetly released publicly the *Smyth Report* with its detailed description of how the A-bomb was developed, attempted to cover up for this major blunder by encouraging Congressional investigating committees and government officials to embark "upon spy hunts unparalleled in our history, whipping up in the country an emotional frenzy in which the word of every perjurer, if he testified about an alleged spy, was accepted as gilt-edged truth and virtually every man accused was convicted by the accusation."

There is no doubt in Mr. Cook's mind that the advancing Juggernaut which he describes has made enormous inroads on the proper functioning of representative government in the United States. "The real issue is whether American democracy is to be preserved—whether the most crucial decisions are to be determined by a military-industrial partnership not elected by or responsible to the people, or whether they are to be made by the civilian representatives elected for that purpose."

Regarding the most crucial decision of all—declaring and making war—the author is clear that Congress, which alone under our Constitution has that power, has become "a figurehead body." For "we recognize that, in the missile age in which obliteration from launching bases on the other side of the world is only thirty minutes away, there is no time for Congress to meet, to debate, to declare war. There is time only to react." Even the President does not have time. And that leaves the fateful decision in the hands of the trigger-happy military, to perhaps some "division commander—with the rank of brigadier or major general and not necessarily even an American."

The Ordeal of Soviet Russia

In his *Russia: What Next?* written shortly after Stalin's death in 1953, Isaac Deutscher predicted with a considerable degree of accuracy some of the main trends that have taken place in the Soviet Union since that time. In his most recent book (*Russia in Transition and Other Essays*, New York: Coward-McCann, 1957) Deutscher continues his analysis of Soviet developments and gives a lucid and realistic appraisal of the USSR on the threshold of its fortieth anniversary. His is a middle-of-the-road approach which recognizes that Soviet socialism has been and is a complex mixture of good and bad.

Mr. Deutscher is perfectly clear as to the tyrannical nature of the Stalin regime and its widespread violations of basic civil liberties and ordinary human decency. Even before the Khrushchev revelations, he had no illusions about Stalin's ruthless character. But the author does not follow the familiar pattern which utilizes the terrible shortcomings of the Stalin era as justification for roundly denouncing the whole Soviet enterprise.

Mr. Deutscher's recognition of Stalin's vices does not blind him to the enormous contributions that Stalin made to the upbuilding of the Soviet Union. Not even an anticommunist government in the USSR, he argues, could afford to renounce the system of economic planning and collective farms established under Stalin. Industrial growth, in a half-ruined economy after the close of the Second World War and while Stalin was still alive, was so remarkable that future historians may well describe it as the "most momentous feat in social technology achieved in this generation."

Source: New World Review, *February 1958.*

Mr. Deutscher sees three main reasons underlying the evolution of Stalin's harsh dictatorship. First, there was the general backwardness of the country when the communists took power and set out "to impose on the Russia of the *muzhiks* an ideal and a way of life for which Russia was not prepared, either materially or mentally. The primitive magic of Stalinism, the deification of the Leader, and the bizarre and elaborate rituals of Stalinism had all sprung from Russian backwardness and all served to tame that backwardness. Since the vast and swift transformation of the whole social outlook of Russia, undertaken by Stalin, was not based on the will and understanding of the people, its origin had to be traced to the superhuman wisdom and will of the Leader."

Second, the author states that the relative weakness of the Soviet working class, especially in numbers, at the end of the exhausting civil war and foreign intervention paved the way for the rise of a powerful, hard-driving, dictatorial bureaucracy. "A social vacuum arose," Mr. Deutscher declares, "in which the new bureaucracy was the only active, organized and organizing element. It filled the political vacuum and established its own preponderance."

Third, the policies of the Stalin regime were of course much affected for the worse by the isolation of the Soviet Union in an encircling capitalist world. The capitalist nations constantly kept Soviet nerves on edge through economic embargoes, sinister diplomatic maneuvers and massive military attacks capped by Hitler's aggression in the Second World War.

If I may spell this out a little further, it has always seemed to me that a conscious part of capitalist efforts to destroy and discredit Soviet socialism has been to put such pressures on the USSR that, even if it did not collapse, it would be forced into a Draconian dictatorship in order to survive. This has certainly been a prime capitalist motive in the Cold War and the armaments race. The intent has been to increase tension within the Soviet Union by compelling it continually to step up the pace in armaments production and so divert effort from general industrial growth and from raising the standard of living by increasing production of consumer goods.

While the capitalist elements of the Western democracies have ever outwardly lamented the lack of political freedom in Soviet Russia, inwardly they have rejoiced because this state of affairs gives them a most potent propaganda weapon against both the Soviets and the new socio-economic system of socialism. To maliciously paint socialism as inherently bound up with an austere garrison type of government has been especially effective in capitalist countries with a democratic tradition.

The first reason Mr. Deutscher gives for the development of the oppressive Stalin dictatorship is no longer operative. A country can hardly be called "backward" when it has been able to abolish all student tuition fees from the elementary school up through the university and graduate school levels and has produced two successful earth satellites. The second reason for the extremes of the Stalin era is, according to the author, on the way out.

The third reason has been considerably modified because the isolation of the USSR ended when the communists won control of mainland China in 1949. In this connection Mr. Deutscher argues convincingly that Stalin tried to dissuade the Chinese Communists under Mao Tse-tung from launching their final offensive against the Nationalist Government. But contrary to Stalin's advice, Mao and his associates decided to go ahead, and were completely successful. Here is another important consideration that belies the notion that the present Chinese Government is a puppet in the hands of the Kremlin leaders.

There remain the Cold War and capitalist nuclear threats, emanating principally from the United States, as serious factors holding back the growth of democracy within the Soviet Union. Mr. Deutscher feels sure, however, that today "it is the twilight of totalitarianism that the USSR is living through."

I do not have the space to analyze some of the author's best essays in this volume: "Post-Stalinist Ferment in Ideas," "Stalin's Last Word," "Marx and Russia," "Two Revolutions" (which makes a brilliant comparative study between the French and Communist Revolutions) and "1984—The Mysticism of Cruelty" (which shows the tremendous harm done to East-West understanding by George Orwell's popular novel and demonstrates that "the plot, the chief characters, the symbols and the whole climate of his story" were borrowed from a little-known Russian emigré writer, Evgenii Zamyatin).

I do, however, want to add a special comment on Mr. Deutscher's perceptive dissection of "The Ex-Communist's Conscience," in which he takes as representative examples James Burnham, Whittaker Chambers, Ruth Fischer, André Gide, Arthur Koestler, Ignazio Silone and others. These problem children of contemporary politics, as the author calls them, all claim, in Koestler's words, that "We ex-Communists are the only people who know what it's all about." To this Mr. Deutscher retorts: "One may risk the assertion that the exact opposite is true. Of all people, the ex-Communists know least what it is all about. . . . Most of them (Silone is a notable exception) have never been inside the real Communist movement. . . . As a rule they moved on the literary or journalistic fringe of the party. . . .

"Worse still is the ex-Communist's characteristic incapacity for detachment. His emotional reaction against his former environment keeps him in its deadly grip and prevents him from understanding the drama in which he was involved or half-involved. . . . Whatever the shades of individual attitudes, as a rule the intellectual ex-Communist ceases to oppose capitalism. . . . Having once been caught by the 'greatest illusion,' he is now obsessed by the greatest disillusionment of our time. . . . He advances bravely in the front ranks of every witch-hunt. His blind hatred of his former ideal is leaven to contemporary conservatism. . . . He contributes heavily to the moral climate in which a modern counterpart to the English anti-Jacobin reaction is hatched."

Mr. Deutscher points out that the ex-communist "may no longer be concerned with any cause except one—self-justification. And this is the most dangerous motive for any political activity." Now endless self-justification is one of the chief varieties of preoccupation with self. And I have noticed that most of the liberals and radicals with whom I have been acquainted who have turned into professional anti-Soviet-eers seem to be colossal egotists. They tend to lose the larger vision and the long-run perspective on Soviet affairs in their bitter feeling that they have been personally betrayed by the course of history. And having become used to appreciative—and sometimes adulatory—audiences when they were sympathetic to the Soviet venture, they must at any cost build up appreciative audiences to maintain the nourishment of their egos when they transfer their allegiance to the anti-Soviet crusade. This means that they are compelled to become more and more extreme in their denunciations of Soviet Russia and the other communist states, for they must somehow outdo the larger tribe of long-established specialists in the ever flourishing business of anti-communism.

In their attempts at self-justification, many ex-communists evidently feel that the only way they can expiate their former passionate love for all things communist is to give expression to a fanatical hate for the communist world—a hate so intransigent that they are willing to risk the extermination of the whole human race in a nuclear war if only the communists can be exterminated in the process. Lord Macaulay a century ago described in universal terms the obsession to which I refer when in the *History of England* he spoke of "that peculiar malignity which has, in all ages, been characteristic of apostates."

Mr. Deutscher goes on to quote a significant aside by Koestler that answers some of the latter's own attacks on the Soviet Union. Koestler asserts: "If we survey history and compare the lofty aims, in the name of which revolutions were started, and the sorry end to which they came, we see again and again how a polluted civilization pollutes its own revolutionary offspring." In the case of Soviet Russia, this means that the Communist Revolution was "polluted" from the start by the

Tsarist civilization from which it sprang. In other words, newborn societies no more than newborn individuals can escape the bad effects of a bad inheritance. And the Soviet Republic was bound to inherit a large measure of the backwardness, cruelty, corruption and despotism rampant in the old Tsarist empire.

As Professor Paul A. Baran puts it in *The Political Economy of Growth*: "Socialism in backward and underdeveloped countries has a powerful tendency to become a backward and underdeveloped socialism." This formulation, I believe, provides a key to understanding much that on the surface has seemed unintelligible or unprogressive in the socialist commonwealths of the USSR, the Eastern European People's Republics and China, the new giant looming on the world horizon.

The Crime Against Cuba

Walter Lippmann, dean of American columnists, has referred to the Kennedy Administration's support of the anti-Castro military venture in Cuba as an appalling and colossal mistake. But the abortive April invasion at the Bay of Pigs was worse than that. It was an outright crime against the Cuban people; and it was also a crime against the American people, against the United Nations and against world peace.

President Eisenhower must share the responsibility with President Kennedy for this enterprise in international immorality. As columnist William V. Shannon said in the *New York Post* of April 9, 1961: "Back in late 1959, the Eisenhower Administration decided to apply to Cuba 'the Guatemala treatment.' That is, the National Security Council gave CIA Director Dulles the go-ahead to organize the Cuban exiles, train a military force and plan an invasion of Cuba." On January 3, 1961, Eisenhower, partly in furtherance of this plan, severed diplomatic relations with Premier Fidel Castro's Government.

In his 1960 election campaign, President Kennedy, on October 20, issued a special statement about Cuba, claiming that the Russians had established a "new satellite" there, and suggesting that the United States Government should help to strengthen the "democratic anti-Castro forces in exile, and in Cuba itself, who offer eventual hope of overthrowing Castro."

This statement by Kennedy aroused considerable misgivings among liberals and progressives, including myself, who had supported his candidacy. But most of us felt that his tough attitude towards the Castro

Source: Basic Pamphlet, 1961.

regime was political eyewash designed to catch right-wing votes. Subsequent events made it clear that we were guilty of wishful thinking.

In the early, predawn hours of April 17, 1961, some 1,500 Cuban exiles and refugees—recruited, organized, subsidized and armed by the Central Intelligence Agency, a subdivision of the American Government—invaded Cuba. This army came in boats supplied by the CIA, with guns and tanks supplied by the CIA, and with fighting planes supplied by the CIA. The aim was to secure a beachhead in Cuba, trigger a mass rebellion against Castro and set up a provisional government, which would then get official American recognition and aid. The U.S. Joint Chiefs of Staff approved the military aspects of the blueprint for invasion, which was given the code name of Operation Pluto by the CIA-Pentagon strategists.

The April 28th issue of *Time*, a magazine distinctly hostile to Castro, stated: "The invaders—all Cubans—were trained by the U.S., supplied by the U.S., and dispatched by the U.S. to carry out a plan written by U.S. military experts. President Kennedy knew D-day in advance and approved." To handle the anti-Castro forces, there were "six main training bases in Guatemala" and "two staging bases at Puerto Cabezas, Nicaragua, and tiny Swan Island off the Honduran coast.

"In recent weeks, the equivalent of fifty freight carloads of aerial bombs, rockets, ammunition and firearms was airlifted into Puerto Cabezas by unmarked U.S. C-54s and C-47s, in such quantities that on some days last month planes required momentary stacking. During Easter week, twenty-seven U.S. C-124 Globemasters roared in three or four at a time to off-load full cargoes of rations, blankets, ammunition and medical supplies at the U.S.-built airstrip at Retalhuleu, at Guatemala City and at Guatemala's San José airbase."

The U.S. Navy, at least, rendered direct aid to the expedition against Cuba. One of the Cuban invaders who later escaped to Miami writes in his diary, published in the *New York Herald Tribune* of May 5: "April 14—The flotilla is steaming toward our date with destiny. Two destroyers—I think they are North American—flank us." This information was confirmed from other rebel sources.

U.S. News and World Report (May 15) gave further details: "U.S. destroyers escorted the ships to within six miles of shore. A U.S. aircraft carrier was in escort, as well, but remained about thirty miles offshore. . . . The B-26s of the anti-Castro forces flew from bases 600 miles away. They were escorted by U.S. Navy jets which peeled off about five miles from the beach, and left the B-26s on their own."

As history will permanently record, the Cuban Army and civilian militia smashed and smothered the invasion within three days, capturing more than 1,000 prisoners. Castro's tiny air force drove off or downed the enemy bombers, and sank most of the ships that had brought the invaders to the shores of Cuba. The entire Cuban people rallied to the support of the Government, and no sign of an uprising could be detected. Thus the long-heralded invasion to "liberate" Cuba ended in complete fiasco, with the Kennedy Administration that had backed this madcap venture discredited throughout the entire world.

The extent to which the U.S. Government was in charge of the invasion is further shown by the fact that just before it began, the CIA hustled off José Miró Cardona, President of the Cuban Revolutionary Council, and the other leaders of this principal anti-Castro organization, to an isolated and abandoned airbase in Florida where they were held incommunicado. The CIA then issued news releases in the Council's name, but without its knowledge.

According to *The New York Times* of April 26, these Cuban leaders "were kept from using the phone or from communicating with anyone on the outside. . . . Enraged, several of the Council members announced that they were leaving even if it meant being shot by the armed guards." Finally, Adolf A. Berle, Jr., President Kennedy's coordinator of Latin-American policies, and Arthur M. Schlesinger, Jr., another close adviser to the President, flew to Miami to calm down the Revolutionary Council. Apparently the CIA thought that the Council leaders could not be trusted to be discreet.

Earlier the CIA had also kidnapped seventeen anti-Castro volunteers because it considered them too Left politically, and held them in a remote jungle camp in Guatemala for eleven weeks before and during the invasion (*New York Times*, May 7). This episode reinforces our general knowledge that the CIA, in lining up recruits for and organizing the Cuban expedition, was partial to right-wing elements, including former supporters of Batista. And the two "kidnapping" incidents together prove beyond doubt that the assault on Cuba was masterminded by the CIA, and that the Cubans involved, whether leaders or rank-and-file, were essentially captives of U.S. imperialism.

On the very day of the invasion, Dr. Raul Roa, Cuba's Foreign Minister, charged before the Political Committee of the United Nations that his country had been invaded "by a mercenary force which came from Guatemala and Florida and which was organized, financed and armed by the Government of the United States of America." Ambassador Adlai E. Stevenson categorically denied these accusations and declared: "The United States has committed no aggression against Cuba. . . . I wish to make clear also that we would be opposed to the use of our territory for mounting an offensive against any foreign government."

Thus, as in the incident of the U-2 spy plane flight over the Soviet

Union on May 1, 1960, the U.S. Government was caught red-handed in the Big Lie. Everyone who heard Mr. Stevenson speak in the U.N. knew that he was telling a diplomatic falsehood—one that turned out to be most undiplomatic. For only a week later the White House gave out an official release on the Cuban affair, saying that "President Kennedy has stated from the beginning that as President he bears sole responsibility for the events of past days."

The participation by the United States in a military assault on a country with which it was officially at peace was a dishonorable action totally opposed to the best in our traditions as a democracy. It constituted a cynical violation, not only of America's ideals of international peace, but also of our laws, our Constitution and at least six international treaties, including our solemn agreements under the United Nations and the Organization of American States.

One of the neutrality laws violated went into effect on June 25, 1948, under Title 18, Section 960 of the U.S. Code, Annotated: "Whoever, within the United States, knowingly begins or sets on foot or furnishes the money for, or takes part in, any military or naval expedition or enterprise to be carried on from thence against the territory or dominion of any foreign prince or state, or of any colony, district or people with whom the United States is at peace, shall be fined not more than $3,000, or imprisoned not more than three years, or both." Sections 956 and 959 of Title 18 are also most relevant.

With President Kennedy's assent, the CIA took such complete command of the Cuban invasion that it became in reality a U.S. act of war, if not *de jure*, at least *de facto*. However, under the Constitution (Article I, Section 8, Item 11) Congress alone has the right to declare war. Thus in the Cuban situation the Kennedy Administration—the Executive branch of our Government—usurped the power of the Legislative branch and went ahead on its own to involve the United States in military hostilities that conceivably could have led to a worldwide nuclear conflict.

The aggression against Cuba was also contrary to the United Nations Charter, Chapter I, Article 2, Sections 3 and 4. Section 3 states: "All Members shall settle their international disputes by peaceful means in such a manner that international peace and security, and justice, are not endangered." Section 4 requires: "All Members shall refrain in their international relations from the threat or use of force against the territorial integrity or political independence of any state, or in any other manner inconsistent with the Purposes of the United Nations."

Likewise, the Cuban venture violated Article 15 of the Charter of the Organization of American States, signed at Bogotá in 1948 by both the United States and Cuba: "No state or group of states has the right to intervene, directly or indirectly, for any reason whatsoever, in the internal or external affairs of any other state. The foregoing principle prohibits not only armed force but also any other form of interference or attempted threat, against the personality of the state or against its political, economic and cultural elements."

The American Government's disregard of the U.N., OAS and other international obligations of the United States is itself a violation of our Constitution under Article VI, Section 2: "This Constitution and the laws of the United States which shall be made in pursuance thereof and *all treaties made, or which shall be made, under the authority of the United States, shall be the supreme law of the land,* and the judges in every State shall be bound thereby, anything in the Constitution or laws of any state to the contrary notwithstanding." [Italics mine—C.L.]

It was ironic that just two weeks after the landing in Cuba President Kennedy, signing a resolution that proclaimed May 1 as Law Day throughout the United States, said in part: "Law is the strongest link between man and freedom, and by strengthening the rule of law we strengthen freedom and justice in our own country and contribute by example to the goal of justice under law for all mankind."

The official reasons that the U.S. Government gave for its disregard of legal commitments, domestic and international, in the Cuban situation were that Premier Castro had created a communist dictatorship in Cuba, that international communism had set up a base of operations in that country and was thereby violating the Monroe Doctrine, that Cuba—only ninety miles from American shores—had become a Soviet satellite, and that all this gravely threatened the national security of the United States.

An objective examination of the facts demonstrates that these charges against the Cuban Government are specious and mere pretexts for foreign intervention by means of force and violence. Nobody in his right mind can believe that the Castro regime, governing a little country with a total population of about 6,500,000—less than that of New York City—aims at military aggression against the United States. And Castro has repeatedly declared that he will work out the problem of the U.S. Naval Base at Guantanamo Bay through peaceful negotiations.

Since, therefore, Cuba does not represent any real menace to the security of the USA, the American enemies of the Castro Administration are compelled to manufacture excuses for the most drastic action, including military invasion, against the Castro regime. These excuses must sound sufficiently plausible to delude the American people and world opinion. This explains the tremendous efforts—on the part of newspapers, magazines, radio, TV and the Government itself—to whip up hysteria in the United States over the subject of Cuba. In this age, *nations as well as individuals can be victims of a frame-up.*

The revolutionary Government of Cuba came into power in January 1959 as the result of an indigenous, noncommunist movement led by Fidel Castro to overthrow the reactionary and bloody dictatorship of Fulgencio Batista. The small Cuban Communist Party had long looked upon Castro as a well-meaning but blundering adventurer, and gave support to his 26th of July Movement only as it was nearing its final triumph. Throughout the Castro regime's brief existence of two-and-a-half years it has remained independent, while going steadily to the Left and experimenting with a socialist economy especially adapted to Cuban conditions and the Cuban people.

In this leftward trend Premier Castro's Administration was stimulated to a considerable degree by the hostile actions of the American Government and American business interests. Furthermore, when the Eisenhower Administration treated the Castro regime as a pariah and finally ruled out all American-Cuban trade except in food and drugs, the Cuban leaders decided—with the very survival of their nation at stake—to fill in the void, especially in the absolutely essential trade in oil and sugar, by large-scale commercial agreements with Soviet Russia and Communist China. It was at this point that American Government officials and most organs of public opinion in the United States started labeling the Castro Government as "communist" and to talk wildly of "the communist bridgehead in Cuba" and "Soviet domination."

But it is important to remember that in our era former colonial or semicolonial peoples throughout the world, from Indonesia in the Far East to Ghana and Guinea in Africa to Cuba in the Caribbean, have been winning national independence and at the same time setting up dynamically led republics that institute socialist programs in order to bring about rapid economic, social and cultural progress. It is essential to understand that when such regimes put into effect radical measures, as well as establishing close diplomatic and economic relations with the communist bloc, this does not mean that they necessarily are communist-controlled or are becoming communist.

As Mr. Bella Doumboya, the representative of Guinea at the recently concluded session of the United Nations, said in a speech on Cuba before that body on April 17:

> States engaged in the decolonization of their structure always discover, and are appalled by the fact that their economy is not adapted to the needs of their national life owing to foreign exploitation. Single crop economies are an essential characteristic of underdeveloped countries. A revolutionary government, in order to foster comprehensive economic development, is bound to alter the colo-

nial shape of the productive system if it wishes to foster national output and the industrialization of the country.

Contrary to accusations of Communist infiltration which circulate everywhere as soon as an underdeveloped country engages in bold reforms, it should be known that the acts which succeed the assumption of power are the ineluctable consequences of a life of dependence and frustration and derive mainly from the paramount claim of people hitherto subjected to a feudal regime. In countries where the national economy is under the control of foreign interests, misery and wretchedness is the lot of the indigenous population, all of whose labor power is occupied in the production of raw materials required for the continued expansion of the trusts.

In the field of production, in order to facilitate new crops in line with the needs of the people, and to put an end to the exploitation of the peasantry, in order to call a halt to the inevitably catastrophic repercussions of this general situation on national output—in a word, in order to remedy the irrational utilization of land and bring to an end social injustice and misery, fledgling governments must always engage in historic acts which sometimes become the cause of ill repute for them.

Every word of Mr. Doumboya's address applies to what the Castro regime has been trying to do. If the American people and the American Government persist in misunderstanding the situation in Cuba and in other nations that have recently emerged into freedom, the effects on United States foreign policy and international peace will continue to be disastrous. For to ascribe home-grown movements towards national independence and socialism to some sort of communist conspiracy directed from Moscow or Peking not only vastly exaggerates the power of the communist bloc, but also leads to provocative claims of communist intervention or aggression when it does not exist.

It is to be remembered that the United States has a big base at Guantanamo in Cuba, and maintains scores of other military bases fairly close to Soviet Russia and China, often in countries bordering upon them. As James Reston wrote in *The New York Times* of April 23: "Turkey, for example, has been getting from the United States far more power than Castro ever dreamed of getting from the Russians. The United States power, including even rockets with nuclear warheads, has been situated in Turkey for a long time, but the Russians, while annoyed by this fact, have not felt obliged to use their power to invade Turkey."

A flagrant attempt to inflame American public opinion against Castro is shown in the many reports published about the Cuban Air

Force utilizing Soviet MIG jets against the invaders. *Time* even stated that some of them were flown by Czech pilots. That these stories were untrue is indicated by the United States Navy itself in a dispatch from the U.S base at Guantanamo, reported in *The New York Times* of April 20: "The sensitive radar on Navy ships here has picked up no trace of high-speed Cuban or Communist aircraft. Officials, therefore, are confident that there have been no MIG fighters in this area of Cuba at least. Nor has the Navy sighted any foreign submarines." This paragraph was omitted in a later edition of the *Times*.

During May, Senator Wayne Morse (D.) of Oregon, Chairman of a special Senate subcommittee on Latin American affairs, reported that this body had heard "not a bit of evidence" that there was a single MIG plane in Cuba. According to Senator Morse, the Cuban planes that proved so effective in thwarting the rebel landing were of U.S. manufacture and had been sold to the old Batista government.

Castro's own comment on the makeup of his air force during the invasion crisis was "Would that we had had a few MIGs in those days!" In any event the Castro regime has a right to purchase for its own self-defense MIG planes, or any other kind, from a foreign government.

Much of the American propaganda barrage against Castro has centered around Cuba's admitted lack of civil liberties and political democracy. This propaganda, in the first place, naturally fails to mention that the Cuban Revolutionary Government has rapidly developed full racial democracy, complete equality between the whites and the Negroes, who make up one-third of the population. Economic, social and political discrimination against colored people, a pervasive evil under the Batista and earlier tyrannies, has disappeared. As Joseph Newman reported in the *New York Herald Tribune* (March 23): "Castro and Guevara are literally adored by the large number of poor and humiliated Cubans, especially the Negroes. They see these two leaders as saintly and honorable men, dedicated to removing injustices and discrimination."

In two and one-half years the Castro regime has made far more progress towards unqualified civil rights than the United States, particularly in the South, during the entire 100 years since the Civil War began. Actually, many of the Americans who cry out against "the Castro dictatorship" hate and fear racial democracy, and are scared stiff that it might spread from Cuba to the continents of North and South America.

In the second place, our American propagandists do not point out that the Cuban Government has a democratic mandate in the sense that it is supported by the overwhelming majority of the people. This support stems from the fact that the Government has brought to the workers and peasants—the massive legion of the underprivileged—a higher standard of living, release from economic exploitation, vastly increased educational and cultural opportunities, the promise of continued progress, and a feeling of dignity and freedom at no longer being in bondage to U.S. imperialism. Had the CIA, the State Department and President Kennedy known these things, they would not have made the miscalculation that the recent invasion would set off a popular uprising.

U.S. propaganda, in the third place, leaves out of the picture any reference to the relentless political and international pressures that have driven the Castro regime to certain dictatorial actions and policies. The outstanding foreign factor here has been the hostility of the United States, including its far-reaching economic embargo and culminating in April's military assault.

That aggression was hardly the sort of episode that could be expected to encourage democracy in Cuba, or in any other country confronted by similar circumstances. And the Cuban Government was certainly justified in putting into effect throughout the island far-reaching measures on behalf of public safety. It is well to recall that the National Emergency proclaimed by President Truman in 1950 during the Korean War is still in effect in the United States and has been utilized constantly for the curtailment of civil liberties.

There is, in truth, a large element of both inconsistency and hypocrisy in the American Government's call for "free elections" and political democracy in Cuba. It never made any such demands on Batista when he was in the saddle, nor on a number of other Latin American dictatorships that have been classified as part of "the free world," nor on various other dictatorships allied to the U.S., such as those of Pakistan, Thailand, Saudi Arabia, Franco's Spain, Salazar's Portugal and Chiang Kai-shek's Taiwan.

The real reason for the bitter opposition of the United States to the Castro regime is that it has put through radical social and economic reforms, nationalized the huge American property holdings in Cuba, freed the country from U.S. imperialist exploitation, established racial democracy and instituted a planned socialist economy that is functioning successfully. Above all, the Eisenhower and Kennedy Administrations have been afraid that revolutionary Cuba would serve as an example for other Latin American peoples to follow, and that it would inspire dangerous ideas even among the population of the United States.

So far as democracy is concerned, history has demonstrated the following principle of drastic economic and social change: When a progressively oriented revolution takes place in *any* country, the new regime may feel obligated to put into effect Draconian laws and procedures to ensure its survival and the success of its program. This is especially true when the nation in question—like Cuba—has had little or no functioning democracy in the past, is throwing off a reactionary bureaucracy or tyranny, or is threatened by internal counterrevolution and military incursions from abroad.

This principle clearly applies to the noncommunist Castro Government's efforts to build an indigenous form of socialism geared to the welfare of the Cuban people as a whole; it applies to the various revolutions towards socialism that have occurred elsewhere in the twentieth century; and it applies to the American Revolution of 1776 against colonialism, when we were very hard on the Tories, some 100,000 of whom fled the country and suffered the confiscation of their property. In the chaotic and difficult conditions that faced it subsequent to victory in 1781, the new American Republic was quite weak on democracy and civil liberties, even after the adoption of the Bill of Rights in 1791.

It would be well for historian Schlesinger to remind President Kennedy that no presidential elections were held in the United States until 1789, more than seven years after the end of the Revolution; that even then George Washington was unopposed for the office, as he was again in 1792; that the theory of our Founding Fathers, as written into the Constitution, made no place for political parties; and that two distinct parties did not come into existence until a good twelve years after the close of the Revolutionary War.

The eminent philosopher, William Ernest Hocking, Professor Emeritus of Philosophy at Harvard, in his book *Strength of Men and Nations*, stresses a consideration that is most pertinent to the Cuban situation: "In the world-wide effort to meet the needs of under-developed regions, it must be realized that a degree of dictatorship is inescapable for the first steps. . . . A people uneducated and uninformed, devoid of the habit of thinking out their own destiny, must proceed toward self-government under responsible guidance." And in such circumstances the people in general may well want "no gentle looseness of rein but a strict and determined command," just as midshipmen prefer a captain who "keeps a taut ship."

This discussion brings us back to the statement by Mr. Doumboya of Guinea that "fledgling governments must always engage in historic acts which sometimes become the cause of ill repute for them." As to such acts by the Castro regime, as well as its obvious errors and excesses, the words of Lord Macaulay in his *Essay on Milton* (1825) are remarkably relevant:

We deplore the outrages that accompany revolutions. But . . . the final and permanent fruits of liberty are wisdom, moderation and mercy. Its immediate effects are often atrocious crimes, conflicting errors, skepticism on points the most clear, dogmatism on points the most mysterious. It is just at this crisis that its enemies love to exhibit it. They pull down the scaffolding from the half-finished edifice: they point to the flying dust, the falling bricks, the comfortless rooms, the frightful irregularity of the whole appearance; and then ask in scorn where the promised splendor and comfort are to be found. If such miserable sophisms were to prevail, there would never be a good house or a good government in the world.

I said at the beginning of this essay that the U.S.-backed invasion of Cuba was a crime against the American people. This is true not only because it greatly increased international tensions and the danger of nuclear war, but also because it set at naught long-recognized democratic principles and Constitutional safeguards in the United States.

In relation to Cuba, President Kennedy and his close associates acted as a tight little group of conspiratorial bureaucrats, in violation of parliamentary procedures and the Constitutional principle of separation of powers among the three branches of the U.S. Government. Prior to the invasion, Congress was not given the slightest opportunity to debate the Cuban issue; nor was it submitted to the Senate Committee on Foreign Relations, of which J. William Fulbright (D.) of Arkansas is Chairman, nor to that committee's subcommittee on Latin American Affairs. However, Senator Fulbright, who knew about Operation Pluto in advance, almost alone among high government officials opposed it in a memorandum to the President.

Of course the American people had no chance to express their opinion on the question of Kennedy's plunging them into the Cuban maelstrom. As Senator Morse put it in a speech on the Senate floor: "There is grave doubt as to the legality of the course of action our country followed last week in regard to Cuba. . . . Freedom is worth too much as a human system of government for us to surrender any of our freedom to *a police state system in the field of foreign policy*, dictated by denying to the people the knowledge of the facts of their own foreign policy." [Italics mine —C.L.]

Kennedy's Cuban adventure constituted an Executive action running directly counter to the pronouncement in the Declaration of Independence about governments "deriving their just powers from *the consent of the governed.*" [Italics mine—C.L.] As Mr. David Wise, White House correspondent for the *New York Herald Tribune*, wrote on May 2: "If a major foreign policy action—carrying with it the risk of war—must be prepared in secret, then should it be undertaken at all? And a corollary question being asked is how far down the road a democracy can go in emulating the tactics of its enemies before it wakes up one morning and finds it is no longer very different from its foes?"

After the invasion as well as before it, the Kennedy Administration pursued its undemocratic policy, endeavoring to stifle a free and full debate on the crime against Cuba in Congress and in American organs of public opinion. The President arranged interviews with the highest ranking Republican leaders such as former Presidents Eisenhower and Hoover, ex-Vice-President Nixon, Governor Rockefeller and Senator Barry Goldwater. The aim was to secure Republican acquiescence in the Cuban assault and a bipartisan blackout on the whole business. In fact, during the first weeks after the invasion only Senator Morse spoke out in the halls of Congress against Kennedy's reversion to "the law of the jungle," as he called it. There was plenty of criticism in the press about the inefficient handling of the Cuban attack, but precious little criticism of its unethical and hypocritical character.

In a talk April 20 before the American Society of Newspaper Editors, President Kennedy compounded his past mistakes by indicating that there would be new ones in the future. "Let the record show," he declared, "that our restraint is not inexhaustible. Should it ever appear that the inter-American doctrine of non-interference merely conceals or excuses a policy of non-action; if the nations of this hemisphere should fail to meet their commitments against outside Communist penetration, then I want it clearly understood that this Government will not hesitate in meeting its primary obligations, which are the security of our nation. Should that time ever come, we do not intend to be lectured on intervention by those whose character was stamped for all time on the bloody streets of Budapest."

These fighting words seemed to contradict the President's pledge of April 12 that "there will not under any conditions be an intervention in Cuba by United States armed forces"; and they were everywhere interpreted as not only a threat to the Latin American allies of the United States, but also as a warning that Kennedy might set in motion unilateral military intervention to encompass the destruction of the Castro Government. It is no wonder that *The Nation* condemned this speech as "one of the most belligerent and reckless . . . ever made by an American President."

Developing even further his undemocratic techniques, President Kennedy, in an address to the American Newspaper Publishers Association on April 27, urged the press to censor itself on behalf of national security. Angry at newspaper exposures of the CIA's cloak-and-dagger plot against Cuba, Kennedy asserted: "Every newspaper now asks itself, with respect to every story: 'Is it news?' All I suggest is that you add the question: 'Is it in the interest of national security?' And I hope that every group in America—unions and businessmen and public officials at every level—will ask the same question of their endeavors, and subject their actions to the same exacting test." To buttress his position, the President referred approvingly to the fact that in these "times of clear and present danger the courts have held that even the privileged rights of the First Amendment must yield to the public's need for national security."

In this manner President Kennedy expressed his approval of the current tendency in Supreme Court decisions to weaken civil liberties by making sweeping exceptions to freedom of speech as guaranteed in the Bill of Rights. The goal of every tyrant down the ages has been precisely to pressure and frighten the individual into *self-censorship*, so that he will not dare to speak up and protest publicly on controversial issues. When this happens, a spirit of conformity and fear engulfs the nation, as in the United States at the height of McCarthyism. And if America's organs of public opinion adopt the President's recommendations, this country will indeed be in a bad way.

In criticizing the President's speech, the *New York Post* (April 30) stated in an editorial: "Mr. Kennedy said 'no war ever posed a greater threat to our security' than the present crisis and that 'the danger has never been more clear and its presence has never been more imminent.' Such language usually foreshadows the suspension of civil liberties. That, of course, is not now the case; Mr. Kennedy explicitly asserted that he has no desire to establish the 'wartime discipline' under which the Communists continuously operate. Yet the surface impact and logic of his words is to encourage those who would create such a climate here." The *Post* was right.

President Kennedy's suggestion about newspapers censoring themselves aroused other strong comments in the press. Under the heading, "When the Government Lies, Must the Press Fib?" *I. F. Stone's Weekly* (May 8) stated: "The national interest in a free society is supposed to lie in the fullest dissemination of the facts so that popular judgment may be truly informed. It is the mark of a closed or closing society to assume that the rulers decide how much the vulgar herd shall be told."

In an editorial of similar purport entitled "The Right Not To Be Lied To," *The New York Times* (May 11) said: "A dictatorship can get along without an informed public opinion. A democracy cannot. Not only is it unethical to deceive one's own people as part of a system of deceiving an adversary government; it is also foolish." *The Christian Century*, a nondenominational and liberal religious weekly, assailed Mr.

Kennedy's proposals to the press and claimed that they "carried an overtone of panic."

To summarize, the Kennedy Administration has dealt a heavy blow to civil liberties through its intimate involvement in the invasion of Cuba, its brink-of-war policy towards the Castro regime and the President's two unfortunate speeches of April 20 and 27. At the same time, our Government has given new heart and hope to every right-wing chauvinist in the USA, and to every frenetic, anti-freedom group in the land, from the American Legion to the John Birch Society.

Plainly, the attack on Cuba was not only contrary to American ideals of fair play and the abolition of war, but also to our basic self-interest as a people and a nation. For the Cuban debacle seriously set back President Kennedy's genuine endeavors towards international peace and lost the United States an enormous amount of prestige in every corner of the earth, including Canada and Latin America, and among our allies as well as our foes.

Joseph Barry summed up the matter well in the *New York Post* of April 23:

> Whoever wins in Cuba, we have lost. The Cuban catastrophe has become an American tragedy. In its first 100 days the Kennedy Administration has virtually drained its initial favorable balance in the world's books. . . .
> Everywhere our principle of self-determination has been compromised by Kennedy's defense of intervention, however limited, in Cuba's destiny, and the promise—which to the world is a threat—to intervene heavily should its destiny not be the one we prefer. . . .
> The neutrals of the world, from Nehru to Tito, have been shocked. The new nations of Africa are fearful of what some already refer to as "American neo-colonialism." From Delhi is heard the dismaying doubt that "the New Frontier may after all be just the old familiar brink."

In a letter to *The New York Times* printed May 13, Cyrus Eaton, well-known Cleveland industrialist, pointed out the international implications of the American Government's failure to obtain dependable factual information concerning Cuba: "If our intelligence on Cuba, only ninety miles away, could be so erroneous and misleading, how much better is it likely to be on Czechoslovakia, East Germany, Hungary, Poland, Rumania, Bulgaria and the Soviet Union?

"From first-hand observation in Eastern Europe, I know that our diplomatic personnel deliberately maintain the most limited contact with government officials and practically none with the common man. . . . By seeking out the most extreme anti-communist elements wherever it operates, the CIA has largely cut itself off from reliable and useful intelligence."

Meanwhile the Soviet Government had taken a firm and consistent stand on the Cuban situation. Premier Khrushchev in his note of April 22 presented to President Kennedy a series of reasoned arguments opposing the American attitude: "You simply claim," Mr. Khrushchev said, "some right of yours to employ military force when you find it necessary, and to suppress other peoples each time you decide that their expression of will constitutes 'communism.' But what right have you, what right has anyone in general, to deprive a people of the possibility of choosing their social and political system of their own free will?" Khrushchev concluded his message by urging once more that the Soviet Union and the United States work towards peaceful coexistence, with stable agreements on disarmament and other international problems.

In the United Nations on April 26, Valerian A. Zorin, head of the Soviet delegation, repeated his Government's pledge to come to the aid of Cuba if it was subjected to military intervention and asserted that this promise "was given seriously, more seriously than the British pledge of help to Poland that helped to draw the Western allies into World War II." (New York Times, April 27).

As for open U.S. military intervention in the future to get rid of Castro, Senator Morse was correct when he asserted on April 24: "I say to the Senators today that it is my judgment that if the United States seeks to settle its differences with Cuba through the use of military might, either direct or indirect, we shall be at least half a century recovering, if we ever recover, the prestige, the understanding and the confidence of one Latin American neighbor after another. . . . Cuba is not a dagger pointed at the heart of the United States, but is instead a thorn in our flesh."

However, Cuba need not have become even "a thorn in our flesh" had the Eisenhower Administration offered economic cooperation and assistance to the Castro regime when it took over early in 1959. America should have been glad that there was a noncommunist revolution in the Western Hemisphere, with far-reaching social goals and intelligent idealists leading it. Here was a chance for the American Revolution to catch up with and participate in the great social revolution that has been sweeping the world during the twentieth century, a chance for the United States to befriend a struggling new regime and give guidance to a democratic reconstruction of the Cuban economy and political system.

Instead of grasping this unique opportunity, the American Government followed its usual policy of hostility towards a new order dedicated to radical social and economic reform, and did everything possible to weaken and undermine it. For the United States this was an extension of the attitude Walter Lippmann described when he said: "We have used money and arms in a long losing attempt to stabilize native governments which, in the name of anti-Communism, are opposed to all important social change."

But it is not too late to retrieve the Cuban situation. Only a week after the American-supported invasion had been repulsed, Premier Castro and President Dorticos said in a statement about Cuba and the United States: "We are willing to hold whatever discussions may be necessary to find a solution for the tension existing between the two countries and to arrive at a formula of peaceful coexistence, diplomatic relations and even friendly relations, if the Government of the United States so desires."

The U.S. State Department brusquely, foolishly and childishly dismissed this conciliatory gesture with the rejoinder, "Communism in this hemisphere is not negotiable."

However, this need not be the final word if the Kennedy Administration will reconsider the whole matter in the spirit of reason and in the light of what is to the greatest advantage of the American people and lasting peace. In my opinion, President Kennedy should:

1. Issue an unqualified pledge that the United States Government will not at any time in the future undertake military intervention against Cuba, either directly or indirectly.

2. Cease all further support to those Cuban exiles and refugees, on American soil or anywhere else, who are planning another invasion to attempt the overthrow of the Castro regime.

3. Announce that henceforth the United States Government will respect in full all international treaty obligations regarding Cuba.

4. Arrange the speedy resignation from the Central Intelligence Agency of those officials who had primary responsibility for the CIA's ignominious role in the Cuban fiasco. Also, replace Adolf A. Berle, Jr., the Administration's coordinator of Latin American policies, who has displayed an abysmal ignorance concerning Cuba.

5. Accept the Cuban Government's proposal for the reestablishment of diplomatic relations between the United States and Cuba.

6. Agree to negotiate the chief political and other problems that exist between the two countries, including the questions of normal trade relations and proper financial compensation for the American property nationalized by the Castro regime. (Congressman Frank Kowalski, a Connecticut Democrat, made proposals along these lines in a speech in the House of Representatives on April 27.)

7. Agree to submit disputes on which agreement cannot at present be reached to the United Nations or the World Court.

8. Lift the ban against American citizens going to Cuba, reestablishing the precious right to travel.

9. Send to Cuba a special fact-finding commission of distinguished Americans to make a complete, impartial study of the situation there so that the U.S. Government will have reliable information on the developments that have taken place under the Castro regime.

An Open Letter to President John F. Kennedy

Dear President Kennedy:

As individuals who believe that the only security for America lies in world peace, we wish to ask you why at present the United States is sending its Army, Navy and Air Force to bring death and bloodshed to South Vietnam, a small Asian country approximately 10,000 miles from our Pacific Coast.

In other words, since you have the ultimate responsibility in this matter, we want to raise with you the question of the American Government's massive military intervention in South Vietnam to bolster up the corrupt and reactionary dictatorship of Ngo Dinh Diem. According to reliable newspaper reports, the United States has sent nearly 5,000 troops to South Vietnam, together with enormous quantities of small arms, machine guns, artillery and helicopters to transport the soldiers of the Diem Government. In addition, Mr. President, you have set up a special U.S. Military Assistance Command for Vietnam.

All of these measures are calculated to thwart the will of the South Vietnamese people, who have been fighting year after year in a broad, countrywide movement, made up primarily of peasants, to get rid of the tyrannical Diem Government. While a proportion of communists are active in this movement, and there may be some support from North Vietnam, there is substantial participation in it by noncommunists. And considerable opposition to dictator Diem is anticommunist, as witness three attempts by the military to overthrow his Government, and two exiled political groups, the Democratic Party and the Free

Source: The New York Times, *April 11, 1962.*

Democratic Party, both with headquarters in Paris.

The United States intervention in Vietnam is in specific violation of the 1954 Geneva Agreements, which marked the final defeat of France in Indochina and which established Cambodia, Laos and Vietnam as independent countries. These treaties prohibited foreign troops and foreign military bases in Vietnam, limited military advisers to 685, banned fresh military supplies except for replacement, and provided for national elections in 1956 to establish a single, unified government for both North and South Vietnam. The American Government through its intervention has clearly violated the military prohibitions of the Geneva pacts; and it supported President Diem in his illegal refusal to go through with the promised plebiscite.

United States troops have been definitely taking part in military operations in South Vietnam; and U.S. casualties are piling up, including the ninety-three Army men who lost their lives when a Super Constellation crashed on March 16 while flying them from San Francisco to Saigon. It is evident that the United States is involved in a real, though undeclared war. Yet, neither Congress, which under our Constitution alone has the power to declare war, nor the American people have had an adequate opportunity publicly to air and debate the present policy of your Administration in South Vietnam. And you yourself, Mr. President, have given out only the scantiest information about this dangerous situation. We must agree with the Republican National Committee, in its offical publication *Battle Line*, that you have a "clear responsibility to make a full report to the people" as to the extent of American intervention in South Vietnam.

The most persuasive statement that we have found about the need for more information in such a perilous situation as this nation confronts in South Vietnam was made by you, Mr. President, in a speech on the floor of the United States Senate, April 6, 1954, about the Vietnam crisis of that time. We are taking the liberty of quoting a few passages from your address as printed in the *Congressional Record* of that date:

> The time has come for the American people to be told the blunt truth about Indochina. . . . But the speeches of President Eisenhower, Secretary Dulles, and others have left too much unsaid, in my opinion—and what has been left unsaid is the heart of the problem that should concern every citizen. For if the American people are, for the fourth time in this century, to travel the long and tortuous road of war—particularly a war which we now realize would threaten the survival of civilization—then I believe we have a right—a right which we should have hitherto exercised—to inquire

in detail into the nature of the struggle in which we may become engaged, and the alternative to that struggle. Without such clarification, the general support and success of our policy is endangered. . . .

To pour money, matériel and men into the jungles of Indochina without at least a remote prospect of victory would be dangerously futile and self-destructive. . . . I am frankly of the belief that no amount of American military assistance in Indochina can conquer an enemy which is everywhere and at the same time nowhere, "an enemy of the people" which has the sympathy and covert support of the people. . . . For the United States to intervene unilaterally and to send troops into the most difficult terrain in the world, with the Chinese able to pour in unlimited manpower, would mean that we would face a situation which would be far more difficult than even that we encountered in Korea. . . .

The facts and alternatives before us are unpleasant. . . . But in a nation such as ours, it is only through the fullest and frankest appreciation of such facts and alternatives that any foreign policy can be effectively maintained. In an era of supersonic attack and atomic retaliation, extended public debate and education are of no avail, once such a policy must be implemented. The time to study, to doubt, to review and revise is now, for upon our decisions now may well rest the peace and security of the world and, indeed, the very continued existence of mankind. And if we cannot entrust the decision to the people, then, as Thomas Jefferson once said: "If we think them not enlightened enough to exercise their control with a wholesome discretion, the remedy is not to take it from them but to inform their discretion by education."

It seems to us, Mr. President, that all of your comments as a Senator in 1954 apply to what your Administration is doing in 1962 in regard to South Vietnam. In 1954 you expressed the belief that "no amount of American military assistance" could bring victory for the United States in Vietnam, where there exists "the most difficult terrain in the world." We must have the same doubts about American victory today; and some high Washington officials have themselves conceded that it might take years—perhaps as much as a decade—to defeat the guerillas of South Vietnam.

Most important of all, as you said in 1954, "the time has come for the American people to be told the blunt truth . . . We have a right to inquire in detail into the nature of the struggle in which we may become engaged, and the alternative to that struggle." Both Communist China and the Soviet Union have warned the United States Government that its "undeclared war" in South Vietnam constitutes a peril to world peace. Are we running the risk of becoming embroiled in another large-scale conflict such as the Korean War, Mr. President, or even a nuclear-bomb war?

Frankly, we believe that the United States intervention in South Vietnam constitutes a violation of international law, of United Nations principles, and of America's own highest ideals. We urge, Mr. President, that you bring this intervention to an immediate end and that you initiate a special international conference to work out a peaceful solution to the crisis in Vietnam, as you have endeavored to do in Laos.

The people of South Vietnam have suffered enough. Having fought eight long years to win independence from France, they have been compelled to fight seven more years, 1955-1962, to achieve independence from dictator Diem and the United States, which has maintained him in power. It is time to end the ordeal of the South Vietnamese people and to permit them to enjoy the fruits of liberty and the pursuit of happiness.

(The Open Letter to President Kennedy was written by Corliss Lamont and signed by sixteen American citizens.)

The Undeclared War: The U.S. Army vs. the People of South Vietnam

We must go back to the year 1954 to understand why in 1962 the United States Government has deeply involved the American people in a bitter civil war that has been raging for the last seven years in South Vietnam, a small Asian country approximately 10,000 miles away from our Pacific coast.

It was in April of 1954 that Secretary of State John Foster Dulles and Admiral Arthur W. Radford, then Chairman of the Joint Chiefs of Staff, brought forward a plan that called for United States intervention in the Indochina war by an air strike of 500 planes to help the French forces besieged in the fortress of Dienbienphu. With President Eisenhower's approval, an actual date was set for this madcap bombing. The project did not go through, both because of popular opposition in the U.S. and the last minute refusal of the British Government, of which Winston Churchill was then Prime Minister, to approve or cooperate. Dienbienphu fell on May 7, marking imperialist France's final defeat in its eight-year "dirty war." In July a special conference at Geneva formally ratified the independence of the Indochinese states of Cambodia, Laos and Vietnam.

The Geneva Agreements divided Vietnam temporarily into two parts, north and south, but provided for nation-wide elections in 1956 to unify the country under one government. An International Control Commission, composed of representatives of Canada, India and Poland, was set up to supervise both these elections and the other provisions of the Geneva Accords. The treaties also stipulated that after

Source: New World Review, *May 1962.*

France had evacuated its military forces, there should be no foreign bases or foreign military troops in any part of Vietnam and that no further military supplies should be brought in except for replacements. However, 685 foreign military *advisers* were to be allowed in South Vietnam.

In addition to the Indochinese Governments, France, Great Britain, the People's Republic of China and the Soviet Union signed the Geneva Agreements. Great Britain and Soviet Russia were cochairmen of the conference. The United States participated through an official delegation, but did not sign the pacts. Instead it pledged that it would "respect" the treaties and that in accordance with the United Nations Charter, it would "not use force to disturb the settlement."

Actually, Dulles and the U.S. Government never gave up their opposition to the Indochinese settlement, and supported Ngo Dinh Diem, who in 1955 had established himself as President of the South Vietnamese Republic, in his refusal to carry out the promised 1956 plebiscite for the unification of the nation. President Diem, a right-wing Catholic, set up a dictatorial regime that violently suppressed its opponents, whether communist or noncommunist, abolished freedom of the press and civil liberties, and rapidly earned the hatred of the South Vietnamese people in general. Diem's attempts to maintain a democratic facade through rigged elections became known as "Diemocracy." Columnist Walter Lippmann has stated about Diem: "Our man is extremely unpopular, his Government being both reactionary and corrupt." The Kennedy Administration has tried, but failed, to bring about basic reforms in the Diem regime.

One reason for Diem's unpopularity is that he has established probably the world's record for nepotism in government. Brother Nhu and his wife live with Diem in his bachelor palace and wield enormous power. Nhu has the title of Advisor to the President, and controls both the state finances and the secret police. Diem's brother Can is Governor of Central Vietnam; his brother Thuc is Archbishop Vinhlong and oversees all Catholic churches, missions and schools; a fourth brother, Luyen, is Ambassador to England, Belgium, the Netherlands, West Germany and Tunisia. Mrs. Nhu's father, Than Van Chuong, is Ambassador to the United States, Canada, Argentina, Brazil and Mexico; her mother is Ambassador to the U.N.

It is clear that what is going on in South Vietnam today is a broad popular revolt against a fascist-type dictatorship, a revolutionary upsurge that frequently takes the form of guerilla warfare and is especially strong among the peasants, who make up more than 80 percent of the population. The left-wing Vietcong and a small proportion of communists are active in this movement, and of course communist North Vietnam, under the leadership of President Ho Chi Minh, is sympathetic to it. But the movement would go on even if all communist influence were eliminated.

U.S. Government officials keep on saying, however, that North Vietnam is guilty of aggression against South Vietnam and that the whole anti-Diem guerilla movement would fade away without support from the North. These two statements are palpably false. There is no proof or sign that Ho Chi Minh's Government has invaded the South. As for military supplies, *The New York Times* reported on March 6 that "perhaps a small trickle of arms is reaching the Vietcong from North Vietnam, but this supply route is painfully difficult. Most Vietcong weapons are obtained by raids or are crudely manufactured in jungle arsenals." The insurgents are now obtaining more and more U.S. arms, which they take from dead or captured Diem soldiers.

The main reason why the 300,000 heavily armed troops of the South Vietnam Army are losing the civil war to some 25,000 poorly armed guerillas is that an overwhelming majority of the peasants are sympathetic to the anti-Diem rebels. The villagers willingly cooperate with the guerillas in every way, giving them food, shelter and important information about the disposition of the Government forces. According to reliable estimates, only three out of thirty-five provinces are safely in the Diem camp.

The anticommunist and noncommunist opposition to despot Diem was dramatically revealed in November 1960 when a military coup led by paratroopers took place against him. The coup came within a hair-breadth of success. Its leaders had announced that they planned to set up a more liberal regime in place of the "totalitarian, authoritarian and nepotistic" Diem Government.

Again, in February 1962 the military went into action against Diem when two nationalistic pilots of the South Vietnam Air Force flew their fighter-bombers repeatedly over the presidential palace, attacking it with bombs, rockets, machine guns and napalm, the jellied gasoline produced in the United States and usually reserved for burning dissident Vietnamese villages and the peasants in them. One wing of the palace caught fire. President Diem and two brothers who were with him escaped injury, but Mrs. Nhu was seriously hurt.

Many of the most able men and women in the anti-Diem movement live in exile in Paris. Here, for example, we find the headquarters of two political groups outlawed in South Vietnam: the Democratic Party and the Free Democratic Party. The head of the Democratic Party is Nguyen-Thai-Binh, whose informative book *Vietnam: The Problem and a Solution* was recently published. Nguyen-Thai-Binh and his party are not only bitterly anti-Diem, but likewise bitterly anticommunist.

What all this adds up to is that the American Government, claiming that its large-scale economic and military aid to the shaky Diem regime is saving South Vietnam from the communists, is in fact propping up one of the most ruthless and corrupt tyrannies on the face of the earth and is preventing any true democratization of the country. During the past seven years the United States has poured close to $2.5 billion into the coffers of the Diem Government. Thus the Kennedy Administration continues the discredited policy described by Walter Lippmann in these words: "We have used money and arms in a long losing attempt to stabilize native governments which, in the name of anti-communism, are opposed to all important social changes."

During the past few months the Kennedy Administration has established a U.S. Military Assistance Command for Vietnam and has sent into South Vietnam nearly 5,000 troops or other military personnel, together with vast quantities of carbines, rifles, machine guns, artillery, trucks and bombers. The U.S. is also providing Navy vessels and helicopters for the transport of Diem's forces.

In *The New York Times* of March 18, 1962, Homer Bigart reported from Saigon that "United States Army helicopters . . . carried 171 troops on a secret mission to the vicinity of An Phu, where the An Giang Province bulges into Cambodia. This region is the haunt of Hoa Hao, a Buddhist sect often in arms against the Government of President Ngo Dinh Diem. . . . The American pilots of the helicopters said the plan worked well. . . . The fight was commanded by Maj. Milton Cherne of South Holland, Ill."

When American pilots fly U.S. Army helicopters carrying Diem's soldiers and the whole operation is under the command of a U.S. Major, I say there is no doubt that direct U.S. military intervention is going on. And when those pursued may be "dissident Buddhists," to quote Mr. Bigart again, the deep roots of the anti-Diem movement among the masses of the South Vietnamese people again becomes evident.

Secretary of Defense McNamara has admitted that American G.I.s have been fired upon during their air missions in combat areas and that in some instances they have fired back. There have been American casualties in these hostilities. On March 16 a Flying Tiger Line Super Constellation crashed between Guam and Saigon while carrying ninety-three U.S. Army men from San Francisco to South Vietnam. These American troops are all presumed dead and must be considered casualties of the dirty Vietnamese war.

In *The New York Times* of March 29, Bigart describes U.S. participation in a brutal plan which Diem's Government has been carrying out for some time. It involves removing Vietnamese villagers on a large scale from their homes and resettling them in stockades, or concentration camps, in order to isolate the rural population from the Vietcong guerillas.

The plan, called "Operation Sunrise," is now being tested in a rubber-plantation area near Bencat before applying it on a comprehensive scale throughout South Vietnam.

In this area, which Mr. Bigart visited, "1,200 families are to be removed, voluntarily or forcibly from the forests controlled by the Vietcong" and resettled in "strategic villages." The abandoned villages are to be burned down. The operation began with the military encirclement of a half-dozen villages. A hundred villagers managed to escape before the ring closed. The authorities were able to persuade only seventy families to leave voluntarily; the other one hundred thirty-five families were herded forcibly from their homes.

Compensation money is withheld by the U.S. until it is clear that the victims will not run away.

"Operation Sunrise," writes Mr. Bigart, "is subsidized directly with U.S. money, military planning and technical aid."

The massive American intervention in South Vietnam in terms of manpower and matériel clearly violates those provisions of the Geneva Agreements that bar foreign troops from Vietnam, that limit foreign military advisers to fewer than 700, and that prohibit fresh military supplies except for replacements. The fact that the United States has built scores of big airfields and other military installations in South Vietnam is a violation of the treaties' ban against foreign bases on Vietnamese soil. Finally, the U.S. Government, by undertaking outright military operations, is violating its pledged word not to employ force to disturb the Geneva Accords. Once more, as in the invasion of Cuba, the United States is showing a callous disregard for international law and morality. And the Kennedy Administration has obviously returned to the sort of militaristic brinkmanship that Secretary Dulles approved in relation to Vietnam.

All of this has meant a terrible ordeal and tragedy for the people of South Vietnam. Having fought eight long years to win independence from France, they have been compelled to fight seven more to achieve independence from dictator Diem and the United States, which stands behind him and maintains him in power. His Government would not last a week, probably not a day, if U.S. aid were withdrawn.

Meanwhile, we must ask whether President Kennedy and the Executive branch have not violated the U.S. Constitution by going far beyond a so-called police action to a large-scale involvement of this country in a real, though undeclared, war in which American troops have already been killed and which may develop into a conflict of continental proportions. The Constitution gives Congress alone the power to declare war (Item 11, Section 8, Article 1). But in the South Vietnamese situation the Executive branch of our Government is bypassing the constitutional separation of powers and usurping the functions of Congress in respect to war.

It is true that earlier Presidents have embarked on similar ventures in what has been well called "Marine diplomacy." But the dangers of foreign intervention have now become much greater, and we run the risk that a President, through the *fait accompli* of some reckless military intervention abroad will commit America to a major war or even to a disastrous nuclear-bomb world war. What Senator Wayne Morse (D.) of Oregon said about U.S. participation in the Cuban invasion is most relevant: "Freedom is worth too much as a human system of government for us to surrender any of our freedom to *a police state system in the field of foreign policy*, dictated by denying to the people the knowledge of the facts of their own foreign policy." [Italics mine— C.L.]

Senator Morse's statement prompts me to note that one great advantage for our democracy in the system of requiring a declaration of war by Congress is that it gives any existing situation a chance to be publicly aired and debated. In reference to South Vietnam there has been no opportunity for adequate public and Congressional discussion. Hardly a single voice has been raised in the Senate or the House of Representatives, even to question the Administration's position. And President Kennedy has given out only the scantiest information concerning his hazardous policy.

The Republican National Committee was certainly justified when on February 1, 1962, in its official publication *Battle Line*, it charged that the President had been "less than candid" on the extent of U.S. involvement in South Vietnam. *Battle Line* raised the natural question of whether the United States was "moving toward another Korea which might embroil the entire Far East." The Republican policy organ stated that President Kennedy has a "clear responsibility to make a full report to the people" on how many American troops are in Vietnam. The article concluded: "The people should not have to wait until American casualty lists are posted before being informed about the real nature of the nation's commitments." On February 17 Senator Kenneth B. Keating of New York, a Republican voice again, declared that a "made-in-Washington smoke screen" was keeping the American people from knowing what was happening in South Vietnam.

In the meantime, both Communist China and the Soviet Union have warned the United States Government that its continued intervention in South Vietnam constitutes a peril to world peace. The Chinese

Foreign Ministry stated on February 24 that the "undeclared war" is "a direct threat to the security" of North Vietnam and "seriously affects the security of China and the peace of Asia." A similar charge against the United States was made by China in the fall of 1950, just before the Chinese intervened in the Korean War.

American officials, however, have pooh-poohed the idea of Chinese counterintervention in South Vietnam. In Saigon Admiral Harry D. Felt, Commander in Chief of U.S. forces in the Pacific, has referred slightingly to the Chinese communists: "They are not 50 feet tall. We are taller than they are and they have reason to be cautious." Nonetheless, the chance of the South Vietnam war flaring into a much bigger and more critical conflict still remains.

What we need imperatively in Washington is an agonizing reappraisal and reversal of the U.S. policy in South Vietnam, with President Kennedy giving attention to what Walter Lippmann wrote about him after the Cuban fiasco: "The more he engages himself directly while the Soviet Union and China keep a free hand, the more he will weaken his influence." The United States could well take the initiative on Vietnam by calling a special international conference to deal with the crisis and to work out a peaceful solution, as we have endeavored to do in Laos. An alternative step would be to bring the entire matter before the United Nations.

Whatever sort of international conference may be held, one of its chief objectives must be to so reactivate the International Control Commission that it can efficiently fulfill its function of preventing foreign military supplies and troops from coming into South Vietnam from North Vietnam, the United States or any other nation whatsoever. Our own country has the obligation, in line with its constant protestations on behalf of world peace and the self-determination of peoples, to call an immediate halt to our war and intervention in South Vietnam. It is time that the long-suffering South Vietnamese people were permitted to enjoy the fruits of liberty and the pursuit of happiness.

Vietnam: Corliss Lamont vs. Ambassador Lodge

FOREWORD

For some five years I have been active in opposing United States military intervention in Vietnam. In 1962 and again in 1963 I helped to organize Open Letters, signed by prominent Americans, to President John F. Kennedy, urging him to make peace in South Vietnam and to withdraw all American military forces. I have signed protests to President Lyndon B. Johnson against his waging war on all Vietnam, have written letters to the press along the same line and have made numerous speeches on the subject.

President Kennedy's policy towards South Vietnam was bad enough; President Johnson's bombing of North Vietnam, starting in February 1965, and his general escalation of the war, made the situation immeasurably worse. I have been critical of many aspects of U.S. foreign policy ever since we refused to join the League of Nations after World War I. But never before in my lifetime has the United States Government committed such far-reaching violations of morality, international law and ordinary human decency as in its conduct in Vietnam. And never before has a President of this country so continually and consistently deceived the American people about U.S. foreign policy or been so hypocritical in his pretense of seeking peace.

For example, no sooner had the Johnson Administration (December 19, 1966), through United Nations Ambassador Goldberg, requested Secretary General U Thant to make extensive new efforts towards a

Source: Basic Pamphlet, 1967.

Vietnam peace, than news reports revealed that a week earlier U.S. planes had dropped bombs within the city limits of Hanoi. These air raids destroyed sizable residential areas and killed or wounded more than one hundred civilians. In dispatches to *The New York Times*, its crack reporter Harrison E. Salisbury described the vast bombing damage he had seen in both Hanoi and its nearby suburbs.

In the *Times* of December 27 Mr. Salisbury states: "Whatever the explanation, one can see that United States planes are dropping an enormous weight of explosives on purely civilian targets ... President Johnson's announced policy that American targets in North Vietnam are steel and concrete rather than human lives seems to have little connection with the reality of attacks carried out by United States planes.

"A notable example is Phuly, a town about 25 miles south of Hanoi on Route 1. The town had a population of about 10,000. In attacks on October 1, 2, and 9, every house and building was destroyed. Only forty were killed and wounded because many people had left town and because an excellent manhole-shelter system was available."

In another dispatch, appearing in the *Times* of January 2, 1967, Mr. Salisbury tells about U.S. bombings of Phatdiem, a complex of Roman Catholic villages near the Gulf of Tonkin: "In the district as a whole, officials said, there have been more than 150 attacks since 1965. . . . A half dozen Catholic churches in the village complex have been damaged, some severely. . . . The big central cathedrals are no longer used ... because of danger to the congregations from air attacks. . . . Phatdiem has no visible military objectives."

The Salisbury reports clearly show, I think, that the Johnson Administration was concealing the facts when it kept repeating that U.S. bombers were strafing only military targets in North Vietnam. No "mistakes" and inaccurate bombing on the part of American pilots can account for their killing large numbers of civilians, destroying hospitals, schools and churches, and laying waste to residential areas on a wide scale. The conclusion must be that the United States Air Force in North Vietnam, as in South Vietnam, has been guilty of terror tactics against women, children, peasants and civilians in general.

I have known personally only one important official directly involved in the United States aggression in Vietnam. That is Henry Cabot Lodge, U.S. Ambassador to the South Vietnamese Government during both the Kennedy and Johnson Administrations, and my classmate at Harvard. The crisis in Southeast Asia is so extremely serious for both the American people and the world at large that I have taken the unusual step of writing two Open Letters on the matter to Ambassador Lodge, one in November 1965 and another in October 1966. He did not see fit to answer either Open Letter.

My public debates with Henry Cabot Lodge started back in 1923 when we were both members of the Harvard Debating Union and often crossed swords there. In June 1923, I wrote an article for the college monthly, *The Harvard Advocate*, entitled "Ideas for Irreconcilables,"* which argued in favor of the United States entering the League of Nations. Mr. Lodge opposed this proposition. My article was partly an answer to his "Political Sentimentalists" in an earlier issue of *The Advocate*. I claimed that he had grown "morbidly sentimental about sentimentalism."

It is worth noting that in my undergraduate days I also disagreed drastically with Mr. Lodge's grandfather, the first Senator Henry Cabot Lodge, regarding his hostile attitude towards the League of Nations. My parents, too, Thomas W. and Florence C. Lamont, thought that the senior Lodge did a great disservice to America and the cause of world peace by leading the fight against the League in the U.S. Senate. Thus, the Lamont-Lodge dispute stretches over three generations.

My two Open Letters to Ambassador Lodge overlap to some extent, but for the record it seems worthwhile to print both of them in full.

*See pages 157-161.

November 1, 1965

Ambassador Henry Cabot Lodge
U.S. Embassy
Saigon, South Vietnam

Dear Cabot:

You will recall that as classmates in the great Harvard Class of 1924 we both helped to found the Harvard Debating Union during our college days and that you and I had brisk exchanges of opinion at its meetings. Ever since that time, more than forty years ago, we have carried on a running debate concerning basic issues that have confronted our country and the world. You consistently maintained a conservative position, and before long became a prominent member of the Republican Party. I must say that in my judgment you were always one of the better Republicans.

Now our disagreement has become more far-reaching and fundamental than ever because of your active support, as American Ambassador to South Vietnam, of the Johnson Administration's cruel, illegal and immoral war of aggression in Vietnam. Furthermore, you were willing to become Ambassador a second time precisely when Marshal Ky, the new Premier of the South Vietnamese Government, had proclaimed that his great hero was Adolf Hitler.

Like Secretary Rusk and the U.S. State Department, you have pretended that South Vietnam was established as a permanent independent state in the Geneva Accords of 1954, whereas you well know that the division of Vietnam into South Vietnam and North Vietnam was designed as a temporary measure and that the Accords provided for all-Vietnam elections in 1956 to unify the country. You must be aware, too, that it was the United States and its puppet, President Diem of South Vietnam, that refused to permit these elections and thus clearly violated the Geneva treaty.

As Walter Lippmann has pointed out, "While our government endorsed the Geneva agreements, and especially the provision for free elections, it opposed free elections when it realized that Ho Chi Minh (President of North Vietnam) would win them. General Eisenhower states this frankly in his memoirs. Since that time we have insisted that South Vietnam is an independent nation." (*New York Herald Tribune*, April 20, 1965). What all of this adds up to is that in this matter the United States has been guilty of double-dealing and a failure to honor its pledged word.

The inscription on the seal of Harvard is *Veritas,* a motto that has deep meaning for Harvard men. Do you really think, Cabot, that you are serving Truth when you join in distorting the meaning and history of the Geneva Accords that are so basic to understanding the situation in Vietnam?

Again, every objective observer knows that the National Liberation Front in South Vietnam, with its military arm—the so-called Vietcong—is leading a nationalist uprising supported by the vast majority of the population. The fact that communists strongly back this revolution and share in its leadership does not nullify its indigenous character. What we have here is the resolute and unyielding effort of a former colonial people to assert its freedom. Opposing this is a white Western nation, the USA, determined to reimpose shackles such as France maintained for almost a century. As the noted British historian, Arnold Toynbee, tells us, the Vietcong struggle is part of a worldwide "revolt of the 'native' majority of mankind against the domination of the Western minority."

The Vietcong guerillas possess effective modern weapons in considerable quantity, but only a trickle of arms reached them from North Vietnam (at least up to February 1965). It is the United States that has been the main source of supply. For the guerillas have obtained their guns chiefly from deserters bringing in American-made arms or by capturing such arms from the apathetic troops of the South Vietnamese Government.

In spite of these well-recognized facts, the U.S. Government last February, when it realized the Vietcong was winning the civil war, suddenly started intensive bombing of Communist North Vietnam on the specious ground that that country all along had been invading South Vietnam and bore the major responsiblity for the troubles there. Johnson and his military advisors invented this line in order to justify their own savage aggression against North Vietnam.

This crass propaganda issuing from the White House you, Cabot Lodge, have supported all the way in public statements. In your heart of hearts, can you possibly think that this is *Veritas*? U Thant was right when he said in reference to Vietnam: "In times of war and of hostilities, the first casualty is truth."

You have also misled your fellow-Americans by claiming that the U.S. Government's purpose in Vietnam is to save freedom and establish democracy. In fact, starting with the brutal dictator Diem, the United States has bolstered up one puppet dictatorship after another in Saigon—nine different governments in the past two years—as successive military coups have taken place. These South Vietnamese governments rule through police-state methods of crude violence, terror and torture. None of them would have lasted a week without the military support of the United States.

Actually, the main purposes of the President and the Pentagon in Vietnam seem to be experimentation with new military weapons and strategy, arresting the epic struggle of the colored races to throw off the burden of the white man's rule, and setting up a huge military and air base in Southeast Asia. Such a base, of course, would be a constant threat to Communist China. Incidentally, it is absurd to claim, as some Administration spokesmen have done, that China is responsible for the revolutionary upsurge in South Vietnam and for the continuance of the war.

In all frankness, Cabot, how can you sleep nights when you sanction the horrible and wholesale slaughter by U.S. bombers of women, children and peasants—of noncombatant civilians in general—throughout Vietnam? In the past few months American planes have repeatedly dropped napalm and heavy-duty bombs indiscriminately on South Vietnam villages where a few Vietcong were "reported" to be. Here is what a U.S. Air Force officer recently told the Associated Press: "When we are in a bind, we unload on the whole area in order to save the situation. We usually kill more women and children than we do Vietcong." In North Vietnam, our bombers have destroyed hospitals and patients, schools and schoolchildren, residential houses and civilians. Owing to the terrific bombings in South Vietnam, more than 600,000 destitute refugees have fled to the coastal cities.

You are among those responsible, not only for the killing of scores of thousands of Vietnamese, but also for the death of more than 1,000 American soldiers who have resolutely given up their lives in this futile, useless war 10,000 miles from our Pacific Coast—a madcap adventure in which the United States has already wasted billions of dollars collected from American taxpayers. The probabilities are against our winning this conflict even if our trigger-happy President sends 1,000,000 troops to Vietnam. We cannot win because of the jungle terrain, because the overwhelming majority of the Vietnamese people is opposed to the U.S. intervention and because no stable, effective government can be established in Saigon.

Yet the United States buildup increases at a rapid rate. Some 150,000 U.S. ground troops are in South Vietnam, while thousands more Americans participate in the war from carriers, warships and planes located outside of the country. On June 30, 1964, a well-known U.S. diplomat was asked what he thought would be the consequences of massive American involvement in Vietnam. His answer was: "Well, that means we become a colonial power and I think it's been pretty well established that colonialism is over. I believe that if you start doing that you will get all kinds of unfortunate results: you'll stir up anti-foreign feeling; there'll be a tendency to lay back and let the

Americans do it and all that. I can't think that it's a good thing to do."

My dear classmate, do you know who said that? Why, it was none other than the Honorable Henry Cabot Lodge, then serving his first term as Ambassador to South Vietnam. So now that long-suffering country is, as implied by your own words, fast becoming a U.S. colony. Are you hoping soon to become governor of the fifty-first American state—South Vietnam?

Please consider carefully that if the President keeps on escalating this Vietnam conflict, and grabbing more and more Asian real estate, the Soviet Union and Communist China will surely react with far more effective countermeasures than they have used hitherto. Herein lies a terrible danger. For continuing escalation could finally erupt into the Great Nuclear War that would bring untold devastation to the USA and many other countries. Johnson and you, Cabot, are gambling with the survival of our nation and of the human race itself.

Addressing you now as a former Senator, there is a special point I want to make: As a member of the U.S. Senate for many years, you ought to be much concerned with the prerogatives and powers of that august body as set forth in the American Constitution. Today, President Johnson is usurping the functions of both the Senate and the House of Representatives by taking this country into a *de facto* war in Vietnam and thus bypassing the Constitution's pronouncement in Article I, Section 8, that Congress alone has the power to declare and make war.

You, as an ex-Senator, should be one of the first to protest against the President's dictatorial flouting of the Constitution—an obvious illegality that is contributing towards the breakdown of democratic government in the United States. Another example of Johnson's dangerous misuse of the Executive function was his dispatching of 20,000 Marines to the Dominican Republic last spring to prevent a liberal regime from coming to power. (See Senator Fulbright's notable speech of September 15, 1965.)

I should think that you, Cabot, as a former U.S. Ambassador to the United Nations, pledged to uphold its Charter and international law in general, could not but suffer many qualms of conscience in upholding the President's current foreign policy. For the Administration's brutal course of action in Vietnam flagrantly violates the Charter of the United Nations, the Geneva Accords of 1954, the principles laid down at the Nuremberg Trials of Nazi war criminals, and the 1949 Geneva Conventions of the International Red Cross dealing with the "rules of war."

As a member of the United States diplomatic corps, you cannot be unaware that President Johnson's Vietnam venture has seriously set back American influence and prestige virtually everywhere in the world. Johnson has been able, through judicious arm-twisting, to obtain token support here and there, but even America's own allies are really appalled at our Vietnamese policy. On the shelf for the duration are the pressing tasks of working out disarmament agreements regarding both nuclear and conventional weapons. And in general, to cite Walter Lippmann again, "the war in Vietnam is blocking the progress of the nations, including that of Red China itself, towards the peaceable coexistence and accommodation which is the predominant need of all the peoples." (*New York Herald Tribune,* October 12, 1965.)

The way out of the Vietnam mess is clear. There must be a cessation of U.S. bombings in all of Vietnam and a general cease-fire; a peace conference that includes the National Liberation Front as an independent authority, as well as the various nations directly involved; and a settlement that returns to the original Geneva Accords. This would mean the complete withdrawal of the United States Army and all other foreign troops from South Vietnam, a guarantee against any foreign military bases in that country, and elections to enable the Vietnamese people freely to choose their own government in accordance with the long-established principles of self-determination.

It is often said that America would lose face if it gets out of Vietnam without winning a clear-cut victory. But the United States has already lost so much face because of its barbaric conduct in Vietnam that this argument has little merit. In all truth, our country would gain great prestige by retiring from Vietnam, just as did France and President de Gaulle when they finally agreed to Algeria's independence.

Of course, a negotiated settlement in Vietnam would be helpful to the communist countries as well as the capitalist. The self-interest of every nation is served by peace. Thus, the position I have presented is essentially pro-American and pro-humanity. It is a position shared in general by millions of American teachers, students, writers, clergymen and workers, as well as such eminent individuals as President de Gaulle, Senator Gruening, Senator Morse, Professor Linus C. Pauling, Bertrand Russell and Arnold Toynbee.

In conclusion, then, I urge you, Cabot Lodge, to stop abetting President Johnson's evil actions and designs in Vietnam. It would be an enormous pity at this advanced stage of your career for you to fatally tarnish your reputation by qualifying as a leading War Hawk. Resign your ambassadorship and rebuild your public image before it is too late! The highest patriotism is not militaristic; it is to strive for justice and peace and that international amity which is the best assurance for America's national security. Come home and help transform the Republican Party into the great American party of peace, opposed to U.S.

military intervention in Asia, Latin America or anywhere else. On that platform you and the Republicans might well win another election.

Sincerely yours,
Corliss Lamont

P.S. Because of the pressing importance of the Vietnam issue, I am treating this communication as an Open Letter and am sending it to our fellow Harvard classmates.

LODGE ON VIETNAM

On September 13, 1966, the World Journal Tribune *of New York printed a letter from Ambassador Lodge on Vietnam. I sent a reply refuting his statements to the* World Journal Tribune; *but this newspaper, which in general supports the Lodge-Johnson position on Vietnam, refused to publish my communication. This is what prompted me to write my second Open Letter. Lodge's letter to the* World Journal Tribune *is as follows.*

In sending best wishes to the new *World Journal Tribune,* I am sure I speak for many Americans who realize what this newspaper can mean to the nation as well as to New York. The fact that I am an old *Herald Tribune* man gives me a special interest.

This may be an appropriate time, too, to summarize why the suppression of aggression in Vietnam is important—especially so important as to justify the present active involvement of the United States.

To give a brief answer to a big question. I submit, first, that to suppress aggression is morally right since the suppression of aggression has a high priority on the list of the purposes of the United Nations which are embodied in its Charter. And the United Nations Charter is the most widely adhered to code of behavior for nations.

Then, to the United Nations Charter should be added the Southeast Asia Treaty and the numerous acts by Congress on the subject which give our involvement in Vietnam not only a moral but a legal base.

Finally, our involvement is a matter of prudence and wisdom, sagacity and self-defense.

If the Communist aggression against Vietnam were to be successful and we were to be expelled and they were to seize the country, a situation of danger would be created which could scarcely be exaggerated and which would make our present situation seem as safe as a church.

No one recognizes this more than the leaders of the other Asian countries. They know if Vietnam goes under, the repercussions would come soon in Thailand, the Philippines, Malaysia and Taiwan. History shows that aggression feeds on itself and that one aggression encourages another.

Do we want to wait until the aggression is lapping at the shores of Japan and Australia, bringing on the worldwide holocaust which a threat to these countries would involve?

Clearly such a defeat would shake confidence in us, not only in Asia, but also in the Atlantic community. It would thus endanger peace everywhere.

Clearly, the United States is not trying to be policeman for the whole world. We are not making our stand on the peaks of the Himalayan Mountains. But neither should we wait to defend our country until the enemy is either on the sands of Waikiki Beach or on the sands of Cape Cod.

For this great Vietnamese sweep of coast, with one of the greatest food producing areas of the world at its southern end, to fall to the aggressor would be a direct threat to our security in this shrunken world. If you look at the map, you can see this country is in the middle of Southeast Asia—a sort of strategic keystone. What happens to it affects all of Southeast Asia. But it also has a direct and vital effect on us.

The American fighting man who is here today is quite simply and plainly fighting for his country.

> Henry Cabot Lodge
> U.S. Ambassador to South Vietnam
> Saigon

LAMONT TO LODGE, 1966

October 6, 1966

Ambassador Henry Cabot Lodge
U.S. Embassy
Saigon
South Vietnam

My dear Cabot:

For over forty years, ever since we graduated together in the great Harvard Class of 1924, we have been corresponding on public issues. Our letters have been frank and hard-hitting. We have almost always disagreed, but sometimes have learned new facts or viewpoints from each other.

Today, continuing with our lifelong debate, I write you in great distress of mind because I am so concerned over President Johnson's illegal and immoral war in Vietnam, and your own active role in it as Ambassador to the South Vietnamese Government. Recently, in a letter printed in the *World Journal Tribune* of September 13, 1966, you make an unqualified defense of American policy in Southeast Asia on the grounds that our nation must halt "communist aggression" in Vietnam. But as Senators Gruening and Morse point out, the real aggressor there is the USA.

Your letter, dear classmate, virtually achieves a world's record for inaccuracy. You talk loosely, for instance, of the United Nations Charter justifying the U.S. venture in North and South Vietnam. As a former American Ambassador to the U.N. you know perfectly well that this claim is not true. You also know that U Thant, the Secretary General of the United Nations, is firmly opposed to American military intervention in Vietnam, that he has called the war "one of the most barbarous in history," and that he is on record as asserting that if the American people "only knew the true facts and the background to the developments in South Vietnam," they would agree that "further bloodshed is unnecessary."

You give no indication that you have read U Thant's important statement of September 2, 1966, about Vietnam: "The cruelty of this war and the suffering it has caused the people of Vietnam are a constant reproach to the conscience of humanity. Today, it seems to me, as it has seemed for many months, that the pressure of events is remorselessly leading towards a major war, while efforts to reverse the trend are lagging disastrously behind. In my view the tragic error is being repeated of relying on force and military means in a deceptive pursuit of peace. I am convinced that peace in Southeast Asia can be obtained only through respect for the principles agreed upon at Geneva in 1954, and indeed for those contained in the Charter of the United Nations."

Your letter to the *World Journal Tribune* attempts to bamboozle the readers of that newspaper by omitting any mention of the Geneva Accords of 1954 to which U Thant refers. It is impossible to understand the situation in Vietnam without knowledge of these agreements that divided the country into South Vietnam and North Vietnam only on a temporary basis, provided for all-Vietnam elections in 1956 to unite the nation, and stipulated that there should be no foreign military bases or foreign armed forces in either South or North Vietnam. The United States Government promised to respect this treaty and to make no effort to subvert it by violence.

When the American Government and its puppet, the dictator Diem, refused to let the 1956 elections take place, a thoroughly indigenous revolution led by the Vietcong started against the South Vietnamese Government. It soon became a popular movement of wide proportions. Massive American military intervention to suppress this revolution and bolster faltering dictatorships has not only clearly violated the Geneva Accords, but also has transformed the United States into an outright aggressor. If Ho Chi Minh's Government finally retaliated by sending substantial forces into South Vietnam, it was only after Johnson in 1965 had begun the ruthless bombing of North Vietnam and had landed tens of thousands of U.S. combat troops in South Vietnam.

You, Cabot Lodge, like President Johnson, Secretary Rusk and Secretary McNamara, would like to erase from the memory of man the Geneva Accords and the other facts I have cited. The aim is to attempt the frame-up of a whole country, to mislead the American people and the world into believing that North Vietnam is the aggressor instead of the power-mad big bully—the United States of America. Do you really think that such disingenuous tactics on your part conform to *Veritas,* the motto on the seal of Harvard that you and I in our college days swore to uphold?

The reason why all of Johnson's peace proposals are dishonest and phony is precisely that, instead of being directed to the main contestant in the South Vietnamese civil war—the National Liberation Front and its military arm, the Vietcong—they are directed to the Government of North Vietnam and throughout make the false assumption that it is an aggressor state. Unfortunately, you have strongly supported the President's position here. It is obvious that Hanoi will never approve or attend a Peace Conference that at the outset assigns Ho Chi Minh's regime a criminal status.

In modern times many ambassadors have been mere messenger boys for their governments. But as Ambassador to South Vietnam you have been much more than that; you have played a major role since your first appointment by President Kennedy in 1963 in both formulating and effectuating policy. Utilizing your own special study of counterinsurgency as taught by the U.S. Army, you have helped plan military strategy. You have advised American generals on how to combat the Vietcong, and Vietnamese generals on how to stage coups to install new U.S. stooges. Indeed, you have functioned a good deal of the time as a Major General, your rank in the U.S. Army Reserve Corps. And you have consistently taken "the hard line."

So I say to you, Mr. Major General, that you bear prime responsibility for what Walter Lippmann has called "the escalation of frightfulness" in Vietnam; for the indiscriminate napalm and saturation bombing of innocent women, children and peasants in South Vietnamese villages; for the defoliation of the countryside by noxious chemicals dropped from the air; and for the cruel and extensive bombing of North Vietnam. The reckless and inhuman nature of U.S. air strikes becomes tragically clear in the repeated "mistakes" of American planes in killing scores of Vietnamese in "friendly" villages and even annihilating our own troops.

You share responsibility, too, for the flourishing of U.S.-sponsored prostitution wherever American troops are quartered in South Vietnam. The American military has transformed the beautiful city of Saigon into one of the biggest brothels in history. Commenting on the prostitution the Americans have created, a Catholic Sister in Saigon has stated: "I think the Vietnamese resent this more than anything else about the expanding of the war, more even than the bombing." (*New York Times,* August 4, 1966). There is no sign, sir, that you as U.S. Ambassador have said anything or done anything to halt this crime against morality and the women of Vietnam.

Meanwhile, the total American military commitment in Vietnam goes up and up, with well over 315,000 troops there now, not to mention 60,000 sailors of the Seventh Fleet off the coast. U.S. casualties likewise become higher and higher, with the official figure now at more than 5,400 men killed in combat and more than 30,000 wounded. The cost to the American taxpayer mounts correspondingly, with the Vietnamese war taking now at least $15 billion a year to finance. The April 1966 issue of *Fortune* magazine, for which you were once a consultant, estimates that as the conflict escalates, the total expense annually will rise to $21 billion. At the same time our domestic inflation also escalates, and our enormous expenditures in Vietnam further increase the growing deficit in the U.S. international balance of payments. There can be no doubt, either, that the colossal costs of our madcap venture in Southeast Asia are seriously handicapping the Great Society program.

No matter how many soldiers Johnson pours into Vietnam, and how much of our treasure he spends for the killing of Vietnamese, the United States can never win this war. The Pentagon estimates that in a guerilla operation of this kind the United States must have for victory a manpower ratio of ten to one against the enemy. Even if Johnson sends over 1,000,000 men, it is not too difficult for the Vietcong and North Vietnamese to provide 200,000 additional fighters to match them in the jungle terrain. And if the U.S. raises the ante to 2,000,000, then China will come in and easily marshal 400,000 men. This is why General MacArthur and all our military experts have in the past warned against the United States becoming involved in a major land war in

Asia. What we are doing in Vietnam is to sink deeper and deeper into the worst military trap in our history.

You, General Lodge, are caught in this same trap and are throwing your reputation, earned in peaceful and useful public service, down the drain in a futile effort to put across Johnson's evil designs in Vietnam and Southeast Asia. And as the brutal American attack on Vietnam continues, the danger steadily increases, as U Thant warns us, of a major conflict involving China, the Soviet Union and nuclear weapons. Such a nuclear war would be the greatest catastrophe that has ever come to America and the human race.

It is no wonder that peace-loving people and peoples all over the world are aghast at what the militarists of Washington are doing. It is no wonder that Pope Paul is greatly worried and exclaims, "We cry to them in God's name to stop." Even America's official allies are horrified. I should think that the plan of the Bertrand Russell Peace Foundation to try as "war criminals" you and other members of the Johnson Administration would give you pause. It is well to remember what our Declaration of Independence says about having "a decent respect to the opinions of mankind."

Pro-consul Lodge (as they call you in Europe), you are directing a U.S. colonial administration in South Vietnam and yet you pretend all the while that you are trying to save democracy in that country and guarantee its right of self-determination. No government in Saigon since the days of Diem could have lasted one week without the military protection of the United States. That is true of the South Vietnamese Government today, led by Premier Ky, the dictator who had such kind words to say of Adolf Hitler.

And what about the other members of the ruling junta? Here is what Senator George S. McGovern of South Dakota revealed about them on June 30, 1966: "I call attention . . . to the blunt fact that all but one of the South Vietnamese generals who represent the military junta fought with the French against their own people in the war for independence which followed World War II. Would not this be roughly comparable to having eight or nine Benedict Arnolds attempting to run the United States in the years that followed our own war of independence 175 years ago?"

Of course Senator McGovern's suggestion is entirely sound. And how can you, Ambassador Lodge, a veteran of World War II and a 100 percent American—how can you, sir, endure being the boon companion and faithful partner of the Benedict Arnolds of Vietnam? Is this the way to carry on the spirit of our great American Revolution of 1776?

Way back in our student days you had a special appreciation of

French civilization and French culture, and I admired your command of the language. Today you are a member of the French Legion of Honor. Why, then, do you fail to appreciate the wisdom of President de Gaulle and his associates, who have repeatedly stated that the only road to lasting peace in Vietnam is for the United States to carry out a phased and total withdrawal of its forces so that the long-suffering Vietnamese can settle their own destiny without outside interference? A U.S. agreement on such a withdrawal, on a general cease-fire with both the Government of North Vietnam and the National Liberation Front, and on a return to the 1954 Geneva Accords is the intelligent, sane way out for America, for President Johnson and for you, Cabot Lodge. It is the only sure way of your getting rid of the albatross that you so heedlessly hung around your neck three years ago.

When in 1962 de Gaulle, defying the imperialists and reactionaries, withdrew the French Army from Algeria and gave that country its independence, practically the entire world applauded. And France gained mightily in prestige. The United States could win equal prestige throughout the earth if it brought home its army, navy and air force from Vietnam.

If you yourself could see the light sufficiently to support this move and try to persuade Lyndon Johnson of its merits, you would go far in rebuilding your public image that has been so tarnished by your role as a leading War Hawk. Since the American people are daily growing more and more fed up with the Vietnam war, they would feel grateful to any U.S. official who made a real and honest attempt to terminate the conflict. It is time for our beloved country permanently to halt its military intervention in foreign lands and steadfastly to uphold again the traditional American ideals of international peace and cooperation. World peace is the best guarantee of the national security of the United States and the welfare of the American people.

Because of the transcending importance of the Vietnam issue, I am treating this communication as an Open Letter and am sending it to various interested persons. Over the years I have been your chief antagonist in the Harvard Class of 1924, and am today its only member, indeed the only Harvard alumnus in general, who feels it necessary to condemn openly your part in America's aggression against Vietnam. I believe that I am fulfilling a patriotic duty in doing so, both as regards the Harvard community and the public at large. It is possible that eventually our correspondence may prove to have some historic importance. And I am confident that in judging between us, history and the conscience of America will find you to have been terribly wrong about Vietnam.

Sincerely yours,
Corliss Lamont

AFTERWORD: FEBRUARY 1967

My two Open Letters to Ambassador Lodge received considerable publicity in the press, both in the United States and abroad. I presented and commented on the 1966 letter at the Sunday forum of the Boston Community Church on December 11. The minister of the church, the Reverend Donald G. Lothrop, had invited Ambassador Lodge to debate me in person, but Mr. Lodge declined. Mr. Lothrop then asked Ambassador Lodge's son, George Cabot Lodge, to represent his father, but he also declined. Accordingly, in order to have the Ambassador's viewpoint fairly presented, Mr. Lothrop drafted Edmund C. Berkeley, a Harvard graduate and well-known businessman, to read to the audience Mr. Lodge's letter in the *World Journal Tribune*. Mr. Berkeley made it clear, however, that he did not agree with Ambassador Lodge.

To update some of the statistics in the 1966 letter, I find that as of this writing over 465,000 members of the United States Armed Forces are taking part in the Vietnam conflict—405,000 on land and 60,000 at sea. This is exclusive of men in the Air Force involved in bombing flights from Guam and Thailand. The American casualties have risen to more than 7,000 killed in action and more than 40,000 wounded. And the latest reliable figure for the cost of the war to the United States is $25 billion a year. As Walter Lippmann says, President Johnson, because of these tremendous expenses, "has all but brought the so-called Great Society to a stop."

Mexico and Its Painters

MEXICO IN THE SUMMER

My first trip to Mexico has been one of the most exciting and fruitful experiences of my life. The vast majority of Americans who have the chance to travel abroad make a beeline for Europe and will return there again and again if they are able to do so. But here is a country closer and more accessible than any nation of Europe, and one that offers magnificent opportunities for recreation and for acquaintance with a foreign culture rich in political and social history, in archaeological monuments, in artistic achievement, in scenic beauties and in colorful variety of population.

Although it is only eleven hours by plane from New York to Mexico City, I distrust air travel and much prefer the train. For me there is nothing more refreshing and relaxing than to get on an air-conditioned car in the middle of the summer's heat and to lean back and read, completely insulated from the telephone and all the other pressures of city existence. So I did not begrudge at all the three days' journey to Mexico City on the direct railway route through St. Louis and San Antonio.

And for more than a day after we had crossed the Mexican border, I was able to study this new land searchingly from the window and to watch the native Mexicans bustling to and fro wherever we stopped. At some of the larger stations, such as Monterrey, I got off the train and mingled with the crowd. So it was that I obtained my first glimpse of those warm, genial, impressive-looking Mexican Indians descended

Source: Daily Compass, *August 26-31, September 2, 1951.*

from the Aztecs and other early peoples of Central America.

Mexico City, with its fine buildings, broad boulevards, spacious quarters and attractive parks, is somewhat reminiscent of Paris. I have made my headquarters here, making numerous side trips by automobile to fascinating towns and villages in the surrounding territory. Mexico City stands proudly in a beautiful valley with mountains and high hills in the distance in every direction. So it is with each town I have visited. To reach Cuernavaca or Puebla, for instance, you drive over mountain divides 10,000 feet high. Suddenly, just beyond the top, a new vast valley, with its own blue-green mountain ranges, appears shimmering in the sun, the town nestling far below.

Mexico City and these other places are all situated on this country's huge central plateau, which ranges in altitude from about 4,000 to 8,000 feet and has one of the most perfect climates in the world. In the City itself, more than 7,000 feet above sea level, it is perpetual spring the year round—warm and sunny during the day, cool during the night and the atmosphere pure and dry. The rainy season is on now and extends throughout the summer, but that only means it is likely to rain an hour or two late in the afternoon or in the evening. I have hardly noticed this rain and regard the weather as close to Paradise.

Though I have been here for only two weeks, I have done so much, seen so much and heard so much that it seems more like two months. Like any important national capital, Mexico City can keep the alert visitor busy almost indefinitely. Cheap transportation is available by trolley or bus. And taxis are not expensive, the average fare running to about three pesos or approximately thirty-five cents in American money, with no tips required or expected. In general, due chiefly to the favorable exchange rate for the American dollar, living costs for an American tourist or student are as low, I am reliably told, as in a European country like .France. Some Americans say they are lower.

During the summer in Mexico City bullfights take place in a large stadium on the outskirts every Sunday afternoon from 4 o'clock until about 6, with six or seven bulls successively in the ring. I have been to two bullfights. With my humanitarian American instincts and my natural opposition to cruelty to animals, I attended in the first instance with a definite prejudice against the whole business. But before I came away on the second occasion, I had changed my mind and felt able to understand why Latin peoples look upon the bullfight as an art comparable to the ballet or a ritual dance. Bullfighting will never be one of my favorite sports, but I shall not now join the crusades against it.

The Mexicans claim that the noble fighting bulls live longer and happier lives than most cattle; and that during their last fifteen or twenty minutes on earth, while becoming very angry at those who are engaging them in mortal combat, they do not actually suffer much. In fact, the battle is not altogether one-sided; the matadors are frequently injured and sometimes killed by the embattled, charging bull. One slip, one false step, and the matador is lost.

Twice I saw matadors, doing their dancing sidestep in front of the bull and trying to make the enraged animal charge the red cape they waved before him, tossed over the bull's head. They slid off his haunch, fell to the ground, and lay prone with their faces downward. Immediately, assistant matadors rushed into the ring and, waving their own red capes at the bull, attracted him towards themselves. In each case the matador picked himself up miraculously uninjured, and resumed the battle.

The picadors, who from on horseback stick short barbs in the bull's back, also run considerable danger. The bull invariably charges the horse, which is blindfolded and amply protected by heavy padding. I saw two picadors unhorsed and thrown to the ground during this part of the fight, but neither was hurt.

One bull ran into the ring, sniffed the air and looked around, and forthwith jumped clear over the protective wooden stockade into an area where various attendants were walking about. They quickly got him back into the ring. Another bull came in fast and charged up against the stockade so hard that he broke off one of his horns. Thereby he prolonged his life indefinitely, since he was promptly replaced by another bull.

It is not difficult to comprehend why the matador, with his splendid costume—which always includes pink stockings and black ballet shoes—and the other participants in a bullfight receive such enthusiastic applause from the audience. Their skill and daring is a sight to behold. If the matador has mastered his profession, his every movement throughout the fight will be graceful, even in the moments of most danger.

The other night I met an old Mexican friend who over thirty years ago went to the same school with me in the United States. He is a ranch-owner of considerable means, and has a handsome, well-built son of sixteen. For several years it has been this son's ambition to become a bullfighter. "Father," he said, "I shall bow to your wishes, but you will break my heart if you don't let me be a bullfighter." Recently his father reluctantly, but wisely, in my opinion, gave assent to his son's training for the career of matador.

This incident indicates the importance and standing of bullfighting in this remarkable country.

THE GREAT MEXICAN PAINTERS

In Mexico City I have definitely concentrated on art and artists. And it has been my profoundest joy to see at last in their original setting the great mural paintings of Diego Rivera, David Alfaro Siqueiros and the late José Clemente Orozco, who died in 1949. These three men, while using somewhat different techniques, have all done their main work in frescoes in public buildings of one sort or another, have all aimed at reaching the masses of the people through this medium, have all believed that art should embody a realistic social viewpoint and have all been radical in their social, economic and political opinions.

I have expended much effort in trying to track down the many murals of these three painters in Mexico City and its vicinity, but have simply not had the time as yet to see all of their work. Rivera is the most prolific of the trio and probably the most well-known in the United States and the world at large. He has always been a controversial figure and has encountered constant and bitter opposition to his painting in both Mexico and the United States. His frescoes adorn and beautify such important edifices in this city as the National Palace, where the President of the Republic has his executive offices, the Ministry of Education, the Palace of Fine Arts, the Federal Health Department and the National University of Mexico.

In his murals Rivera has pictured, according to his own provocative interpretations, the entire history of Mexico from the ancient Indian tribes who inhabited the region down to the present. In their ideological conception and practical execution, in their extraordinary range and sense of detail, in their magnificent coloring and dynamic spirit, Rivera's frescoes rival the best of such painting in the Americas and Europe.

Among other things, I have been constantly astounded at his knowledge of science. For instance, the two Rivera murals at the Institute of Cardiology show a remarkable grasp of medical progress in the control of heart disease from the ancient Greeks to the modern Americans. In the huge and imaginative mural at the Fine Arts Palace entitled "Man at the Crossroads, Looking With Uncertainty But With Hope to a Better World," Rivera includes a factually accurate treatment of biology, physiology, embryology, physics and astronomy. This is the notable fresco painted for Rockefeller Center in New York in 1929, destroyed by the American barbarians who could not bear its radicalism, and fortunately reproduced here by Rivera in 1934.

Five dominant themes run through Diego Rivera's murals. First, there is his burning antagonism towards the role of supernatural religion and the part played in Mexican history by the Catholic Church, including its responsibility for the horrors of the Inquisition in Mexico.

Second, there is his hatred of the Spanish Conquest and his stress on the brutality of the Spanish invaders led by Cortes. Rivera does not, like some historians, forgive cruelty, torture, slavery and mass murder, all of which the Spaniards brought in abundance to the native Indians, because these things happened far back in history.

Third, there is his unceasing ridicule of the upper classes, of the close tie-up between political power and economic privilege, and of money-mad capitalist civilization in general.

Fourth, there is Rivera's complementary emphasis on the successive revolutions which have resulted in increasing freedom for the Mexican people, and his additional sympathy towards the international communist movement and Marxism.

Fifth, there is his realistic and sympathetic portrayal of the common people of Mexico, of the workers and peasants laboring in mine, factory or field, of the Indians in their fiestas and in the simple enjoyments of family life.

In his larger murals Rivera often skillfully combines four or five of these themes. For example, the controversial 1947 mural in the main dining room of the Hotel Del Prado, starts by showing the agents of the Catholic Inquisition beating and burning to death agonized heretics, goes on to the revolutionary movements led by Benito Juarez, Emiliano Zapata and Francisco Madero, and then savagely satirizes dissolute and decaying high society, symbolized by a luridly attired female skeleton and corrupt Mexican politicians greedily fingering safety boxes full of American dollars. All along the bottom of the fresco are portraits of the underprivileged who generation after generation endure the villainy of the rascals at the top.

It is no wonder that Rivera's murals are continually getting him into trouble. In the painting just described, beneath the figure of Juarez, there is a man holding up a small placard on which originally appeared the following quotation from a nineteenth-century Mexican thinker by the name of Igneus Ramirez: "*God Does Not Exist*. I affirm and demonstrate this logically and experimentally."

This statement caused a storm of protest. Catholic students raided the Del Prado and scratched out the three last words of the opening sentence, leaving only "God." They also badly scratched the face of Rivera's self-portrait in the fresco. In Mexico as well as in the United States there are still barbarians.

The taxi-drivers of Mexico City entered the controversy, one group putting up signs on their cars reading "God Does Not Exist" and another group putting up "God Does Exist." A Mexico City newspaper published a letter from a religious fanatic recommending that Rivera be delivered over to the flames in a fire of green wood which would take a long time to burn.

Rivera then went back to the hotel and repaired the mutilated sections of the mural. But the vandals were soon on the loose again, and scratched out the same two parts for a second time. And this is the way the fresco appears today, hidden six days a week by a big wooden partition and open to the public only on Sunday mornings. It was, of course, a scandal that neither the Mexico City administration nor the Mexican Government was willing to provide the painting with adequate protection or to prosecute the mutilators of art.

Yet, even the enemies of Rivera must concede that his work is brilliant. I believe that he is perhaps the greatest painter, and the one with the greatest mind, that the twentieth century has produced. It is an indication of what counts most in Mexican culture that Rivera and his fellow-painters whom I have mentioned are considered in this country as more important than even presidents and generals. The well-earned fame of these artists will in all likelihood endure for centuries.

AN INTERVIEW WITH DIEGO RIVERA

Hearing that Diego Rivera was finishing up some murals at the new Mexico City waterworks on the outskirts of town, I drove out there one morning about 11 o'clock. Sure enough, there was Rivera, a huge figure of a man, directing the workers on a large, symbolic mosaic in front of the small building in which he had almost completed the new frescoes. He had on brown trousers and coat, a light brown sombrero and short rubber boots. Paint was abundantly spattered over his clothes.

Rivera had designed this mosaic himself and held the plan of it under his left arm. With his right arm he pointed here and there with a long stick and occasionally daubed some paint on the mosaic. For about twenty minutes I watched him walking around and talking to the workers. When finally he seemed to be through with his immediate job, I went up to him casually, said "Good morning" in English, explained that I was a correspondent for a New York liberal daily and asked whether he would mind my interviewing him. He spoke excellent English and said he wouldn't mind at all. We walked over to a nearby tree, which gave some shelter from the sun, and I took out my notebook.

Mr. Rivera was most pleasant and exceedingly generous with his time, talking as fast as I could write. Ever so often a workman on the mosaic would call out "Maestro" in pleading terms, but Rivera paid no attention. At one point a group of American ladies looking for all the world like a DAR delegation approached closely and asked permission to take some photographs of the Maestro. He said "all right," but kept on talking to me—and I didn't budge. So those poor ladies had to include me in their photos; and I rejoice in imagining their reactions should they ever identify me!

I began by inquiring about the trouble over the mural at the Hotel Del Prado and Rivera went into some detail over the matter. He asserted that the Mexican Government allowed the suppression because he put in the fresco the figure of a Mexican President fondling lovingly with his right hand American money running into the millions and with his left hand, the hand of a pretty blonde. Next to the President, Rivera explained, is a priest looking on benignly; and below the President are the initials of a big and well-known Mexican capitalist corporation that greases the palms of the politicos.

Rivera called the terrific uproar over the mural "a very dirty commercial proposition." Through the resulting publicity, he claimed, the Del Prado received free advertising reliably estimated as worth $3,200,000. Rivera also cited the fact that the Catholic Archbishop of Mexico, because of the content of the fresco, refused to give the customary benediction to the building.

Hereupon Rivera launched into a long story about the reactions to his mural of Cardinal Dougherty, then Archbishop of Philadelphia. The Cardinal, he said, looked at the painting fifteen times and gave it high praise, justifying the "God does not exist" statement as an historical quotation from an eminent thinker. According to Rivera, the Cardinal then added:

"The attempted destruction of this painting is not only an act against civilization and culture, but also against the will of God, who is the Creator of the artist and permits him to perform his work, no matter what his opinions about Deity. I respect Mexico City very much and know how ardent is its faith, but I am obliged to assert that the actions against this mural were not in line with Catholic tolerance and understanding as followed by the Pope and the Church."

Rivera then took obvious pleasure in telling me that the Archbishop of Mexico, who had actually encouraged the suppression of the mural, had hoped that he would soon be promoted to a Cardinal. Shortly after the Del Prado episode this Archbishop headed a Mexican delegation to Rome for the Holy Year and was received by the Pope. But he was not made a Cardinal.

I took time out here to ask Rivera what the great prone figure in the mosaic represented. He explained that it symbolized the God of Water in Mexican mythology and he pronounced the name in Spanish. Seeing that I was stumped at this point, he very obligingly took my pencil and himself printed in my notebook the name "Tlaloc." In the design Tlaloc is planting in the earth four grains of corn and then, after they have germinated and grown, presenting four corn stalks to the people. "Corn," stated Rivera, "is the basic food of us, the Mexicans."

The next question I put to Rivera concerned his striking and splendid mural "Man at the Crossroads" in the Palace of Fine Arts in Mexico City. This is a reconstruction of the original fresco which he painted for Radio City, New York, more than twenty years ago and which was later completely destroyed at the direction of the Rockefeller interests. I wanted to know Rivera's version of this downright act of vandalism. Here is the story in his own words:

Because I included a portrait of Lenin in the mural, they told me they could not accept the painting unless I rubbed out Lenin and put in his place some other noted leader of the human race. As the controversy developed, several of the left political parties in the United States met and passed a resolution requesting me to substitute Lincoln for Lenin on the grounds that it was most important to preserve the fresco, that in the next twenty years fifty million people would then see the painting and receive its stirring message, and that anyway everybody would remember the outrageous demand of the Rockefellers in regard to Lenin.

I refused to accede either to the Rockefeller demand or the left resolution. There were several reasons for my position. In the first place, at a closed session of 200 wealthy New York art lovers, who were enthusiastic about the painting, I asked Mr. John D. Rockefeller, Jr., which part of the fresco he liked the best. Without a moment's hesitation he pointed to the far corner showing a workers' demonstration in the Soviet Union and said: "The red flags you have painted there remind me of the reds in my most beloved tapestry which, God forgive me, is the only personal possession I really care for and the only thing that gives me real joy in life. Next, I like most the portrait of Lenin, because it represents a man who tried to do what he could for humanity in his own way and according to his own beliefs.

In the second place, if I let Rockefeller destroy the painting, I would demonstrate that despite his own opinion of the picture's worth, the power of capital had pushed a rich man down and made him abase himself before his own money and under pressure from the contractors of the building. And there would then be the contrast between Rockefeller and someone who does not have the power of money behind him, but simply the integrity of his own ideas, backed by millions of workers and peasants in every land.

In the third place, if I erased Lenin and changed the mural, this would be a concession to capitalistic power, which does not have the right to stop the free expression of human ideas as guaranteed by the Rights of Man and the American Constitution.

In the fourth place, if, as the left resolution stated, fifty million persons would see the altered mural in twenty years, then it would take a very long time for all the 2,000 million inhabitants of the earth to see it. But if Rockefeller destroyed the fresco, then every single paper in the world would print the news and my 2,000 million fellow-men would know about it in twenty-four hours. This would be much better for me and much worse for Rockefeller and capitalism.

Soon after the destruction of my painting, Franklin D. Roosevelt confirmed my judgment by stating: "In my opinion, my friend Mr. Rockefeller made a serious political mistake by doing away with Rivera's mural. For this act speaks not in favor of its authors, but in favor of the ideas which they tried to suppress."

Rivera then told me that in reproducing the mural in Mexico City he made two changes. First, he painted in a half-length portrait of John D. Rockefeller, Jr., at a fast upper-class party, sipping a glass of champagne and holding hands with a glamorous lady. ("Revenge is sweet," saith the Lord).

Second, he played up Trotsky and his revolutionary movement organized under the banner of the Fourth International. Rivera stated that he included Trotsky in this manner, not because he agreed with him, but because his importance in Mexico where he was living in 1934 was an historical fact. Actually, Rivera went on, although he joined the Trotskyites for a short time, they soon expelled him and he quarreled bitterly with Trotsky, who claimed he had become an agent of Stalin. Rivera now considers the Trotskyite movement as basically counter-revolutionary and hails the victory of the followers of Marx, Lenin and Stalin over fascism in the Second World War.

Rivera finally gave me some account of his tangling with Gestapo agents in Mexico during the first part of World War II and of his efforts to reveal Nazi plotting during the same period.

I looked cautiously at my watch and found that we had been conversing for an hour and three-quarters. So I made a little speech about how much his art meant to me and went back to my hotel for lunch, feeling happy but exhausted.

AN INTERVIEW WITH SIQUEIROS

The day after my long talk with Diego Rivera, I went with two tourist friends, schoolteachers by profession, to the Palace of Fine Arts to look again at the controversial Rivera mural and also to study more closely the frescoes in the same great hall painted by David Alfaro Siqueiros and the late José Clemente Orozco. This is the only place in the world where murals by these three famous painters appear side by side. Ordinary paintings by them also hang on the walls here, showing the versatility of these artists.

In the great hall Rivera has one fresco, Orozco one, and Siqueiros four frescoes, one half-finished. As I wandered up and down the corridors, I noticed a man up on a wooden scaffold busying himself with an unfinished fresco. Inquiring of an attendant, I discovered that this · was none other than Siqueiros himself painting away on his mural. As I watched him, he filled in the colors of the helmet on a Spanish cavalryman riding towards the scene of the torture of an Indian prince named Cuauhtemoc. The Spaniards, representing Christian civilization of the sixteenth century, had kindled a fire near the prince's feet. In the mural Cuauhtemoc was bearing the horrible pain with stoical endurance.

The companion fresco to "The Torture of Cuauhtemoc" was completed some time ago by Siqueiros and is called "Cuauhtemoc's Return." It symbolizes the eventual throwing off of the Spanish yoke by the Indians and their ability to stand off any invader, of whatever nationality. These two murals demonstrate clearly that Siqueiros, like Rivera, does not harbor kindly feelings towards those Spaniards who originally ravaged Mexico and butchered its people in the lustful search for gold.

Since naturally I had no intention of asking Siqueiros to come down off his stand to talk with me, I obstinately hung around for hours just waiting for a break. It finally came when a slight, pretty, dark-haired woman in a black dress emerged from a door in the wooden partition which separated the unfinished mural from the rest of the hall. She started talking in English with two Americans and the attendant informed me that she was Mrs. Siqueiros. So I edged over and at last got the chance to tell her that I represented New York's great liberal newspaper, *The Daily Compass*.

Mrs. Siqueiros was most gracious and in no time at all was giving me all kinds of valuable information about her husband. She told me that he had won second prize at the international exhibit in Venice last year and that he would be well represented at Paris' first all-Mexican exhibit, which is to be held in 1952. She explained that Siqueiros follows a technique somewhat different from Rivera's, since in painting his murals he uses primarily a modern plastic medium known as pyroxilyn and employs both brush and spray.

He is now working very hard on the Torture fresco, sometimes as late as three in the morning, in order to finish it in time for the scheduled dedication in another week or so. At last I summoned up my nerve and asked Mrs. Siqueiros whether she thought there might be an opportunity to interview her husband. She said, "Certainly," and invited me to lunch with both of them the next day.

Accordingly, I met Mr. and Mrs. Siqueiros at two o'clock the following afternoon at a restaurant near the Palace of Fine Arts. They had with them Siqueiros's younger brother, an actor, and two old friends. Siqueiros is a well-knit man about my own size, with alert blue eyes and bushy black hair. His obvious intelligence, sincerity and strength of character impressed me. He speaks English even better than Rivera.

Siqueiros stated that the Mexican muralists are a product of revolution and therefore necessarily social-minded. He himself was in the army during his earlier years, and took part in the successful revolt against the military dictator, General Huerta. The mural painters earn less on public frescoes than they can on private commissions, but they prefer the fresco work because it gives them a better opportunity to express their social ideals and reaches a wider audience.

A few days previously an American who had met Siqueiros had told me that he was rather startled when the painter suddenly exclaimed, "Well, the war has begun!" It turned out that Siqueiros was not referring to World War III, but to the battle against those in Mexico and elsewhere who uphold the abstract in art. As Siqueiros explained to me, the school of art to which he, together with Rivera and Orozco, belongs is one which supports realism and social content as opposed to abstractionism.

Siqueiros went on to say that when he and Orozco were painting the murals on the walls of the patios and staircases of the National Preparatory School in Mexico City, the more conservative students objected strongly to both their realism and social content and started to mutilate the frescoes. Five or six years later Orozco went back and did his over, but Siqueiros did not think it worthwhile to combat the student vandals in this way. Siqueiros asked me whether it was true that the New School for Social Research in New York had recently covered up the Orozco murals there because of their revolutionary implications. I replied that the New School had been under considerable pressure to take this step, but thought that it had not succumbed to the reactionaries.

When I remarked to Siqueiros that the subject matter of his paintings seemed to be more concentrated and easier to grasp than that of Rivera or Orozco, he laughed and cited the following formula: for the murals of Rivera there is needed a great deal of explanation; for the murals of Orozco there is no explanation; for the murals of Siqueiros there is needed no explanation.

259

With a touch of bitterness Siqueiros recounted how in 1943 an American commission headed by Nelson Rockefeller had invited him to come to the United States to paint a large-scale mural on the theme of democracy versus fascism. He happened to be making the trip to the U.S. by plane from Chile and had a stopover in Cuba. He never got any farther, for there the American authorities informed him that he would not be permitted to enter the land of the free, presumably because he was a communist. Siqueiros attempted to visit the United States again two or three years ago, but was denied entrance.

He recalled with pleasure the days when he lived in New York City and ran the Siqueiros Experimental Workshop for painters. That was back in 1936. Siqueiros makes no secret of the fact that he is a member of the Mexican Communist Party and has been so for many years. He is a more consistent radical than Rivera, although his frescoes embody less out-and-out leftism than Rivera's.

Siqueiros is not now as well known as Rivera, but judging from his brilliant and original murals in the Palace of Fine Arts there is some indication that he will eventually outstrip Rivera in the quality of his art and in public esteem.

I continued talking with Siqueiros until 3:40 p.m., when it had become time for him to return to his important work. We all walked over to the Fine Arts Palace together. At the entrance, Siqueiros and I shook hands and said goodbye. Then I drove off in the light rain, which had come earlier than usual that afternoon.

TOWNS, SQUARES AND FIESTAS OF MEXICO

Within easy automobile range of Mexico City, there are an endless variety of interesting and delightful places to visit. Usually you find it convenient to have lunch at the town or place that is your destination.

I have twice been to the town of Xochimilco, known as Floating Gardens, where you leisurely glide along willow-bordered canals in large punts poled by Indians. Each punt is decked out in front with flowers and each has its own name spelt in flowers. The first punt I rode in was called "Alicia," the second, "Love and Glory." Indian bands follow you around in their own smaller punts and play Mexican tunes for three pesos (thirty-five cents) apiece. It is all very gay and pleasant.

Twice, too, I have taken the hour-and-a-half drive to lovely Cuernavaca, where many people from Mexico City spend their weekends and where a number of Americans live permanently. Here the late Dwight W. Morrow had his country house when he was U.S. Ambassador to Mexico, and it is still maintained, with its beautiful gardens and swimming pool, by Mrs. Morrow. In 1930 Mr. Morrow commissioned Diego Rivera to paint a set of murals in the Cortes Palace at Cuernavaca and presented them to the city. They are a fine group of frescoes. The citizens of Cuernavaca liked Ambassador Morrow so much that they finally named after him the street on which his house stands.

My favorite occupation at Cuernavaca has been to sit in the main square, or (with a drink) on a hotel porch bordering it, just watching the people go by. Every city and town in Mexico has a plaza or square which is the center of civic life, where everyone likes to stroll and where concerts and fiestas are held.

At Cuernavaca the people drift by, some clearly of Spanish descent, others, the darker-skinned Indians. Many are barefoot or wear sandals. Here is a whole Indian family of six walking through the square, the mother carrying a baby in her ample *rebozo* or shawl. These Mexican Indians, with their broad faces and deep-set eyes, take life calmly and never seem to be in a hurry. There is a strength, dignity and serenity about them which sets them off from any other people I have known. Yet, considerable prejudice still exists in this country against the full-blooded and mixed-blooded Indians who make up about 40 percent of the population.

Some fifty miles beyond Cuernavaca lies the fascinating town of Taxco nestling in the mountains and clinging to a hill. Founded in the eighteenth century, the town retains much of its old colonial atmosphere, with red-tiled roofs, narrow cobbled streets and an ornate parish church. By law all new buildings must conform to the old style of architecture. Beneath and around Taxco there have been, and still are, rich silver mines; I saw a truckload of the steel-helmeted miners coming back from work.

For a time I wandered through, and up and down, those intriguing winding steps of Taxco. Then I came to the Square of the Fountain and stood quietly leaning against the wall of a house. Little boys and middle-aged women and old men came to get water from the fountain, carrying it away in buckets or large bottles. A funeral passed through the square, with four strong men carrying the black coffin. They and the mourners were on foot and slowly disappeared down a side street.

Then there appeared an attractive lady of Spanish origin and her escort. It seemed to me that I had never seen such a colorfully dressed woman. She had green sandals, a yellow shirtwaist, a red sash, a blue handkerchief, a red pocketbook, a gold bracelet, silver earrings and a green and red dress with various artistic designs in yellow. Her eyes and hair were a deep brown. All these colors blended harmoniously and I admit that I was spellbound. There is nothing like a Mexican square for viewing the full richness of life.

261

Finally, I must mention the fiesta at Milpa Alta (Spanish for "high cornfield"), an old agricultural village dating back to the sixteenth century. Every year in August the people of Milpa Alta have a week-long festival in honor of their special saint, the Virgin Mary. I arrived about 6 o'clock in the evening and found the village square crowded. There were five bands of local talent playing alternately on different stands and a sixth was playing for dancers at the nearby marketplace. I counted five merry-go-rounds for the young and very young. Some gambling was going on for small stakes and I bet a few pesos.

Again, there were those marvelous Indian faces on every side. Sweethearts wandered through the square hand in hand. I saw an Indian grandmother gently kiss the little fingers of a baby lying in its mother's *rebozo*. Laughing children were running about in droves and hopping on and off the carousels. Dogs, which are numerous in Mexico, gobbled up small pieces of food that people had dropped. A few of the men were slightly drunk in a genial sort of way.

I became hungry and bought a bag of crackers. There were too many for me and I offered some to a handsome Indian boy of about sixteen standing next to me. He took a couple and expressed his friendliness by trying to talk to me in Spanish, which I hardly understand at all. So we just smiled at each other. In a completely masculine way this boy was truly beautiful.

Darkness fell and the fiesta went on. They lit alcohol lamps and the faces of the villagers shone in the glow. All of them looked "muy contentos" (very happy). Deep inside I sensed the human warmth of these joy-feeling and joy-giving Mexicans. Their warmth surrounded me and my warmth went out to them. I too was "muy contento."

THE GLORY OF MEXICO

Today, on the eve of my departure from Mexico, I viewed what in my judgment is the greatest single work of art that exists in this country.

Having tracked down the scattered murals of Diego Rivera in no less than ten separate buildings in Mexico City, I drove out early this morning to the eleventh and last place. This was the Government Agricultural College at the small town of Chapingo, which I reached in forty-five minutes from Mexico City.

In the old days the whole town used to be owned by a high-living Mexican general who, according to repute, staged there continual Bacchanalian orgies unrivalled in splendor and riotousness. The Revolution of 1910-20 put an end to this, and the new government transformed the place into a serious educational institution, with modern experimental laboratories and fine dormitories. When I arrived, a number of the students were strolling around between classes. The vast majority of them were of Indian descent. This is natural, since it is the Indians who carry on the greater part of Mexico's agricultural work.

I entered the main building to look at the frescoes which Rivera, from 1923 to 1925, had painted in the hall and stairway. They were a most impressive group of murals portraying the recent development of agriculture in Mexico and showing how closely it has been bound up with the progress of the social revolution. On one of the murals Rivera had painted the legend: "Here we teach how to exploit the earth, not man." And this thought is the underlying motif of these notable frescoes as a whole. The coloring in all of them was superb, especially the blue backgrounds and a soft orange that is indescribable.

Already thanking heaven that I had not allowed myself to miss these paintings, I went around to the small chapel next door which had been decorated entirely by Rivera. As I stood at the entrance looking in, I realized instantly that here was something most unusual and stirring. I walked slowly down the length of the chapel—about eighty feet—and up to the altar, in order to get an immediate total effect. Then I leisurely studied those marvelous murals one by one.

There is no doubt in my mind that as a complete unit Rivera's work in this chapel surpasses anything that he has ever done. He has painted both walls and ceilings, and also made the striking designs carved on the wooden doors and benches. In every detail of conception, color and composition, this chapel seems to me to reveal Rivera at his most talented, forceful and imaginative. The typical themes are there: the oppression by the inseparable trio of church, state and upper class; the revolutionary movement against the exploiters who operate by whip, gun and superstition; the workers and peasants at their daily tasks. And a new, powerful theme is added: the immense creative forces of Nature, symbolized particularly by the magnificent nudes along one wall and on the ceiling.

Viewing this monumental outpouring of genius, I thought at once of the Michelangelo paintings that adorn the Sistine Chapel in Rome. In this little-known town of Chapingo, Rivera has accomplished, with a very different subject matter, something of the same sort. For me henceforth Michelangelo's chapel and Rivera's chapel stand together as the two greatest artistic creations of this kind that I have seen.

I sat down on a bench to look around once more and to think. For me this was a deep-going aesthetic experience, and strong emotions welled up within me. I felt that I had at last entered the portals of the blessed and that for a long time this chapel would remain journey's end for me in my search for the inner beauty of life.

Only a handful of the Americans who visit Mexico take the time to visit Chapingo. Only a small proportion of them seem to care much about the Mexican murals in general. The travel bureaus here give very little attention in their literature and tours to Mexican painting. Evidently they believe that most Americans would be bored by looking at frescoes and would be offended by their radical social content.

Yet the outstanding cultural achievement of Mexico today is precisely the work of Diego Rivera, David Alfaro Siqueiros and José Clemente Orozco. There are no painters in the United States who, in my opinion, measure up to the stature of these three humanist artists; and mural painting in our country remains relatively undeveloped.

Mexico is a land of infinite interest, beauty and accomplishment. But at least for me its shining glory in this age of uncertainty and chaos is the creative genius, sure and compelling, of the mural painters.

My Trip Around the World

EUROPE

During eight long years from 1951 to 1958, the American State Department refused to renew my passport because of my publicly expressed dissenting views on domestic and foreign policy. Finally I sued Secretary of State John Foster Dulles in order to regain my natural right to travel, regardless of my political and economic opinions. I automatically won my suit and obtained my precious passport in June 1958, following the U.S. Supreme Court's decision that the leftist artist, Rockwell Kent, be granted a passport.

Since I had not been able to travel across the seas for so long, I decided to make up for lost time and to circle the globe. Then, too, as a humanist philosopher I have taught that the supreme ethical goal in life ought to be the happiness, freedom and progress of all mankind, regardless of nation, race or religion; but there was a lot of mankind I had never met face to face. I viewed my six months' world tour as a chance to come into closer contact with distant countries and peoples, especially in the Far East, where I had not been before.

So, on the first day of spring, 1959—surely a day of happy omen—my wife and I set sail from New York on *La Liberté* across the Atlantic. For me the seven-day voyage was a rebirth into freedom. And when at last I glimpsed once more the familiar coasts of France and England, I felt that I was rediscovering much that had become, in many journeys of the past, an essential part of my being.

Source: Basic Pamphlet, 1960.

It was the greatest pleasure for me to return to England, a land of happy memories for me and one where I have many good friends. It was a delight just to stroll along the streets of London and through the splendid parks of that city. The English accent is always music to my ears, and I loved simply to listen to the English people talking together as I passed them by or they passed *me* by while I sat in the sun on a park bench, looking out upon places where not so long ago Hitler's bombers were creating havoc. Most of the war's debris has been cleared away, but even today a number of burnt-out squares remain as silent monuments to a determination that "it must not happen again."

Our little hotel on Half Moon Street was less than a block from lovely Green Park, which runs into Hyde Park, famous not only for its wide green lawns, but also as a free-speech center where radicals and dissenters and even crackpots can talk their heads off with no interference from the public authorities. There ought to be a Hyde Park of free speech in every city of the world, including our own United States. And as I listened to these orators in *London's* Hyde Park, I couldn't help reflecting how much better Great Britain had preserved *its* civil liberties since the end of the Second World War than had America. To be sure, during this period occasional violations of free speech have taken place in Britain, but that country has experienced nothing comparable to the far-reaching suppressions of our McCarthy era, the consequences of which are still etched deep in almost every sector of American life.

While I was in London, Parliament was in session, and I went over to the House of Commons two or three times to lunch with some of my friends in the British Labor Party. It was especially pleasant drinking coffee with them on the beautiful Commons Terrace overlooking the Thames and with a fine view up and down the river. We discussed at length the political situation.

I was particularly impressed by the program of the Victory for Socialism Council, led by Labor M.P.s such as Harold Davies, Stephen Swingler and Konni Zilliacus. This forward-looking group wants the Labor Party to become more militant in its socialist program, and to declare itself in favor of Britain's unilaterally halting both the further testing of nuclear weapons and their manufacture. But the conservative leadership of the party has rejected these proposals and has been soft-pedaling many important issues. That is one of the main reasons why the Conservative Party won such a sweeping victory in the general election of October 1959. As Mr. Zilliacus summed up the trouble, "Before we can beat the Tories in the country, we must beat the Tories in the Labor Party."

During our last weekend in England my wife and I made a pilgrimage to Oxford University where I studied at New College in 1924-25. That was one of the best years of my life. It was a joy to wander again around the University and to visit my old haunts. The New College garden, bounded on one side by the old city wall built many centuries ago, is as quiet and lovely a place as can be found anywhere. And in general the gardens of the twenty-five or so colleges that make up the University are unexcelled in their beauty, and give to one a rare sense of isolation from the outside world. As everyone knows, the creation and care of gardens in England have long since achieved the status of high art.

From Oxford we drove out ten miles into the rolling countryside to call on Mr. and Mrs. John Masefield, two of my family's oldest and best friends. Mr. Masefield met us at the door of his house and was most cordial. He invited the lady taxi driver in to have some tea, but she declined. John Masefield, Poet Laureate of England and eighty-one years old, is in vigorous health and still turning out first-rate poetry. Only recently he began to make very successful vocal recordings of his poems. I don't know anyone who has a finer voice for reading aloud.

Although I am hardly a conservative in politics and economics, I do happen to be one as regards poetry, and still prefer poems that rhyme or scan. I was glad to find that here Mr. Masefield on the whole agreed with me. He said that our contemporary poetry in England and America lacks discipline and form. He likes very little of it and feels that current poets no longer dwell on themes of love and nobility. I consider John Masefield one of the truly great men I have known. The simplicity, honesty and ruggedness of his character, together with his continuing vitality, remind me of America's own dean of poets, Robert Frost.

I could go on indefinitely discussing England and the English, a wonderful country and a wonderful people. But I have space only to describe some of the highlights of my long trip. And so I now turn to the continent, and especially Italy.

After spending a few days in Paris, ever a joy to the traveler, we relaxed at Nice on the French Riviera. Then on one long rugged day, with sensational views every few minutes, we drove the entire distance to Florence—along the Mediterranean Côte d'Azur, past the cliffs of Monaco, into northern Italy with its steep and mountainous roads, and finally down into the Florentine plain.

We stayed three weeks in Florence, which is, of course, one vast treasure-house of art. Our hotel room looked out over the River Arno to colorful hills where we could see the old city wall and towers that Michelangelo helped to construct back in the sixteenth century. Below us, along the river walk, strolled the people of Florence—buoyant and

267

uninhibited. There were young couples with their arms around each other, old couples enjoying the sun and children skipping along. At our open window we had a splendid balcony seat to watch the world go by. And every so often a singer with a guitar would saunter past and serenade us.

With Florence as headquarters, we made expeditions in all directions to Italy's marvelous hill towns such as Siena, San Gimignano, Volterra, Perugia and Assisi. As you approach these magic cities from a distance, you see their graceful towers rising far away, then disappearing and reappearing according to the curve of the road and the structure of the Tuscan hills. We were living in a pervasive atmosphere of beauty, where the loveliness of Nature was continually merging with that of *human* creation. The hills and valleys were lush and green; and as twilight approached a golden glow suffused everything.

The history of this region is absorbing, but it often makes one sad. For the city-states of Italy, at the height of their artistic flowering during the Renaissance, were continually assaulting one another. Not only were irreplaceable works of art ravaged during this period, but the flower of Italian manhood was killed off. Coming to a much later era, stiff fighting took place in and around Florence during the Second World War when the U.S. Army was driving out the Nazis. The retreating Germans shelled the bridges across the Arno and smashed all of them except the famed Ponte Vecchio. At this moment art lovers held their breath to see whether the Germans would bombard the rest of the city. It did not happen, but it was a close call. War is a terrible destroyer of the good and the beautiful.

The next highlight was Greece, all of it. This historic land was a very special experience for me because I had never gone there before and because as a philosopher I was fascinated at seeing the places where Socrates, Plato and Aristotle walked, talked and lectured. We stayed in Greece several weeks and made Athens our headquarters. At least every other day we went up to the Acropolis, wandered through the half-ruined structures built in the Golden Age of Pericles, viewed from every angle the architectural miracle of the Parthenon, and looked out between its white marble columns, designed by Phidias, to the city lying below and to the shining sea in the distance. It was all the sheerest aesthetic ectasy. And it continued even into the hours of darkness, for every so often the Parthenon was lighted up at night and we could see it from the streets of Athens.

We made many exciting explorations to cities such as Delphi, Corinth, Mycenae and Sunion, where on a headland an ancient and perfectly proportioned temple to Poseidon stands out dramatically. In *Don Juan* Lord Byron referred to Sunion's "marble steep," and we saw there his signature carved into a marble pillar. Then came our five-day boat trip through the Greek Islands of the Aegean Sea, an adventure into the living past and the enthralling present, centering around legend-crusted isles like Crete and Rhodes and Delos.

As in Italy, we were constantly drinking in vast panoramas of history along with the sublime art and the natural beauty. I took particular satisfaction in going out to the battlefield of Marathon and reconstructing from maps just how the Greeks drove back the Persians in 490 B.C. Here I held up a whole busload of hurrying American tourists when I insisted on stopping to see the swamp that protected the Athenian right wing against a Persian cavalry charge. One plump angry lady in the bus demanded that a vote should be taken as to whether I be permitted to look at the swamp. For once I did not wait upon the democratic process, but quickly got out of the bus. There was a plaque at the edge of the ancient swamp and I thought it would tell more about the battle. Instead, it stated that some years ago the area had been filled in as a mosquito-breeding hazard through the funds of John D. Rockefeller, Jr.!

In Greece even more than in Italy the ravages of innumerable wars are apparent. Athens, Sparta, and the other Greek city-states were at one another's throats most of the time. The Persians sacked much of the country; and later came barbarian invasions from the north. The most hideous war episode of all was in 1687 when the Turks placed a powder magazine inside the Parthenon, and the attacking Venetians scored a direct hit on the building with a mortar shell. This transformed the larger part of the Parthenon into a shambles. War is the most frightful enemy of art, as of every other human value.

Yet despite the fact that almost all the architectural splendors of Greece, and much of its ancient sculpture, have been badly battered because of physical violence or plain neglect, what remains is so magnificent that we have in this small kingdom perhaps the greatest concentration of artistic glories in the world. And when I saw American bombers from the U.S. military airfield nearby zooming over Athens and heard talk about setting up a base for long-range ballistic missiles in Greece, I suddenly conceived the idea that the United Nations, with, of course, the agreement of the Greeks, should declare Greece an International Art Sanctuary and a permanently neutral state, something like Switzerland.

It would then be under special U.N. protection, until the danger of war had passed away for all the nations of the earth. Let the United States, the Soviet Union and all other countries keep hands off and place Greece outside the realm of power politics! Then this unique country that marked the birthplace of Western culture would carry on in lasting peace as a great Art Sanctuary, an enduring shrine of beauty where art lovers, students and ordinary travelers could go forever for inspiration and aesthetic enjoyment.

From Athens I took a small but comfortable steamship to Istanbul, passing through the Dardanelles and sailing across the Sea of Marmora. At Istanbul I could look out from my hotel window across the Bosphorus to the green-clad hills of Asia Minor. But I must not stop here to describe what I saw and did during my two days' stay in Turkey's capital, nor to enter into my even more interesting weekend in Warsaw on my way to Soviet Russia.

THE SOVIET UNION

In our long trip around the world we naturally spent considerable time in the Soviet Union, where we had not been since 1938. Shortly after my return to America in that year I wrote: "The very fact that, over a territory far larger than the United States and non-Russian Europe combined, socialist economic planning has for many years been operating on a fairly efficient basis proves that *it can be done*."

Twenty-one years later, in the summer of 1959, what I observed in the USSR shows clearly that my earlier expression, "It can be done," has become a decided understatement; now it is accurate to say that Soviet planning is carried out on so wide a scale and so successfully that the whole world, including the most conservative capitalists and economists, is taking note and reluctantly recognizing Soviet Russia's extraordinary achievements. After enormous setbacks resulting from the Nazi invasion, Soviet socialism has come into its own and is operating with marked effectiveness in almost every sphere. And Soviet productivity not only proceeds with practically no unemployment, but is able to support certain social and cultural accomplishments that are quite remarkable.

I think especially of Soviet Russia's socialized medicine, which capitalist Britain is seeking to rival; of the USSR's impressive educational system, which has abolished illiteracy and forged dramatically ahead both in the field of general education and scientific training; and of recent technological wonders in the exploration of outer space and sending rockets to and around the moon. As to the educational system, it is difficult to work out exact figures for comparison, but I believe the soundest estimate available is that the Soviet Union allocates 10 or 15 percent of its national income to education, while the United States spends about 3 percent for the same purpose.

During June and July my wife and I saw at first-hand the great progress that has been made in the USSR. Moscow was in some ways hardly recognizable because of the tremendous building and municipal planning programs that have been carried through. A whole new city numbering some 250,000 has been erected on what used to be the outskirts. Everywhere as we drove around the Soviet capital there seemed to be beautiful broad boulevards—twice as wide as New York's Park Avenue—and fine new apartment houses. However, when we looked closely at the apartment houses, it was evident that some of them had been shoddily constructed and hurriedly finished to cope with Moscow's ever insistent housing needs.

We found that architectural styles had improved little since 1938 and were, with the notable exception of the unique subway stations, either drab or grandiose. From our hotel window we could see six of Moscow's new skyscrapers, including the University of Moscow, the Ministry of Foreign Affairs and two big hotels. The buildings looked splendid from a distance, but when you got close the gingerbread decorations became obtrusive. The Soviet authorities themselves, including Premier Khrushchev, have become aware of these various defects, and there is now under way throughout the country a movement for the improvement and modernization of architecture.

While we were in Moscow my wife and I talked with many different types of Soviet people, especially in the professions. Soviet individuals did not have the slightest hesitation to visit with us, or with other American travelers and other foreign visitors from capitalist countries. It was a boom year for tourists in the USSR; among our fellow-travelers were ex-Governor Harriman, Vice-President Nixon, and seven governors of U.S. states whom we encountered on several occasions. A record number of Americans—more than 12,000 altogether—visited the Soviet Union during 1959.

One of the persons we saw most of was our old friend Vladimir Kazakevich, a Russian who for many years brilliantly taught and lectured in the United States on Soviet affairs. After the Cold War began, the U.S. Immigration authorities began to get rough with him, and he chose to go back to the Soviet Union rather than to endure insult and persecution from the McCarthy gang. Mr. Kazakevich has a good job in the American section of the Institute for World Economy and International Relations. He is one of the outstanding Soviet experts on America.

Another Soviet citizen who greatly impressed us was Professor of Psychology A. R. Luria, a most able teacher at the University of Moscow. I was particularly interested in his views on psychoanalysis.

He stated that while most Freudian theories have no verification, Soviet psychologists do not discard psychoanalysis completely. They do, however, insist on proof for any psychoanalytic hypothesis. Professor Luria asserted that Freud gave too much emphasis to animalistic and biological factors in man, who also happens to be a *social* being.

During the Second World War Soviet psychologists and physicians expected a great deal of neurosis in the Soviet Army and among the civilian population; but very little developed. Neurosis comes when there is trauma plus internal conflict because you don't know what to do. During the war, Professor Luria went on, there was trauma without much internal conflict, because everyone was part of a group and knew what to do. The pervading sense of We throughout the Soviet Union has been and is a major factor in holding to a minimum the incidence of neurosis and disturbed personality.

Naturally, I enjoyed talking with the alert editors of the Foreign Literature Publishing House, which in 1958 issued a Russian translation of my book on American civil liberties, *Freedom Is as Freedom Does*, in an edition of 25,000 copies. Mr. P. A. Chuvikov, the head editor, told me that this edition sold out quite quickly, and it was only with some difficulty that he was able to find two copies for me. After Mr. Chuvikov had presented me with a handsome author's fee (in rubles), I discussed with him and his associates the whole question of the Soviet Union entering into some international copyright agreement that would cover the rights of foreign authors in the USSR, and Soviet authors abroad. This controversial matter remains in the domain of unfinished business. The lack of any Soviet copyright accord has aroused much resentment among foreign writers, many of whom are not even informed by their Soviet publisher when one of their works is issued in the USSR.

Still another delightful occasion in Moscow was the bountiful luncheon given us by Ludmilla Pavlechenko, the famous woman sharpshooter who disposed of about 400 Germans in the Second World War. She visited the United States in 1942. The party at her comfortable apartment was warm and gay, with many toasts, both flippant and serious, drunk in vodka that flowed somewhat too freely for my limited capacity. Also present were Miss Pavlechenko's attractive husband and several friends.

One of my most interesting talks was with Soviet Foreign Minister Andrei Gromyko, whose office is far up in the new skyscraper where the Ministry of Foreign Affairs is now situated. I had known Mr. Gromyko when he was Ambassador to the United States, and have always had a high regard for him. He had just come back from the

Geneva Conference where he had labored long and arduously. In my opinion, Mr. Gromyko is a most sincere and effective worker for international peace. It has often been stated that while the Soviet *people* really desire peace, their top leadership—"the scheming communists in the Kremlin"—are secretly plotting war and aggression. Nothing could be further from the truth. As my conversation with Mr. Gromyko showed once more, both leadership and people in this nation are completely united in their will for world peace and better American-Soviet relations. I believe that Premier Khrushchev convinced a majority of Americans that this is so on his visit last fall to the United States.

Another current fable about the USSR is that the Soviet people always look serious, troubled and sad. This is nonsense. We carefully observed the Soviet people in their offices and homes, in restaurants, parks and theatres, in the subway and on the streets. I have rarely seen more laughter and gaiety. People in any country are likely to look serious and preoccupied when hurrying to or from work; but when men and women in Soviet Russia relax, they show as much *joie de vivre* as individuals anywhere.

Yet another report sometimes appearing in the American press is that the Soviet Government has been depriving the people of food and other consumer goods in order to produce Sputniks, moon rockets and intercontinental missiles. The fact is that the planned economic system has been functioning so well that both technology and the standard of living have been developing rapidly in all directions. There is plenty of food throughout the USSR today and the people look well fed. In fact the food was so tempting that I myself put on considerable weight. There are plenty of fine beverages, too. Soviet champagne compares favorably with some of the best French champagnes and costs about $3.00 a bottle. The Government recently reduced the price by 23 percent, partly to let it compete successfully with the more potent vodka. Unfortunately, drunkenness is still a problem in Soviet Russia.

Obviously, the Soviet Union has not made nearly as much progress in political democracy as in other fields. Yet there has been considerable relaxation since Stalin died and especially since Nikita Khrushchev became Premier. As Averell Harriman pointed out in a 1959 newspaper series on the USSR, the political prisoners in the concentration camps have been freed and have been rehabilitated into useful work. During my stay in Soviet Russia, I heard a good many criticisms of the Government. However, the Soviets have a long way to go to establish full civil liberties as we English-speaking peoples understand the term. The first step here should be the implementation of the 1936 Constitution, which specifically states: "The citizens of the USSR are guaranteed by law freedom of speech, freedom of the press, freedom of assembly, including the holding of mass meetings, freedom of street processions and demonstrations."

My wife and I have always been a bit nervous about traveling by airplane, and so we felt some trepidation as we boarded the big Soviet TU 104 to go from Moscow to Tashkent on our first jet flight. We did not need to worry. For the Soviet jet operated smoothly and efficiently all the way.

We had long wanted to make a trip to the southernmost section of Soviet Central Asia, both to see the magnificent architectural beauties of the Moslem culture that so long dominated this area and also to study the functioning of the Soviet minorities policy in an enormous region where five major Turco-Tatar peoples intermingle with one another and with the Russians. We were able to fulfill our two main purposes during our fortnight's stay in Tashkent, capital of the Uzbek Republic, with side trips in a 200-mile radius to such places as fabulous Samarkand, ancient capital of Tamerlane's earth-shaking empire, and the Fergana Valley, where a network of irrigation canals has transformed former desert lands into a most fertile agricultural district.

Wherever we went in Central Asia there seemed to be ample food, as in the Moscow area. In the towns and cities crowds of people were busy buying the abundant consumer goods that are available in the stores. The general standard of living, including the spheres of education and health, is fairly high in this vast region, where before the 1917 Revolution a primarily nomadic and Moslem population maintained a precarious existence in poverty and squalor, ever facing the depredations of drought, famine and epidemic disease.

From everything we could observe, the different peoples in Uzbekistan all live together on a plane of equality, with the old racial prejudices and discriminations almost completely eliminated. Among the 444 deputies chosen for the Supreme Soviet of the Uzbek Republic in the last election held early in 1959, thirteen separate nationalities were represented. The most important minority is the Russian, with sixty-two representatives.

Another important fact to keep in mind is that out of the 444 deputies elected, 129 were women. This bears out our impression that in this huge territory the female sex, traditionally held in bondage there by the Moslem male, has made immense strides towards equality with men. Not only has polygamy been abolished by law, but also 99 percent of the women have discarded the heavy, long, black horsehair veil that for centuries the Mohammedan religion demanded all females wear outside the home.

In Uzbekistan we enjoyed meeting and mingling with the dark-skinned and half-Oriental Uzbeks who make up the overwhelming majority in this land. They are a delightful and handsome people, with mobile, expressive faces, and the Uzbek children are a delight to watch. The girls wear their hair in two long braids hanging down their backs, and their dresses are brilliantly colored. The youngsters were frolicking everywhere like kids in any other country. Since it was extremely hot, with the temperature ranging from 85 to 90 degrees Fahrenheit, one of my favorite recreations was to go swimming in Lake Komsomol, in the city's biggest park, where I was able to relax with the Uzbek youth at play.

One of our most enjoyable afternoons in Uzbekistan was when we went to inspect the big Sverdlov Collective Farm (cotton) just outside Tashkent. We found it highly mechanized and operating most efficiently. After we had walked around for quite a while in the broiling sun, with the Chairman of the Collective as our guide, we retired to a shady veranda where we were served "tea" consisting of a small portion of green tea and very large portions of vodka, champagne and plov, a national Uzbek dish of meat and rice. The Chairman of the Collective raised his small vodka glass and proposed a toast to American-Soviet friendship. "Bottoms up," he said. Since my wife and I had chosen champagne, it was a bit difficult for us to drain our larger glasses. Nevertheless, we did it and then went gaily on to the next glass as I offered a toast to world peace.

We drank a lot of other genial toasts, and a final one to the continued success of the Sverdlov Farm. Each time the chairman repeated, "Bottoms up"—and we maintained the pace as best we could. At the end of the "tea" my wife and I and an American newspaperwoman who was present had consumed two whole bottles of Soviet champagne! It is testimony to the high quality of that wine that none of us got either a headache or hangover.

Another afternoon we went to the most important mosque in Tashkent and witnessed an outdoor Moslem prayer service. At a Moslem religious service the men and women are segregated, and on this occasion all of the women were out of sight in the back somewhere. So we walked through the midst of some 1,000 silent, bearded Mohammedan males to the chairs reserved for our small party. Almost all these men were native Uzbeks, many of them very handsome, and some, with their shaved or bald heads, resembled Yul Brynner. It was a real thrill to hear the Muezzin call out repeatedly in a high-pitched voice, "Allah is great," and to see each worshipper, kneeling on his little prayer rug, bow down his head to the ground. I have never been so close to Allah before!

After the service the Mufti, head of the Moslem religion throughout

Soviet Central Asia, gave us tea, fruit and lamb stew at a beautifully set table. We asked him many questions. He said the Moslems had complete freedom of worship in Soviet Russia, that they trained young men to be mullahs in special seminaries and freely distributed the Koran at the mosques. The Mufti was a dignified, charming man with seven children and five grandchildren. He was very sincerely concerned about world peace.

The Mufti explained that according to the Koran, the Moslem religion, wherever it is functioning, should cooperate with the established government. He and his associates, he told us, are cooperating with the Soviet Government and are on good terms with it. This is also the attitude of the Eastern Orthodox Church, by far the most powerful religious body in the USSR. The patriotic services of this Church during the Second World War led to greatly improved relations between religion and state in Soviet Russia. The Orthodox Church now actually supports the socialist economic system, which it does not find inconsistent with Christianity. The Soviet Government, on its part, has eliminated most of the crude antireligious propaganda that was carried on until the Nazi invasion in 1941.

Towards all the people we saw in Uzbekistan I felt a deep warmth and should like to have remained among them indefinitely. But we had set out to circumnavigate the globe and had to move on. On our last afternoon we signed our names in the Tashkent guest book of Intourist, the official Soviet travel agency. By coincidence on the opposite page there was a statement signed by the seven American governors, who had left the day before, July 13. What they said is interesting:

On this day the undersigned have concluded a three-day stay in Tashkent, vital and inspiring capital of the Uzbek Republic. The warm friendship which has been extended to us by the people at every hand, the exemplary courtesy of all public officials, make us feel that our stay has been constructive. It will always remain in our memories as one of the most enjoyable experiences of our lifetime. We leave Uzbek and Tashkent with every wish for the protection of the ancient charm which has been so manifest and at the same time the continued business progress which has also been most conspicuous. [Signed] LeRoy Collins, Governor of Florida; George D. Clyde, Governor of Utah; John E. Davis, Governor of North Dakota; Stephen McNichols, Governor of Colorado; Robert E. Smylie, Governor of Idaho; Robert B. Meyner, Governor of New Jersey; Luther H. Hodges, Governor of North Carolina.

Before breakfast on July 14 we drove out to the Tashkent airport and took another Soviet jet, this time bound for India. Reflecting on my trip through the USSR, I felt more convinced than ever that this socialist country run by communists—with all its defects past and present—is a country with which the United States can and should cooperate in normal international trade, intercultural exchange, the banning of nuclear weapons, general disarmament and the establishment of enduring world peace. The USA and the USSR will continue to disagree fundamentally on issues of economics and politics; but such disagreements need not stand in the way of peaceful, though competitive, coexistence between the capitalist and communist blocs.

INDIA

On a very hot morning in the middle of July my wife and I stepped into a Soviet jet at Tashkent and took off for Delhi. We flew over the towering Tien Shan, meaning "Celestial Mountains," over a part of Communist China's Sinkiang Province that juts out between the USSR and India, then over the Himalayas themselves with their soaring, snowcapped peaks stretching out for hundreds of miles on either side, and finally down to our destination on India's wide northern plain. It was the most thrilling trip by air that we had ever made.

To reach Delhi took only about three hours. As we struggled through the Indian customs and out to a taxi, no less than six porters insisted on helping us to carry our seven bags—a sign of the immense poverty that burdens India—and I felt obliged to tip each one. This situation was in striking contrast to our experience in Soviet Russia where tipping is now definitely frowned upon and where, having been rebuffed on several occasions, I finally gave up this pernicious custom altogether for the remainder of my stay in the USSR.

Delhi became the capital of India only in 1931, and the section that functions as the seat of government is known as New Delhi. It is a spacious and well-planned city, with fine government buildings, parks and apartment houses. The older section of the city, Old Delhi, where we spent much of our time, is more picturesque than the new part and also contains the chief slums in the metropolitan area. The appalling poverty of the Indian people was readily apparent to us when we walked or drove through the streets and alleys of Old Delhi. On every hand there were wretched beggars, both young and old, some of them quite disfigured. It is a horrible fact that beggar parents in this Eastern country will sometimes mutilate their children in order to make their begging more effective.

In Old Delhi, too, we saw at first-hand the meaning of cow worship in India. Often a cow would saunter across a main street along which we were driving in a taxi; the taxi would then have to make a detour, especially if the cow decided to lie down. When we were walking on the sidewalk, frequently a cow would be smack in our path. We watched cows calmly munching vegetables from vegetable stalls along the street; the owners could not interfere because the cow is a sacred animal and *must* be fed. Over all of India wander literally millions of cows, a large proportion of them diseased. They have the right of way over both human beings and vehicles.

There are also plenty of bulls on the loose. A professor who had taught at the University of Calcutta told me that one day a big bull wandered onto the campus. No one was pleased, but no one dared to prevent a sacred animal from munching the grass. A week or so later the bull charged and gored a student who was riding a bicycle through the campus. The young man almost died. Only then did somebody gently usher the bull off the university grounds, still free to roam and gore at will. There have been many instances of such bulls killing Indian men and women.

When we had tea with Malcolm MacDonald, British High Commissioner to India and son of England's first Labor Prime Minister, Ramsay MacDonald, he told us that the cow situation had become worse since the establishment of Indian Independence in 1947. While the British were still in control, they did not interfere with cow worship, but neither did they encourage it. Shortly after Independence, however, the right wing of the Congress Party forced through a law prohibiting the killing of cattle throughout the whole of India. Monkeys, too, are sacred animals and constitute a destructive nuisance in many parts of the country.

Cow worship is of course closely tied up with the belief in reincarnation, which is a fundamental doctrine in the Hindu religion. The Hindus—and there are approximately 320 million of them among India's 400 million people—are reluctant to take the life of any animal. They think that if you kill a cow, you may in effect be killing your grandmother or some other deceased relative.

Indian cow worship and the law against the slaughter of cattle prevent the utilization of what could be a very substantial source of fresh meat. This is a major reason why the vast majority of Indians are undernourished. Furthermore, the cows and monkeys eat tons and tons of food that ought to be going to human beings. I know of no other nation where the dominant religion has such a direct and deleterious effect on nutrition and health as in India.

When I visited Calcutta, I witnessed aspects of Hinduism that clearly belong in the category of primitive religion. One Saturday morning I went to the temple of the Goddess Kali, an important Hindu deity who has three eyes—one each for the past, the present and the future. In the stone courtyard of the temple, fire worship and animal sacrifice were going on. One Hindu family after another came in leading a little bleating goat and turned it over to the burly executioner. He pinioned the struggling animal in a sort of guillotine and quickly cut off its head with a big sharp knife. The head and the body fell to the pavement, and blood gushed out over the stones. Then a priest stepped forward, dipped his forefinger into the goat's blood and put a red blood mark on the middle of the forehead of each worshipper, including the small children.

An old woman squatting nearby took over the head of each goat and cut away, for the priests of the temple, the parts suitable to eat. Dogs lapped up the pools of blood, and the sacrificer carried home the body of the goat to eat. For the Hindus the goat represents animal passion. When you sacrifice him, it symbolizes winning control over your own passions, killing them, as it were.

After I had watched about five or six goats being sacrificed, I felt I couldn't stand any more. I walked out of the temple grounds and down the street outside. It was lined with beggars, some of them stark naked, seeking alms from the crowds who come to worship Kali. When four or five of these beggars spotted me as a foreigner and literally surrounded me, I broke into a run in order to escape.

Of course there is much that is splendid about India, including its magnificent art and historic buildings. The incomparable beauty of the Taj Mahal can scarcely be exaggerated. Then there is this nation's firm stand throughout the postwar period for world peace and disarmament, the intellectual alertness of its educated class, and the economic aspirations embodied in the Five-Year Plans that the Government has been carrying through in order to raise the standard of living and advance towards socialism. The Second Five-Year Plan started in April 1956 and runs through March 1961.

But the economic and social problems are so formidable that I do not see how Prime Minister Nehru—whom I admire as one of the leading statesmen of this century—and his Congress Party are going to solve them. The population of this subcontinent is increasing at the rate of at least seven million a year, and birth control is making only slight progress. One of Nehru's Cabinet ministers was recently quoted as saying that during the next decade probably some fifteen million Indians would starve to death. That is one well-known way in which economic problems are "solved."

Although Prime Minister Nehru and the Congress Party are formally committed to the establishment of democratic socialism, the Indians I talked with told me that to a considerable degree only lip service is being paid to this aim. The Congress Party has not been militant in pushing through its economic and social programs, and many of its members are conspicuous for their apathy and lassitude. While my Indian friends did not look upon the Communist Party as the solution, they thought that the best hope for the ultimate success of Nehru and his associates was for them to acquire some of the militancy characteristic of the communists.

As Walter Lippmann has put it, what is needed above all in India are "the organized pressures of a popular movement under government leadership so dynamic and so purposeful that it can inspire people to do voluntarily the kinds of things that in Communist China are done by compulsion." (*New York Herald Tribune,* December 11, 1959).

A first priority for a truly militant policy on the part of the Congress Party would be the elimination of the graft that is widespread throughout governmental administration, both at the federal and the state level. Another priority would be the general institution of elementary efficiency. As Arthur Bonner, a CBS correspondent who has lived in India for more than five years, states in his informative article, "India's Masses," "entering a government office is like stepping back fifty years or more. There are few filing cabinets and paper clips. Papers are attached by a string threaded through a hole in one corner and then wrapped in a folder tied together by another string. A code letter is pinned to the cover, and the name of the file is registered in a ledger. The file is then tossed on a shelf along with mounds of others. The registers are tossed somewhere else, and how any file is ever found again is a wonder." (*The Atlantic,* October 1959, p. 50).

Looking back now on my globe-circling tour, I feel that my experiences in India were the most significant of the whole trip. For in no major country had I ever seen before such dreadful poverty, such a disease-ridden people, such backward religion and such abysmal and widespread ignorance. To me as an American the whole situation was a great shock, and a valuable shock. And it made me understand more fully the 1917 Communist Revolution in Russia and the 1949 Communist Revolution in China, since in those two countries the living conditions of the masses of people were similar to what exists in India today.

When the Chinese communists won power in 1949, living standards were even worse in China than in India. A United Nations Statistical Bulletin, *National and per Capita Incomes, 70 Countries, 1949,* estimates the per capita income in India, in dollar equivalents, as $57, as compared with China's $27. These estimates do not of course tell the whole story about the comparative standards of living, but there is no doubt that the Chinese level had been declining, owing to disastrous floods, wide-scale famine, civil war and international war.

The important point is that when a people numbering tens of millions or hundreds of millions lives generation after generation in misery and semi-starvation, it is not difficult to comprehend why they may eventually explode into revolutionary violence in hopes that a new socio-economic system will provide for their basic needs and give them a better chance to enjoy the good things of life. News of the dramatic economic upsurge in mainland China over the past decade is not only reaching the Indian intellectuals, but is also seeping through to the masses of the population. And unless India's Five-Year Plans bring about more rapid progress than at present, the example of Communist China will steadily grow more persuasive among the Indians and other peoples of the East.

Another point that India brought into focus for me was the whole relation between a country's economic system and the functioning of democracy. Political democracy in India today is weak and faltering, with Prime Minister Nehru frequently playing the role of an all-wise father. What I want to stress in this situation are the effects of the economic base on the educational prerequisites for democracy. While I was in India I kept thinking of John Dewey's insistence that there cannot be properly functioning democratic institutions unless the people are sufficiently educated to possess the information and understanding for voting intelligently on public issues. Nobody can pretend that this is the case in India. In this huge country there do not exist even the *material* necessities—schoolhouses, college buildings, pencils, paper, book publishing and the wherewithal for teachers' salaries—adequately to educate the electorate. Thus, 74 percent of the Indian population remains illiterate. Only some 50 percent of the children six to eleven years old attend primary school; about 10 percent of children fourteen to seventeen go to high school; and a mere 1 percent of men and women seventeen to twenty-three are students at colleges or universities. Turning to other aspects of education important for political awareness, we find that the daily circulation of newspapers in India is 3.1 million for a population of over 400 million, while radio sets number a little more than 1.5 million. TV was only recently introduced.

Again, reflecting on India's educational situation, I saw more clearly not only why right-wing dictators had been able to seize the governments in nearby countries with similar conditions, such as Pakistan, Burma and Thailand, but also why left-wing dictatorships had come into power in Soviet Russia and China. This statement leaves unqualified my immense preference for the use of democratic and peaceful procedures everywhere in the world for effecting economic and social change.

HONG KONG AND JAPAN

From Calcutta I flew on to Bangkok, Singapore and Hong Kong. These are all fascinating cities, but I have space only to discuss briefly Hong Kong. Ringed with small mountains and on a bay studded with numerous enchanting islands, it is the most beautiful and dramatic harbor I have ever seen. It surpasses even San Francisco. Hong Kong boasts a long waterfront where you can watch Chinese junks and other boats being loaded and unloaded. Since there is a lively trade with Communist China, you can see plenty of communist boats, flying their five-star flag, at the docks. On the myriad junks and sampans—"floating communities," as they are called—live thousands of families in cramped and squalid, though picturesque, quarters.

Since the communist take-over on the Chinese mainland, more than a million refugees have fled over the border to Hong Kong, creating an enormous problem for the municipal authorities. Naturally, these refugees are bitterly anticommunist; but among the city's original Chinese population pro-communist sentiment runs strong, even among some of the wealthier businessmen, who are proud to see China finally a free nation standing on its own feet and no longer subject to imperialist aggression and exploitation. Hong Kong in British hands serves as a valuable trade outlet and transshipment center for mainland China.

This British Crown Colony offers tourists a fine opportunity to buy a vast assortment of intriguing Oriental goods at low prices, and I myself started to purchase a few presents for my family and friends. Then I was stopped short by the discovery that the United States Government had put into effect a regulation that all articles, within at least thirty broad classifications, bought by Americans in Hong Kong would be confiscated by the U.S. Customs unless the buyer could obtain from the seller a Certificate of Origin certifying that the merchandise in question did not originate in Communist China or North Korea.

I was much incensed by this regulation whereby the American Government pushes its unrealistic and out-of-date Far Eastern policy to a ridiculous extreme, interfering with the right of Americans to buy what they want abroad. I also felt surprised that the British Government, which had reluctantly agreed to the U.S. procedures, would allow such an infringement of its sovereignty. The final result was that I bought very little in Hong Kong.

I remained only five days in Hong Kong, but it is a place where I would like to spend five weeks, five months or indeed five years. From Kowloon, on the mainland side of the bay, I drove towards the small Sham Chun River which denotes the border with the People's Republic of China, and was able to climb a little hill that gave me a view of two communist towns a mile or so distant. That was the nearest I got to Communist China. I did not try to enter, because having only recently obtained a passport, I did not wish to have the U.S. State Department take it away from me and bar my traveling abroad for a long time to come.

Early in August I left Hong Kong for Tokyo on a Pan American Stratocruiser. The weather was clear as we flew over the Tokyo airport in the late afternoon, but instead of landing the plane started to circle. I quickly became aware that something was wrong, and when, through a fluke, I heard the captain talking with the airport about his left landing gear, I realized that we might be in for real trouble. Finally, the hostess told the passengers that we must prepare for a crash landing because the left landing gear might not hold.

A number of passengers were ushered towards the rear, where I happened to be sitting. A Chinese mother and her two young children crouched between me and the back of the next seat. The children were frightened and crying, but I quieted them somewhat by singing a couple of American dance tunes. I remained outwardly calm, but felt terribly nervous. Then the plane came in. On the first bump the landing gear held firm, and I said aloud, "It held!" The flight officer opposite me said, "Wait for the second bump!" A moment later the second bump came, and everything was all right. We had made a perfect landing. As we descended from the Stratocruiser, I noticed six or seven fire engines drawn up on the airfield.

In Japan I made Tokyo my headquarters, staying at the Hotel Imperial and frequenting especially the spacious and exotic old wing, which had been designed by architect Frank Lloyd Wright in the early twenties. I went on all-day trips through beautiful Nikko National Park and Hakone National Park, and then on a four-day tour of the lovely temple cities of Kyoto and Nara and the atom bomb city of Hiroshima.

The Buddhist and Shinto shrines in Japan are impressive, but as works of art I did not think that they were as fine as the religious buildings in Thailand and India. The Buddhists, with their belief in reincarnation, are a strong and influential sect in Japan. I was struck by a story in the newspaper that there would probably be at least 1,000 suicides throughout the country when Crown Prince Akihito and his wife have their first baby. Each of those individuals is convinced that if he can arrange to die at the precise moment the baby is born, his soul will be reincarnated in it, and he will in effect become a member of the royal family, and perhaps Emperor.

Surprisingly for me, Hiroshima turned out to be one of the most splendid harbors I have visited—surrounded by jagged mountains and looking off to the colorful islands of Japan's big Inland Sea. Since I had taken an active part in the campaign against nuclear weapons, I was particularly interested in Hiroshima and explored it thoroughly in order to obtain as clear an idea as possible of·what happened when a plane of the U.S. Air Force dropped the first atom bomb in history upon this city, August 6, 1945.

A party of four Japanese took me around. My official guide and interpreter had been a soldier in the Japanese Army and was stationed near Hiroshima when the bomb struck. The following day his unit was sent into the city to render aid. He gave me innumerable grisly, ghastly details. Most helpful also was Dr. Ichito Moritaki, Professor of Philosophy at Hiroshima University and Chairman of the Hiroshima Council Against A- and H-Bombs. He had lost his right eye on A-bomb day. Two girl students who spoke English likewise accompanied us. One of them had been injured when the bomb fell.

I went through three Hiroshima hospitals. The first was the Atom Bomb Hospital, which administers only to patients suffering from the effects of the original explosion. Now, fourteen years later, scores of people are still coming to this hospital for treatment every day. I saw many of them in the waiting room. The director told me that in the first eight months of 1959, twenty-seven Japanese A-bomb victims had died.

The second hospital, run by the Atomic Bomb Casualty Commission and partly supported by American funds, concentrates on research concerning the effects on human beings of the A-bomb explosion. It does not try to cure anyone, but its work is very important in a long-range sense.

The third hospital I visited is a small private institution run by Dr. Shima and built on the ruins of the old Shima Hospital, which happened to be the exact center of the atom bomb strike. The fifty patients and ten staff members that day were simply obliterated in one minute or less. The hospital itself was completely destroyed. I talked at length with Dr. Shima, who fortunately was operating at a hospital in the country when the bomb fell. He told me he came back quickly to Hiroshima to help his patients, but all he could find in the ruins of his hospital was the charred body of the head nurse. The fact that the very center of the bomb's destructive power was a hospital ministering to the sick for the preservation of life seemed to me symbolic of the horror of nuclear weapons. It is a remarkable coincidence that at Nagasaki, too, the first direct center of the American A-bomb attack proved to be a medical institution, the Nagasaki Medical School.

What I saw and learned at Hiroshima was all rather grueling to me. And I came away completely persuaded that the United States made a terrible mistake in letting loose the A-bombs on Hiroshima and Nagasaki. In terms of dead, injured, suffering and long-term effects on human health, these bombings were the most frightful military actions perpetrated against civilian populations in the entire history of human warfare.

During my three weeks in Japan I came to like its people very much. I have never known a people so polite, thoughtful and smiling—so pleasant in general. To everyone, including hotel personnel and taxi drivers, I returned the bows and smiles with equally deep bows and broad smiles of my own. I found this sort of give-and-take an amiable and heart-warming custom.

These Japanese traits I have been describing have often been ridiculed in the United States, but I believe they are sincere expressions of the Japanese character. Here we have an outstanding example of an essentially fine people being misled into nationalist aggression and eventual disaster by an autocratic and ruthless military clique. How could it happen? I have no pat answer to this paradox. Important factors, however, were undoubtedly the long tradition of strict feudalism in Japan, the fanatical Emperor worship and the tendency of the ruling class in recent times to imitate the most hard-boiled features of German militarism and its Prussian code.

I hated to leave Japan just as I had hated to leave Hong Kong, India, Soviet Russia, England and Greece. Indeed, wherever I went on my six months trip, I always wanted to remain much, much longer than I did. Every country, every city had something special to offer in the way of natural beauty or artistic achievement. But above all I liked the people—of every nationality, of every race and color. And the warm feeling I had always had for humanity throughout the earth was constantly reinforced by my day-to-day experiences and observations.

Human brotherhood extending over the globe is no mere dream; and the humanist aim of working for the welfare and happiness of the whole family of man is the greatest and most worthwhile of all ideals.

An Interview with Chile's President Allende

On July 11, 1971, the day after I arrived in Santiago, the Chilean Congress passed unanimously a constitutional amendment for the nationalization of all the copper mines in the country. A few days later, on July 15, President Salvador Allende signed the amendment into law and called it "perhaps Chile's most important action since independence." He proclaimed a Day of National Dignity and stated: "Now we will be the owners of our own future, truly the masters of our destiny."

I was glad to be in Chile during this week—surely one of the most significant in its entire history—since I had long opposed the economic exploitation of Latin American nations by U.S. business and had been in sympathy with the socialist goals of President Allende and his Popular Unity coalition. And I was especially happy to receive, on July 19, an invitation from the President to see him at his office in the Palacio de la Moneda (Government Palace) that same evening.

Since the Palace, like the Hotel Carrera where I was staying, was situated on Constitution Square, I did not have far to go. Waiting in an anteroom for a few minutes, I chatted with a military attaché who had attended West Point for awhile. Then the President walked in and greeted me cordially. He ushered me into his office and first pointed to three framed photographs hanging on the wall, one of him and his family, a second of him and some friends riding horseback in the country, and a third of a Chilean general pinning the highest military medal of the nation on Allende as the new Commander in Chief of the Armed Forces. The President said with a twinkle in his eye that hostile

Source: The Churchman, *October 1971.*

newspapers throughout South America had published this third picture with the caption: "President Allende receiving the Order of Lenin from a Soviet General."

My interpreter for this interview was Dr. Gustavo Molina, Professor of Preventive and Social Medicine and adviser at large to the Chilean Minister of Health. Dr. Molina and President Allende were old friends, since Allende was a physician at the start of his career and had worked closely with Molina.

I opened the conversation by saying to the President that I brought good wishes to his Administration as an unofficial representative of hundreds of thousands of Americans who were sympathetic to its aims and program. Allende replied that such people could be very useful in bringing about understanding between Chile and the United States.

He told me that the Chilean Government would do everything possible to maintain good relations with the United States, but that difficulties might arise over the precise amount Chile could and would pay U.S. companies in compensation for the recent nationalization of the copper mines. He added that some American firms, anticipating full nationalization, had become careless and wasteful in their mining operations. Hence the mines would not be in the best of condition when the Government was ready to take them over completely.

While the Chilean Government obviously faces many difficulties in establishing a planned socialist society, the President, whose term lasts six years (through 1976) convinced me that during that time his Administration would go far in engineering the transition to socialism. He pointed out that an extensive nationalization program is already well advanced.

(The Government, besides its take-over plans for copper, has made substantial progress towards nationalizing the banks; the coal, iron and steel industries; and the larger cement and textile plants. I went through the big Hermas textile factory in Santiago, nationalized by the Government about two months earlier, and found it operating efficiently. The Allende Administration has also announced that it is initiating a skiing program for low-income families at ski centers such as Farellones and Portillo, at both of which I enjoyed fine skiing while I was in Chile.)

President Allende stressed the fact that the Popular Unity coalition has every intention of putting across socialism through democratic procedures. I remarked that if democratic socialism—socialism without dictatorship—could be achieved in Chile, it would be of tremendous significance for the whole world. Allende agrees with this comment and fully realizes that there are far-reaching international implications in what he is attempting to do and that the eyes of mankind are on him and his associates.

The President impressed me greatly. A spry, slender man in his early sixties, he combines firmness of character and keen intelligence with a deep compassion for his fellow humans. Certainly he is the greatest political leader to emerge in South America during the twentieth century.

I asked President Allende whether he was perhaps a Humanist in his philosophy. He answered that he didn't go in much for labels, but that since he was a Marxist, he was naturally a Humanist and that his Administration was doing many things of a humanist nature.

As I rose to go, the President took up a paperback book on his desk and inscribed it. He presented it to me, the title being *The Political Thoughts of Salvador Allende*. The inscription read: "To my friend C.L. from compañero Presidente [comrade President] with hearty affection and faith in the victory of the peoples.—S. Allende."

After thanking him for his book, I remarked that I would like to send him a copy of my book *The Philosophy of Humanism*. He said he would be glad to have it.

As I walked out of the room, President Allende shook hands with me and said warmly, "Come back again!"

South American Sidelights

Although for a half century I have traveled widely throughout North America (including Mexico), Europe and Asia, I had never been to South America prior to the summer of 1971. What initially prompted me to visit that continent was my desire to learn first-hand about the new socialist Government of Chile, with a convinced Marxist, Salvador Allende, as its President.

I arrived in Chile two days after a sizable earthquake had hit the Pacific coast district near Valparaiso, causing a great deal of damage and killing almost one hundred people. During my first night at the Hotel Carrera in Santiago I was awakened at four o'clock in the morning by my bed shaking violently. I heard excited voices in the corridor outside my room; then somebody knocked loudly on my door. When I opened it, a lady in a dressing gown—she was apparently an American—told me I must get dressed at once because "it's an earthquake."

But I was in a reluctant, sleepy mood and decided to phone the desk before I committed myself to drastic action. The desk said in good English: "Do not worry, Señor. There has been merely a slight tremor. After a big earthquake we always have tremors because the earth has to readjust itself." So I went back to sleep.

A week or so later I drove from Santiago to Valparaiso to see this famous port and to view the effects of the earthquake. Many buildings had been badly damaged, and sometimes the entire front side of a house had fallen out onto the sidewalk. Plaster, bricks, stones and

Source: The Churchman, *December 1971.*

wooden beams still littered the sidewalks in much of the city. Few persons, however, were killed in Valparaiso. The main loss of life was among the peasants in villages five or ten miles away from the coast where the houses were built of frail adobe or unburnt sun-dried brick made out of wheat stalks mixed with mud. The earthquake wreaked havoc on such houses.

Driving north from Valparaiso a few miles, I passed through Viña del Mar and Concon on a coastal highway along the edge of the Pacific Ocean. There were beautiful views of surf rolling in on sandy beaches and dashing against rocky bluffs to dissolve into sunlit spray. I had lunch at a beautiful restaurant called Los Lilenes from which you could look through the window at beaches and breakers.

Another well-known Chilean resort that I visited was the great ski center at Portillo, 9,500 feet high in the Andes and only two-and-a-half hours' drive from Santiago. Since Chile's winter comes in the months of June, July and August, I found splendid skiing during my four days at Portillo in the middle of July. (Chileans celebrate Christmas in their mid-summer season.) The weather was freezing at night, but mild during the day. The mountain scenery was, of course, magnificent, with jagged, snowcapped peaks visible in every direction and the beautiful Lake of the Incas in the valley in front of the main hotel. The Allende Administration intends to make Portillo available to skiers from low-income groups.

While I was in Santiago, I walked around the city as much as possible. I liked to sit on a park bench and just watch the people go by, studying their faces for a moment as they passed. In many of those fascinating faces there was clearly an Indian strain. Approximately two-thirds of the Chilean population are of mixed Indian and Spanish descent. Only some 200,000, or 2 percent, are pure-blooded Indians, as compared with about 50 percent in Peru.

One afternoon I was walking with an American acquaintance along a broad avenue in search of the statue of Bernardo O'Higgins, soldier, statesman and outstanding liberator of Chile from Spain in 1817-18. He became head of the country's first permanent National Government. As my friend and I were standing on a street corner feeling more or less lost, a chauffeur-driven car stopped in front of us and an attractive lady in the back seat said in English, "Can I help you?" I replied, "Why yes, we are trying to find the statue of O'Higgins." She countered, "Well, you're going in the wrong direction. You'd better let me give you a lift, because I am going right by the statue." So I said "Fine!" and we stepped into the auto. After we had driven six or seven blocks the car drew up at the O'Higgins statue and I thanked the lady for her thoughtful, humane act. As we got out, she remarked, "By the way, I am the great, great granddaughter of O'Higgins."

From Chile I went on to Argentina and Brazil. When I flew from Buenos Aires to Rio de Janeiro, officials of the Argentine Airlines, which had had several hijacking incidents, thoroughly searched all passengers boarding my plane. Much to my surprise, out of more than one hundred passengers I was the only one who came under suspicion. When a security officer discovered a pair of medium-sized scissors in my briefcase, he asked sternly, "Why do you have these?" "Whenever I travel," I answered, "I carry scissors with me to cut clippings out of newspapers." The officer looked gloomy and I thought for a moment I might be headed for jail. Then he said, "We will have to take them." Accordingly, he appropriated the scissors, but gave me a receipt whereby I could retrieve them when I reached Rio. However, in the general melee of disembarking at the airport and recovering my baggage, I forgot all about my scissors!

With its backdrop of small mountains, its lovely islands in the bay and its miles of sandy beaches, Rio is unsurpassed for beauty among the big cities of the world. While I despise the present military dictatorship in Brazil, I yielded to temptation and spent four days in Rio where I especially enjoyed surf-bathing in the Atlantic just a scant 200 yards from the entrance to my hotel. It is remarkable that Rio, with a population of more than 4,000,000, is far ahead of most American cities in having had such rigorous pollution control that the water is safe for swimming at any one of the several large beaches within the city limits.

My 1971 tour of South America lasted only three weeks, but obviously I could have stayed three months to advantage. It is a continent of enormous variety in peoples, cultures, political systems, scenery and archaeology. Americans in a mood for travel, whether for serious study or plain recreation, ought not to neglect South America.

IV

EPILOGUE

Epilogue I: My First Sixty Years

On March 28, 1962, Casper Citron interviewed Corliss Lamont on his radio program on Station WRFM, New York City. The interview follows.

CASPER CITRON: I'd like to welcome back a person who has been with us a number of times, a man who is well known in America: Dr. Corliss Lamont, a former lecturer at Columbia, a philosopher and author. Dr. Lamont is celebrating his sixtieth birthday today, and we thought it would be interesting to talk to him about what these past sixty years have been all about; how a man, particularly of his background, which is very unusual, has come by some of his beliefs, and why he has done some of the things he has done in the last sixty years. So, Corliss, welcome back and happy birthday.

CORLISS LAMONT: Thank you, Casper. It's a great pleasure to be with you again, and especially to be celebrating my sixtieth birthday with you.

You mentioned my background, and I suppose I should start with that in tonight's discussion, because in my family circle there were a great many influences that have stayed with me throughout my life.

There was in my family a real freedom of discussion for all of the four children. My father and mother were well-educated people; and we were always talking over the great issues of the day, whether they dealt with domestic or international affairs, in which my parents were very much interested.

In addition, they had a wide circle of fascinating friends, both in

Source: Basic Pamphlet, 1962.

America and abroad. Since my father and mother concentrated on England in their trips to Europe, they came to know many of the leading Englishmen of their day. Staying often at our New York house, which became a sort of International Inn, were British M.P.s, statesmen, dramatists, poets, novelists and painters. And I can remember many times being at the dinner table with these persons and actually participating in conversations with them.

Of course this sort of informal discussion gave me a fine education, even before I went to college. I can remember, for example, some of the arguments that H. G. Wells participated in with my parents. Wells and I would take on my father and mother, both of us—Wells and myself, that is—being in favor of some form of socialist economy. That was not only very stimulating but, of course, very informative.

And so it was for a large part of my earlier days, so that when I got to college, I had this very helpful background. Naturally my education at the Phillips Exeter Academy and Harvard University was also very important.

CITRON: Corliss, there's one point that, of course, I wouldn't expect you to mention yourself, but that I should ask about. One thinks of the Lamont family as being a very wealthy family, but you didn't touch on this.

LAMONT: Well, certainly they were never in economic want, one may say. And it is a fact that in spite of my father's and mother's wealth, they were interested in liberal causes—in trade unions, and in the League of Nations, *especially* in international affairs. I would call them, on the whole, liberals in their public positions.

So, when it comes to the matter of economic status, it's perfectly true that I have not been in want at any time during my life. I think that part of my independence and my willingness to take dissenting positions stems to some extent from my feeling of economic security, due to the generosity with which my father and mother treated me.

CITRON: One last question on that, Corliss. Was it from your father or further back that the Lamont wealth came? And how was it made?

LAMONT: My father was actually a rather poor boy to start with, the son of a Methodist minister in upstate New York. He worked his way through school and college. Then he went into banking and became very successful.

He was very generous with the wealth that he acquired, and made important gifts to all kinds of educational institutions.

CITRON: I hate to keep prying on this, but was it your father who was associated with Morgan?

LAMONT: My father was a partner in J. P. Morgan and Company from about 1910 on. He died, however, before Morgan merged with the

Guaranty Trust Company. That firm today is called Morgan Guaranty Trust.

CITRON: Well, let's leave the pleasant topic of how you acquired money. It's much more important to find out what you did with it. When you went to college, I imagine that you must have had some thoughts in your mind about philosophy because you took a Ph.D. at Columbia in philosophy in 1932.

LAMONT: It's true that I became interested in philosophy at a very early age. For one thing, my mother was a student of philosophy, and took an M.A. at Columbia way back in 1898. She talked over these philosophic subjects with me. So there were continuous discussions of philosophical questions in the family circle—questions about God and immortality, the meaning of the Bible and that sort of thing.

Actually, when I was an undergraduate in college, I wasn't quite sure what I was going to concentrate in. But a couple of years after my graduation, I came back to philosophy as the subject that I felt should be my field of concentration, and then went to both Columbia and Harvard graduate schools to study. I took my Ph.D. degree in 1932 at Columbia, with a thesis entitled *Issues of Immortality*, which dealt with the question of personal survival after death. That has always been a fascinating topic to me, especially now that I'm getting a little older and may have to go on to some other place before long.

CITRON: You wrote a book—I don't know if it's still being published—called *The Illusion of Immortality*. Could you tell us a little bit about it?

LAMONT: Well, its still in print. It's in a paperback edition now, sold by Philosophical Library. It has gone into several editions and still sells pretty well because it's one of the few books that tries to give a careful and thorough examination of the case against personal survival after death.

I had started out believing in immortality. But after my studies in philosophy, I came to the conclusion that we could not go on beyond the grave, except by way of lasting influence and through our children and descendants—that is, biological immortality. So I was forced to conclude that this was my one and only life. I have operated on that basis for the last thirty years; and I think it makes a difference because I feel that I am more concerned with what happens here, on this earth, than if I were looking forward to an after-existence. I work a little harder and try a little harder to bring justice and happiness to people in this natural world.

CITRON: Were there any reactions from institutions such as the Catholic Church, or other church groups, to this book?

LAMONT: It has been attacked fairly often by church people and church bodies, but I don't think any particular church ever took it on in great detail. Actually, it has become, if I may say so, something of a reference book in many colleges and universities. At Union Theological Seminary, for instance, the President of that institution, Henry Pitt Van Dusen, a good friend of mine, has used *The Illusion of Immortality* in some of his courses to show his students what he calls "the best argument" against the traditional Christian belief.

It isn't that Dr. Van Dusen agrees with me. But he is one of those teachers who wants to present both sides of the question to his students. This book has been used in that way in many places, including England, where there have been several editions.

CITRON: You mentioned how you feel that immortality must come through one's children. I neglected to ask you in the beginning: what have you done about children through the last sixty years?

LAMONT: Well, I followed the example of my father and mother and, like them, have had four children, three daughters and a son. Two of my daughters are happily married. One of them has presented the family with two wonderful, beautiful grandchildren, whom I see a good deal of. And then I have another grandchild, who was born to my son and daughter-in-law in Boston a year or so ago. I've been very much blessed, I think, in the realm of children. It's a great thrill to have grandchildren—even though it seems a bit queer sometimes to be called "Grandpa."

CITRON: What class were you in at college?

LAMONT: I graduated from Harvard in the Class of 1924. And in my class there were some very interesting, stimulating people: Senator Henry Cabot Lodge—Ambassador Lodge—was one of those I knew well in that class. Even in those early days, when we were both only about twenty years old, Lodge and I were on different sides of the fence; he always was conservative, and I was always liberal or Left. Another gentleman in that class who has meant a great deal to me is Charlie Poletti, who became Lieutenant Governor and, for a very brief period, Governor of New York. We have had writers, too, like Oliver La Farge—who, incidentally, is the President of the Association on American Indian Affairs—a very fine man, a very gifted man, and whose early novel, *Laughing Boy*, I think it was, attracted me soon after I left college.

So that was a fine class. And at Harvard I continued what you might call the liberal education that I got in my family circle; that is, at Harvard all kinds of ideas were presented to us students. I got a chance to hear not just the orthodox viewpoint, but liberal and radical viewpoints as well. I think that Harvard still has that reputation and that sort of atmosphere, perhaps more than most other colleges. It is a place where there is plenty of room for dissenters. And as you will recall, we have had many eminent public men who graduated from Harvard who didn't exactly take the line of least resistance, for example, Franklin D. Roosevelt, not to mention the present President of the United States.

CITRON: After you took your Ph.D. at Columbia in 1932, you started to put into deeds your interest in civil liberties. I believe it was in 1932 that you became a director of the American Civil Liberties Union. What is your recollection of your earliest interest in civil liberties?

LAMONT: Actually that went back to Harvard College, where I was always interested in trying to get unorthodox speakers to address the student body. And at one time I tried to get people like Scott Nearing and W. Z. Foster invited. I didn't succeed, actually, at that moment. But my civil liberties experience started then. It blossomed after I graduated and became one of my main interests. As you mentioned, I became a director of the American Civil Liberties Union, fighting through many crises with them, supporting uncompromising freedom of speech for all individuals and groups in the United States.

And as I went on, I tangled with various government bodies myself. I not only tried to defend the civil liberties of other people, their free speech and their freedom of association, but I tried to help establish civil liberties by speaking out frankly in all kinds of dissenting ways.

CITRON: In the course of your interest in civil liberties you went before Senator McCarthy's famed committee, which led later to an indictment for contempt of Congress. Can you tell us exactly what happened there?

LAMONT: That was, of course, a very remarkable experience for me: to be haled before McCarthy's committee by old Senator Joe himself, who came to New York especially for my hearing. My crime was that, like other authors, I had written a book which Senator McCarthy did not like because it was about Soviet Russia; it was called *The Peoples of the Soviet Union* and was about the racial groups in that country. McCarthy found that the book was on a U.S. Army bibliography. That is why he summoned me before his committee, where he started to ask me a lot of unconstitutional questions about how I had prepared to write the book, whom I talked to about it, what my places of research were and that sort of thing.

I refused on First Amendment grounds to answer most of McCarthy's questions. I told him plainly that my writings were outside the jurisdiction of his committee, which was supposed to look only into government operations. Since I was not an employee of the Government, I did not consider that my books were a proper subject for his committee.

Also, freedom of the press was involved: I had published a book and McCarthy had no right to start asking questions of me about it.

My case went before Congress. In the Senate, I was indicted for contempt, though three Senators voted against the citation, including Senator Lehman of New York.

CITRON: Who were the other two, Corliss?

LAMONT: The other two were Senator Chavez of New Mexico and Bill Langer of North Dakota. Langer was an erratic, wonderful guy—

CITRON: And a Republican.

LAMONT: *And* a Republican. And he voted against the citation.

But anyway, the case went to the courts. I was defended by a brilliant civil liberties lawyer, Philip Wittenberg. We battled it through the District Court and up to the Appeals Court, winning first in the District Court, and then having the indictment dismissed in the Court of Appeals, which ruled that my books were simply beyond the jurisdiction of Senator McCarthy's committee.

I was very happy to be involved in that battle. It was exciting, it was interesting, it was worthwhile. And I think that I helped to put a nail in McCarthy's political coffin. Actually, if you look at his record in the courts, he won practically nothing. Of course, that was at a time when Congressional committees, especially his committee, were riding high, and they still remain a great menace to American civil liberties.

CITRON: You're referring, no doubt, to the House Un-American Activities Committee.

LAMONT: Yes, and also to the Internal Security Subcommittee of the Senate, because both of these committees are still operating today, calling witnesses before them for no good reason, ruining careers, smearing innocent people; and they have constituted the spearhead of reaction and witch-hunting in the United States.

CITRON: Since you brought up the House Un-American Activities Committee, do you think that there are any functions of this committee that are legitimate?

LAMONT: Actually, no. I think this committee is unconstitutional on its face since the very resolution supporting it calls on the committee to expose un-American propaganda—and propaganda is the lifeblood of any democracy. Of course, we call propaganda what our opponents call education, and vice versa. But in a great political campaign, whether it be for the presidency or some other office, propaganda is really the heart of the matter—on both sides. So that when you start to make an investigation of propaganda, you are really investigating free speech and trying somehow to curtail free speech.

Therefore, the House Un-American Activities Committee has no legitimate function and is actually contrary to the Constitution in its functioning. Hence, I stand with those who favor, very strongly, its total abolition.

CITRON: Are you willing to admit the possibility that there could be activity in the United States that is un-American?

LAMONT: Why—I hate that term "un-American."

CITRON: Instead of un-American, against the interests of the United States?

LAMONT: Of course there can be activities against the interests of the United States. There can be treason. There can be murder. There can be sabotage. There can be espionage. And actually, on the statute books, both Federal and State, we have plenty of laws to take care of all those crimes. The Government should go after anyone—whether they're a communist or not—who is guilty of those crimes.

But these committees of Congress actually are going after people who cannot be reached by any statute of the United States, and that is why it is unconstitutional: they pursue them in a sort of extralegal way, acting in reality as courts of justice to condemn these people without their having a chance to defend themselves according to proper legal procedures and regulations.

CITRON: You have admitted that there are possibly certain actions in this country that might be considered un-American, or non-American, or whatever terminology you prefer. Also, we have a Government that is divided into three branches: Executive, Legislative and Judicial. Now, you obviously believe in the right of individuals to have their cases tried in the courts, and you obviously believe in the right of the Executive to look into these cases. But we have a Legislative branch of Government, and if they can't investigate things through the Un-American Activities Committee, how can they look into them?

LAMONT: I happen to believe in this three-way separation established by the Constitution. In fact, I continually stress it. It is exactly that separation of powers that strengthens the case against the House Un-American Activities Committee because it has again and again usurped the functions of the Judiciary and the Department of Justice. Now you ask who is going to look into these things if—

CITRON: From the Congressional viewpoint.

LAMONT: —from the Congressional viewpoint. The purpose of Congressional investigating committees—which I approve of—is to ascertain facts which are useful for legislation. But these witch-hunt committees don't do anything of the sort. They just keep trying to smear people. And they dig up information that everybody knows about already. So that I don't think they have any real function—from the legislative point of view.

But you see, it's not only the Legislative branch that oversteps its powers now and then. The Executive branch can overstep its powers too, as when the President of the United States involves American military might in foreign countries in some war or other without the Congress having had a chance to vote on it.

CITRON: Would you allow the House Un-American Activities Committee to exist if its field was limited and its methods changed?

LAMONT: Not under its present mandate from Congress, and not under the definition of "un-American," which, as I said before, is so vague and sweeping that it can never really be limited to any one idea or group of ideas, or even group of activities.

Actually, if there ever were such a thing as a valid Un-American Activities Committee—which I doubt—it would have to investigate *actions*—illegal actions by groups and people that are not covered by other agencies of the Government. But you see, the Federal Bureau of Investigation takes care of all that.

CITRON: But that's in the Executive branch of the Government.

LAMONT: Yes, that's in the Executive branch, but the Legislative branch is not supposed to deal with uncovering criminal actions.

CITRON: But they are sort of a watchdog.

LAMONT: Well, as I said, they can be a watchdog for legislative action and for digging up useful facts. Now, mind you, I'm in favor of the Congressional power of investigation in general. It's only three or four committees—like the McCarthy committee, the Un-American Activities Committee, the Senate Internal Security Subcommittee—that have gone overboard in these investigations. There is a committee on banking, for example, or a committee on commerce, and most of those committees stick to their knitting pretty well, performing the limited function that has been assigned to them by the House or Senate.

But the witch-hunt committees are sort of roving committees which take the whole world—the whole world of the United States—as their jurisdiction, which I think is unfortunate and actually illegal.

CITRON: Dr. Lamont, we could spend the remainder of our time on this question, but there is too much that I'd like to talk to you about that we haven't yet touched on. One point that you sort of came to yourself a moment ago was the question of foreign intervention on the part of the United States Government through the Executive branch. You're no doubt referring to such things as the invasion of Cuba.

LAMONT: Well, Cuba first. You know, it was just a little under a year ago, April 17—I can never forget that date—when the United States, through the CIA, helped to stage that invasion of Cuba by Cuban exiles who were armed, organized and financed by the United States Government. I thought that that was really a terrible thing and that it went beyond the power of the Executive department because it was involving us in a little war without anybody discussing it in Congress, without Congress exercising its prerogative to declare war.

And I find a similar example today in South Vietnam. There you have the United States Government, again, embarking on a large-scale military intervention, sending troops and machine guns and trucks and now helicopters to aid the tyrannical government of a fellow named Diem, who is an arch-reactionary and a very cruel dictator.

There has been very little discussion of the issue by the people of the United States and practically no discussion in Congress. And again, I think the Executive—that is, President Kennedy—is going beyond a so-called police action to embroil the United States in a real, though undeclared, war that could flare up into a major conflict with the most serious of consequences for the people of the United States.

CITRON: I think that even the President believes that this Cuba situation was an ill-advised expedition in the form that it was undertaken and that the CIA had no business in fighting its own private war. But let's not talk about that.

I'm not going to talk about South Vietnam either because I feel that the action taken by the Executive branch—while it has not had the explicit approval of the Congress—has had bipartisan White House Breakfast approval from the very start of the conflict.

Instead, there are three other situations that I would like to ask you about. What do you think of our intervention: a) helping in the United Nations action in the Congo; b) our action in Lebanon in 1958; and c) the operation in Korea, which was almost entirely American. What about those three?

LAMONT: Well, I think the Congo intervention under the aegis of the United Nations was justified and that insofar as the United States supported it, trying to bring peace and unity to the African Congo, it was a good and justified action.

As for Eisenhower's sending the Marines to Lebanon, I thought that was a great mistake. It was the kind of Marine diplomacy that we have come to frown upon in relation to Latin America, for instance. And it was not only a mistake because of our sending armed forces, but the reasons were also wrong. It was all due to a revolution that took place in Iraq. As soon as that revolution took place, overthrowing a pretty dictatorial king, there was immediately a cry of communism and the charge that it was really a communist front.

Now actually it turned out to be nothing of the kind. These were just military men and nationalists trying to get a better government in Iraq. But on the pretext that the communists were threatening the whole Middle East, Eisenhower sent the Marines there to prevent the communist revolution from sweeping into Lebanon—but there wasn't any communist revolution involved.

CITRON: But didn't the Lebanese Government request our intervention?

305

LAMONT: It may well have, but that does not, it seems to me, necessarily justify such an intervention. Actually, in South Vietnam today the Government has requested our help, but that doesn't make it right.

CITRON: What about Korea?

LAMONT: I don't think the Korean situation is quite as clear as the Congo; but just the same I do think that the invasion of South Korea by the North Koreans was a terrible act of international immorality and that the U.N. cease-fire order should have been carried out by both South Korea and North Korea. Therefore, I think that there was justification for President Truman sending in American troops, though I wish that he had not sort of jumped the United Nations on it. And I also wish that he had dismissed MacArthur earlier, so that MacArthur and the American Army would not have swept on to the Chinese border in North Korea, which brought the Chinese into the war.

In other words, while part of the Korean operation was justified, part of it went in a very wrong direction. Bringing in the Chinese cost us thousands of American lives, and insofar as that happened, it was a mistake.

CITRON: Let's move to the question of international peace. I have a quote from you which says: "I have been active in working for international peace and American-Soviet understanding." Can you amplify that?

LAMONT: Well, I would have to go back again to my parents and to those early days when they took me to Geneva, to look at the League of Nations when it was operating. I have maintained a very deep interest in international organizations for the prevention of war ever since that time, so that when the United Nations was established after the Second World War, I became very much interested in it and have always been a firm supporter of U.N. principles and the U.N. Charter in general.

At the same time, it seemed to me that American-Soviet relations presented the greatest danger of war. Therefore, I early became interested in trying to improve American-Soviet understanding.

I went to Russia two or three times, wrote a couple of books on that country, and tried to get across to the American public—and indeed to the American Government—the fact that the Russians were very anxious to cooperate with the United States to insure peace. I think that was true *before* the Second World War, and I think it's been true *after* the Second World War.

I have maintained that interest down to the present and still believe that understanding and peaceful coexistence between the Soviet Union and the United States are the key to world peace today.

CITRON: There are a number of things that have been going on that serve to amplify what you have said about peace between the East and

West, which is in reality the two countries. What would you have done, if you had been President Kennedy, in the relationship with the Soviets during the last year?

LAMONT: I would need a lot of time to answer that question. I won't take all that time. But I will just outline a couple of things that come to mind. If I had been President Kennedy, I would have sat down with Khrushchev and the Russians. I would have held a Summit Conference.

CITRON: Well, he has met with Khrushchev.

LAMONT: Yes, he met with Khrushchev in Vienna a year or so ago, but it was very informal.

CITRON: Wasn't this sort of an awakening for Kennedy? He had thought that he could sit down with Khrushchev, but according to all the scuttlebutt, he came out a very worried man.

LAMONT: I'm not sure whether that was the case or not. But I think that, instead of boosting American armaments by eight or nine billion dollars, Kennedy should have accepted some of the Russian disarmament proposals. And that—

CITRON: Without safeguards?

LAMONT: *With* safeguards—that the Russians should disarm at the same time—and with other safeguards, too. I believe that Kennedy went a little wild over the Berlin situation and scared the Russians with his threats that we would, if necessary, resort to nuclear war over the Berlin issue. I could never see that the Berlin issue amounted to that much or was that important.

In general I think that the Kennedy Administration's whole attitude towards the Soviet Union is based on a wrong premise: namely, that the Soviet Union and the communist states intend military aggression, if they can get away with it. I don't think that the Soviet Union has ever wished to spread socialism or communism through military aggression or wars. That is, they believe that the capitalist system is doomed anyway and that the workers in each country will bring about the change to a socialist system on their own—in some cases, as Khrushchev said recently, through democratic processes.

In other words, the whole military buildup in the United States has been based all along on the idea that we must work up a mighty deterrent to the Soviet aggression that is always just around the corner. It was never around the corner. The Russians have never intended war. They suffered so in the First and Second World Wars that they are through with war so far as they can express a purpose of their own. And therefore, I think that this is a political myth which has been foisted on the American people to keep us nervous, and even fanatical, over the alleged communist and Soviet menace.

CITRON: How do we know you're right?

LAMONT: It becomes clear from a study of Marxist and Soviet documents, and from observing the Soviet efforts towards world peace and their own principles, as demonstrated in, for example, the League of Nations—that is, even before the Second World War—where they were firmly in favor of collective security and tried hard to get the other Great Powers to unite on that basis against Hitler.

It is something, I suppose, that it is very difficult to prove. And so far as disarmament is concerned, I don't ask that the United States disarm unilaterally. But I do ask that we try to enter into reasonable disarmament negotiations with the Russians—not only about conventional weapons but about nuclear weapons as well.

CITRON: I'm glad you brought that up. You were on this program not long ago after the Russians resumed nuclear testing. In doing this, they completely destroyed the moratorium that was understood, that we'd been dickering with them about for a number of years—constant meetings where we both had agreed not to test. You yourself condemned the Russian decision to restart nuclear testing. Now, is it out of sorts for Americans to say that we cannot enter into a new disarmament agreement or a treaty on banning atomic testing without adequate safeguards? Isn't this a perfectly normal reaction after what happened?

LAMONT: Well, certainly it is. And I still condemn the Soviet Union for breaking the moratorium and going ahead with those tests. At the same time, I am sorry that the United States responded by going ahead with underground tests last fall, and that President Kennedy has now announced that we will begin atmospheric tests in all probability in April. I think this is a great mistake.

But you see, in addition, you talk about safeguards. All this talk about inspection of the Soviet Union, or the United States for that matter, to prevent nuclear testing has, I think, become quite irrelevant.

I think that, on the whole, both atmospheric testing and underground testing of nuclear weapons can now be detected by foreign countries through new mechanical devices. And I think that has been shown again and again in the last year or so. As a matter of fact, the British in this last round of discussions at Geneva, have been pushing towards that general conclusion.

In other words, an agreement to stop nuclear testing, both above ground and underground, is now pretty much self-enforcing, because as soon as there is a test, a violation, everybody else knows about it. So I don't think that it's necessary to harp on that particular approach. If we would only make a start at stopping nuclear testing, just get the ball rolling, we would be on the road to peace and mankind would be much happier.

CITRON: Well, you mentioned that the Soviets as long ago as before World War II definitely wanted peace. Now, why will they not then allow us to have some kind of an inspection system set up whereby we would immediately forego our testing of atomic devices in the atmosphere?

LAMONT: Well, they did accept the idea of inspection for a while. I imagine they really are, as they have hinted from time to time, afraid of spies. I think that this is unfortunate; I think the Soviet Union should—if the United States insists—accept an inspection system for the stopping of nuclear tests.

CITRON: But they won't budge on this.

LAMONT: On the other hand, if the Soviet Union won't budge on it, I think the United States should make a treaty anyway. It's so terribly important to get that treaty to stop nuclear testing. As I said, a non-testing agreement seems to me to be self-enforcing.

CITRON: Isn't this the situation that the two governments have been in for approximately three years? You talk about "if this" and "if that"— this is the position that they've been in: neither side will give in. We want safeguards; the Soviet Union doesn't want safeguards.

LAMONT: The question is what the safeguards should be—

CITRON: Well, inspection then.

LAMONT: —and how necessary they have become. I think that the whole idea of inspection has become much less necessary than it was earlier because of devices that reveal our underground testing even thousands and thousands of miles away.

CITRON: Let's move on to your attitude towards socialism. What do you think that the future has in store for the United States democracy? Do you think that socialism is in the offing?

LAMONT: Let me go back for a minute to my basic philosophy, Humanism, which is a philosophy that stresses working for the welfare and progress and happiness of all mankind. What I have been moved by, motivated by, during the greater part of my life, is a compassionate concern for humanity. Some people would call it "love of humanity," in Auguste Comte's phrase. And also I rely primarily on the methods of reason and science in solving individual and social problems.

I think it is this feeling for justice and the welfare of all humanity that has led me to the belief in a democratic socialist economy as the best system, not only for countries that are underdeveloped but for countries that are, say, overdeveloped, like the United States.

And when I use my intellect and thinking process to answer the question of how we can bring economic security and justice to the masses of mankind, I feel that some sort of collectivism—whether one calls it socialism or not—is the answer.

We have become increasingly collectivistic in the United States. We have little socialist experiments here and there, as in the Tennessee Valley Authority and the Social Security program. There are a lot of measures dealing with unemployment insurance and social security that were in the old socialist programs that have been adopted by both Democrats and Republicans in the United States. So that we are moving steadily in the direction of socialism. But we're not moving nearly as fast as other countries, where some kind of socialism has been established, as in the Soviet Union, Czechoslovakia and the Eastern European states.

My own feeling is that it's unfortunate that socialism has come into power first in countries like Russia and China, which were terribly backward in a democratic sense and therefore found it easy to move from dictatorial feudalism to dictatorial socialism. I want to see one of the democratic nations like Great Britain or France or the United States vote socialism into power, so that we'd bring this new sort of economy into effect through the democratic process.

CITRON: Abolish the capitalistic system?

LAMONT: It would nationalize the main instruments of production and distribution; and, yes, it would abolish capitalism in general, but the state need not take over everything.

CITRON: What would not be taken over by the state?

LAMONT: A lot of the smaller businesses and perhaps part of the agricultural economy. When I say smaller businesses, I mean people who are employing only three or four workers. I would not be in favor, necessarily, of group ownership of every little industry or every little service in the community.

CITRON: Am I correct in assuming that you would advocate complete state ownership of industry in America except for the very smallest?

LAMONT: Well, not necessarily by the Federal state. They might be owned by the city government, as are the subways in New York.

CITRON: It really wouldn't matter too much whether it was the city, state or Federal Government, would it?

LAMONT: It would matter to this extent: the key concept in the transition to socialism, and in the functioning of a socialist economy, is planning—economic and social planning. I don't dwell on the class struggle at all. But life in our modern economies has become so complex that there must be some kind of overall planning from central positions. One central position is obviously Washington, D.C.

CITRON: Don't they indulge in that?

LAMONT: They already have a good deal of planning. That's right.

CITRON: The Council of Economic Advisors—

LAMONT: That's right. And I would extend it much further. But at the same time, I would allow for plenty of local autonomy in states and municipalities. I don't want everything controlled by the Federal Government under socialism. There's room for State planning in New York, for instance, or city planning in New York City, which could be very helpful.

And already, as you suggest, planning goes ahead to some degree. But under socialism, it would be expanded enormously. Our general economic efficiency would increase, depressions and unemployment would be abolished, and the standard of living would go up much higher than it is even today.

CITRON: Aren't you forgetting what might happen to American initiative though?

LAMONT: I'm not worried about that because I don't think that initiative is brought into play solely by the profit system, the urge to make money under capitalism. All kinds of other things can stimulate individual initiative. After all, we have plenty of good, decent, efficient people working in the government service already whose primary motive is other than making a profit on the stock market. I feel that the motivation of men can be transformed and bettered under socialism, so that they'll work just as hard—if not harder—as under the capitalist system or the feudal system.

CITRON: Wasn't it, though, the capitalistic system that made the industrial might of America?

LAMONT: Certainly it was—because that is the system that has operated here ever since the American Revolution. We were never bothered with feudalism in the United States. We had a form of capitalism from the start. And in many ways capitalism has done a splendid job; let's not forget that. But I think it has performed its task by developing the country technologically, by bringing about big and new industries, and that it is time, finally, for socialism to take over.

CITRON: Corliss Lamont, it's been a great privilege and very informative—certainly to me—to hear your views, after sixty years of life. And I, needless to say, find some of your point of view that I agree with, much that I do not. But it has been interesting to take both sides of these arguments. And I've certainly appreciated your taking time off on your sixtieth birthday to come to talk to us.

LAMONT: I've enjoyed it very much, Casper, and appreciate the chance, always, to talk with you.

AFTERTHOUGHTS

In my interview with Casper Citron, I covered almost all of those fundamental interests and causes that have meant most to me during the first sixty years of my life.

We did not have time, however, to discuss the love of Nature that has played a major role in my life ever since I was a Boy Scout during the happy days of my youth in Englewood, New Jersey. My troop there took long hikes in the nearby woods, often on trails along the top of the Palisades of the Hudson. Thus it was that I early came to know intimately the rugged splendor of those cliffs and the magnificent views from dramatic, rocky lookouts rising sheer above the river.

In the summer of 1914, when I was twelve, my father and mother took the whole family to a Montana ranch in the Rocky Mountains. From our cabins we could see snowcapped peaks in the distance. We rode horseback a great deal and sometimes went on camping trips into the exciting mountain country, our guide always carrying a rifle and constantly on the alert to the danger of a roaming bear. I learned, too, that summer the pleasures of trout fishing while wading down the bed of a rushing stream and casting the fly into deep, eddying pools shaded from the sun.

Again, in July and August of 1915, our family traveled to the West, this time to White Pelican Lodge on the shore of Lake Klamath in Oregon. During these two extended trips to the Rockies, my parents introduced us to Crater Lake National Park, Glacier National Park and Yellowstone National Park. I was thrilled by the beauty of these great outdoor recreation centers, and since that time have visited as many national parks as possible. I am convinced that America's broad network of state and national parks surpasses any comparable public park development in any country in the world. One of my pleasantest assignments was serving as a member of the Committee on the Appreciation and Conservation of Nature of the American Humanist Association.

Returning to the subject of the Palisades, about which John Masefield wrote his splendid poem "The Western Hudson Shore," I should record that in 1929 my parents moved to a big house atop those cliffs near Sneden's Landing, New York, and lived there for close to twenty years. When my mother died in 1952, she willed to my younger brother Austin and me a score of lovely woodland acres fronting on the Palisades, and stipulated that this property should be maintained permanently in a wild and natural state. The Audubon Society of Nyack is the official custodian of this Lamont Sanctuary. I am its supervisor, and I take much pleasure in keeping the trails in good condition, sawing through and clearing away the trees that occasionally fall across them.

Exercise in the open air has always been my chief recreation, and I equally enjoy hiking, canoeing, skating, tennis, sailing, and surf bathing along a sandy beach. The queen of sports for me, however, has for many years been skiing. Since it is a bit dangerous, each December I say to myself that I am getting too old for it. But when the snow starts to fall on those beckoning slopes in New England and the Catskills, I am unable to resist the temptation. Ski weekends with friends or family have been among the greatest joys of my life.

The recognition of Nature's wonder and magnificence is not merely a personal enthusiasm for me, but is also a basic part of the philosophy of naturalistic Humanism. Humanists can find no Divine Father in or behind Nature, but Nature is truly our fatherland. We rejoice profoundly in the inexhaustible beauties and possibilities of this earth which is our home. We feel a deep kinship with the cosmos and with the myriad forms of life upon this planet. In our aesthetic and emotional response to a glorious sunset, to the infinite expanse of shining stars, to a foaming waterfall framed in evergreen, to the simple beauty of white dogwood or red roses, we Humanists attain a sort of naturalistic mysticism.

The appreciation of Nature, however, is by no means the only way in which the ordinary sensitive person can experience a state of what I like to call normal mysticism. With no supernatural explanation necessary, the spiritually alert individual frequently achieves natural ecstasies that bring an exalted and intensified sense of life. Listening to a Beethoven symphony, looking at Michelangelo's frescoes in the Sistine Chapel, viewing the skyline of New York City, reading one of Shakespeare's sonnets, knowing the thrill of artistic or literary creation, or being overwhelmingly in love—these experiences and the many others like them constitute ultimate fruitions of the spirit and give richest meaning to human life.

Just as significant as such experiences is the feeling of joy in work, the deep satisfaction of liking your job and realizing how it contributes to the advancement of your fellowman. As a Humanist, I reject the superficial view that all human actions are motivated by self-interest. To say that a brave soldier willing to give his life for the defense of his country, or a parent glad to make repeated sacrifices for the sake of his children, is moved primarily by personal self-interest is a shallow oversimplification and runs counter to the obvious facts of human nature. All normal people are capable of powerful emotions of altruism that come into play not only during periods of social crisis, but in the day-to-day problems of living in a family and in a society. The fact that you always act *as* a self does not necessarily mean that you must always act *for* self.

My commonsense ethical philosophy, then, is that men and women should intelligently *combine* self-interest and social altruism throughout their lives. Clearly, self-regard in the sense of keeping healthy, acquiring an education and enjoying plenty of recreation is something to be encouraged for the welfare of both the individual and society. But in addition everyone ought to be concerned with the larger social objectives such as the good of his family, his city, his state, his country and the world at large. The ideal of public service is one that the sincere Humanist always adheres to. And when there occurs a definite clash between personal self-interest and the social good, he puts the community first.

Long ago I discovered that the way to achieve happiness is not to seek pleasure directly, but to find work and other activities that are congenial, healthy and socially significant, and then to let pleasure and happiness come as a by-product. If you can lose yourself, as it were, and indeed forget yourself through absorption in an interesting craft or profession important for the community, then the chances are that the *joy in work* I mentioned earlier will overflow into your leisure hours and days, and that you will become a truly happy man. George Santayana phrases the central point with his customary acumen when he talks of interests that "so possessed the self that all thought of self was banished in pursuing them." (*The Realm of Spirit,* pp. 160-161).

As a dissenter in the fields of philosophy, politics, economics and international affairs, I have come into constant conflict with orthodox opinions and orthodox persons, who tend to be dogmatic and intolerant. Bitter and unjust attacks have constantly been made against me, and I have been harassed by inquisitorial investigating committees of both the House and Senate, by the American Legion and by the FBI. Throughout these battles I have kept my eye on my main goals of furthering the philosophy of Humanism and of helping to bring about a better life for all mankind.

Also I am continually inspired by such lion-hearted individuals as Professor Alexander Meiklejohn, ninety-year-old philosopher, former President of Amherst College and outstanding writer and crusader for civil liberties; Dr. Harry F. Ward, age eighty-nine, former Professor of Christian Ethics at Union Theological Seminary and another great civil libertarian; William Ernest Hocking, also eighty-nine, Professor Emeritus of Philosophy at Harvard and still active in the cause of peace; and Bertrand Russell, just turned ninety, internationally famed British peer and philosopher. All of these men, whom I am privileged to know personally, have effectively kept on with the good fight, despite their advanced years. And there are many others, women as well as men, who could be mentioned in this connection.

Looking to the future, I cannot conceive that I shall ever voluntarily retire from working for the significant ideals and causes in which I believe. What happens to me almost daily is that after I have finished reading *The New York Times* at breakfast, I am full of indignation over the cruelties and injustices recorded in the news. This recurring indignation serves as a great spur to action.

Epilogue II: In Retrospect at Seventy-Two*

At age seventy-two I find myself in excellent condition and working almost as hard as ever—as a writer, lecturer (including TV broadcasts) and organization executive. I believe that lots of exercise has been a big factor in maintaining my health, and I am still skiing, skating, hiking, dancing and playing tennis.

Looking back on the fifty years since I graduated from Harvard College and forward to the twenty that may remain to me, I feel that my life has gone by with incredible speed and that even a life that lasts into the nineties is all too brief. With Shakespeare's Hotspur, I cry, "O gentlemen! the time of life is short." Much as I would like to believe in conscious survival after death, with the chance to see dear departed relatives and friends again, I think that personal immortality is impossible.

I hold to an ethics that combines self-interest and personal pleasure with altruism and service to the community. I have enjoyed my work in teaching and writing, and hope that it has been of some use to my fellow humans. I have been able to fit in long, pleasant vacations that have often included fascinating travel to different countries in Europe, Asia and Latin America. At the same time I have waged an unceasing struggle on behalf of my main objectives in public affairs: democracy and civil liberties in politics, democratic socialism in economics, Humanism in philosophy, international peace throughout the world and the conservation of Nature, including the extension of ecological values.

*For the Harvard Class of 1924 50th Anniversary Report, 1974.

On the civil liberties front, I have engaged in continuous battle against the many different kinds of government repression since the end of World War II. When in 1953 Senator Joseph McCarthy and his Senate Committee came after me, I refused to answer McCarthy's unconstitutional questions. He had me indicted for contempt of Congress, but a United States Appeals Court squelched this dastardly demagogue by dismissing my indictment. I won another significant civil liberties victory in 1965 when the U.S. Supreme Court upheld my challenge of a Congressional statute that directed censorship of foreign mail entering the United States. In *Lamont v. Postmaster General* the Court unanimously declared the law unconstitutional on First Amendment grounds.

For a number of years I was Chairman of the Bill of Rights Fund and am currently Chairman of the National Emergency Civil Liberties Committee. In 1972 the Corliss Lamont Foundation was established as a tax-exempt institution that receives financial contributions for the legal servicing of important civil liberties cases.

Ever since I was an undergraduate at Harvard, I have been active in endeavors to establish enduring world peace. I backed the League of Nations, and since World War II, I have vigorously supported the United Nations. Starting in 1962, I became a militant opponent of United States military intrusion in South Vietnam and Southeast Asia and wrote an Open Letter, published in *The New York Times*, to President John F. Kennedy calling upon him to halt the American intervention—an abysmal folly from the start. Under Presidents Johnson and Nixon this unconstitutional war of aggression, with its accompanying danger of developing into a nuclear world conflict, became the most cruel, immoral and altogether evil business in the history of U.S. foreign policy.

In waging the war, these two iniquitous Presidents constantly deceived the American people and at the same time extended the sway of executive power to unconstitutional extremes unprecedented in our history. Except for corruption in government, the most critical political issue of these times is how Congress can regain and maintain lawful control over the President, preventing him from becoming a virtual dictator in initiating wars and in other important aspects of foreign policy.

Regarding another front in the struggle for peace—improvement of American-Soviet relations—I have worked for understanding and cooperation between the USA and the USSR for forty years. From the start I condemned the Cold War as a useless and provocative thing initiated by the United States on the basis of the myth that the Soviet Union was planning to spread communism by military attacks on

Western Europe and other parts of the world. Of course I was happy that in 1972 President Nixon softened the Cold War by adopting most of the program on American-Soviet cooperation that I had been advocating since 1932. I also approved of the détente he brought about between the United States and the People's Republic of China. While I am most critical of the lack of civil liberties and democracy in the Soviet Union and China, I believe that socialism in both of these huge countries has brought about enormous economic and social progress.

I have continued to write and publish books and pamphlets, articles and reviews. My book, *The Philosophy of Humanism*, first issued in 1949, is still in print and remains the standard reference volume for naturalistic Humanism. This philosophy (or religion), recently summarized in *Humanist Manifesto II*, rejects belief in God, personal immortality and all other forms of the supernatural. Humanism is an affirmative way of life which holds that the chief aim of human beings should be to seek the this-earthly happiness and progress of all humanity, with reliance primarily on the methods of reason and science, democracy and social cooperation for the solution of problems. In my development of the humanist viewpoint, I published in 1967 *Freedom of Choice Affirmed*, which attempts to present the overall case for human free will as contrasted with the total determinism posited by such thinkers as Professor B. F. Skinner of Harvard.

During the past few years I have tried to work out a philosophy of marriage and sex relations that stands the test of experience and intelligence. I believe that the survival of our country and of the human race demands that the institution of marriage, despite all its shortcomings, be preserved. The most common cause of divorce, I suggest, may be that wife and husband simply see, hear and have too much of each other, so that they become bored with the situation. One possible solution is for marriage partners to enjoy more variety by having ample contacts and warm friendships with members of the opposite sex outside the family circle.

In 1972 I published a book of love poems under the title *Lover's Credo*. One of my main aims was to show that passionate sex love need not descend into the realm of vulgarity and obscenity. I have been appalled by the extent of hard-core pornography in books, magazines and movies, and by the constant debasing and trivializing of sex relations in the United States and other countries.

In this year 1974 I am engaged in various literary pursuits including the publication of *Voice in the Wilderness*. And I have been active in the campaign to impeach President Nixon. He does not like me, either, for my name was on the White House list (second schedule) of special "enemies." I considered this quite an honor. Soon I shall start to write my Autobiography. Continued activity is a good way to keep healthy and to avoid the possible boredom of old age.

I never intend to retire so long as I can wield a pen, tap a typewriter or carry on dictation. My aim is to follow the example of England's famous philosopher Bertrand Russell and keep on fighting for the great human causes until my dying day.

Index